Ma...ing...

WITHDRAWN
19/4/23

Managing Through Organisation offers an excellent analysis of different approaches to work organisaiton. Colin Hales uses an original and coherent theoretical framework to trace ways in which the management process has become separated, extended, dispersed and institutionalised within large-scale organisations. He examines the implications of the idea of 'managing *through* organisations' for managerial work and managerial power, influence and authority.

Based on the author's experience of teaching both students of management at undergraduate and postgraduate level and managers on executive programmes, this new text combines theory and practice. It brings an innovative perspective to bear on traditional approaches to work organisation and offers a useful synthesis of the current literature. The analysis covers the 'classical' approaches of bureaucracy and rationalisation, scientific management, and the more recent alternatives of decentralisation through divisional, professional and 'adhocratic' organisation and 'despecialisation' through work redesign and employee participation. International depth is given to the volume by a discussion of cultural controls on management exercised through Japanese and 'clan' forms of organisation.

The impact of different forms of organisation upon managerial work – managing *within* organisation – is examined and conclusions offered about the effectiveness and desirability of different forms of managing through organisation. Colin Hales's provocative new approach presents a dynamic view of management and organisation as 'process'.

Written in an accessible style, this refreshing analysis will appeal to students in all management disciplines and to academics and managers interested in the organisation context of management.

Colin Hales is Lecturer in Organisational Behaviour at the University of Surrey and Visiting Assistant Professor at the London Business School. He has worked for several years in market and government research and contributes regularly to leading management journals.

Organisational Behaviour and Management Series
Edited by Robert Goffee
London Business School

An understanding of organisational behaviour has become an increasingly important component of modern management education and development. This new series addresses key issues in contemporary organisational studies. It includes rigorous theoretical and empirical analyses of work, organisations and their management from a variety of perspectives. Contributions from well established fields of study – for example, individual change and motivation group processes, theories of organisation and change – are represented as well as those which explore *new* areas – technological change and innovation, corporate culture, strategy and competitiveness, public sector management, gender relations, stress management and career development. Series authors are lecturers and researchers in organisational behaviour and related disciplines: sociology, anthropology, social psychology and industrial relations. All books in the series will be of interest to the practitioner and students on graduate, undergraduate and post-experience courses.

Previous title:

Management in Developing Countries
Alfred M. Jaeger and Rabindra N. Kanungo

Managing through organisation

The management process, forms of organisation and the work of managers

Colin Hales

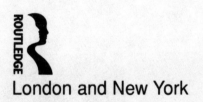

London and New York

First published 1993
by Routledge
11 New Fetter Lane, London EC4P 4EE

Simultaneously published in the USA and Canada
by Routledge
29 West 35th Street, New York, NY 10001

Reprinted 1994

© 1993 Colin Hales

Typeset in Bembo by
Ponting-Green Publishing Services, Chesham, Bucks
Printed and bound in Great Britain by
Mackays of Chatham PLC, Chatham, Kent

British Library Cataloguing in Publication Data
A catalogue record for this book is available from the British Library

Library of Congress Cataloging in Publication Data
A catalog record for this book is available from the Library of Congress

ISBN 0-415-01002-0 (hbk)
ISBN 0-415-01003-9 (pbk)

*For Joan, Alex and Rosanna
and to the memory of my parents*

Contents

Figures

Tables

Preface

This book began life as a series of lectures to undergraduate and postgraduate students at the University of Surrey and elsewhere. However, as I suspect is the case with many other books developed in this way, the process of translating lecture notes and their extemporaneous elaborations, with all their omissions, ambiguities and elisions, into the unforgiving permanence of a text proved a lengthy and painful one. This was so since it involved not only substantial rewriting, but also re-reading of material whose content had, over the course of time, sedimented in my mind into comfortable, selectively-remembered impressions. Therefore to Rob Goffee, the series editor who originally encouraged the writing of the book and then exhibited unflinching patience as it was slowly written, and to Rosemary Nixon, editor at Routledge whose encouragement and patience also seemed limitless, I owe a considerable debt of thanks.

Since the purpose of this book is to synthesise and evaluate knowledge and understanding of how work may be organised, many of the people to whom it owes a debt are people whom I have never met. They are the authors on work and organisation whose work has informed and inspired my own. These authors are too numerous to mention by name, but, collectively, they attest to the truth of the dictum that even pygmies can see a long way, if they stand on the shoulders of giants.

A more personal debt is owed to a number of people with whom I have had illuminating and agreeable conversations about management and organisations over a number of years: David Dann, Rob Goffee, Yvonne Guerrier, Linda Hicks, John Hunt, Gareth Jones, John Machin, Henry Mintzberg, Richard Scase and Rosemary Stewart. I also owe a particular debt to the late Derek Allcorn whose wit and wisdom inspired me as a postgraduate student and have endured ever since. Needless to say, I alone carry responsibility for any deficiencies in the text.

There are no institutions to acknowledge for funding, sabbatical leave or clerical support, since the book was written in the time left over from work and domestic duties and it was typed with skill and care by my wife, Jo. My heartfelt gratitude to her has, I hope, been expressed in other ways, but stands repeating here.

The book is dedicated to the memory of my parents, Jack and Vicky Hales, who never wrote a book but influenced the writing of this one in immeasurable and treasured ways, and to my family, Jo, Alex and Rosanna who remind me, in so many ways, that there are things just as important as writing books.

Introduction

This book is about management and organisation. Like a
gatecrasher at a large, prestigious party, it requires not so much
an introduction as an explanation of why it is here. Essentially,
it grew out of teaching management and organisation to final
year undergraduate and postgraduate students without, as I saw
it, benefit of a single book which would serve as a central course
text. Of the mountain of books on or about organisation, none
seemed to combine a comprehensive, accessible review of
different approaches in a way that was relevant to the practical
concerns of would-be managers, yet also sensitive to the
subtleties of academic theory and research findings.

The book tries to do a number of things. Firstly, it is 'about'
management and organisation, not in the sense of offering a
perspective (or perspectives) for looking at organisations, but in
the sense of considering what different forms of management
and organisation entail in practice. The central question, then,
is: how is management carried out or attempted through
organisation; rather than: how may organisations be viewed?
This means that the concern of the book is with management
and organisation as processes rather than as things. Secondly, in
contrast to many texts which concentrate upon a particular
aspect or type of organisation, the book attempts to be comprehensive in reviewing the range of different approaches to
organisation. Thirdly, it seeks to provide, not a sequential
catalogue of authors and texts, but a synthesis of ideas and
empirical material, whatever their origins, which bear upon
different approaches to organisation. Thus, the book is itself
organised, not by sources, but by topics and issues. Related to
this is an attempt to avoid bland neutrality in the treatment of

the material. Whilst endeavouring to remain faithful to the material from which it draws, the book offers both a critical stance – a point of view – on this material, and offers some new ideas with which the critical reader can engage.

Central to the book is an analysis of different approaches to organisation within a consistent and coherent conceptual framework – the 'managing through organisation' (MTO) framework developed in Chapters 1–3. The purpose of this is to permit a comparison of different approaches to organisation in such a way that their similarities, differences, strengths and weaknesses are thrown into sharper relief.

The book is therefore both practical and theoretical. Whilst it addresses the practicalities of organising, it is also theoretical, in that firstly, it is couched in a theoretical framework and, secondly, it tries to discern general principles in the processes of management and organisation. Whilst these principles are illustrated by reference to examples, the assumption is that the reader will have their own areas of practical or theoretical interest to which they will want to apply the ideas set out here. The book therefore aims to provide a compass, rather than a map of a particular area.

The starting point and the basis for the theoretical framework is the proposition that the management process – the process of planning/decision-making, allocating, motivating, coordinating and controlling work – has become separated from work itself, and has amalgamated with ownership functions to form a distinct extended 'management' function which is dispersed, through a management division of labour, and is institutionalised into organisational arrangements and mechanisms. Hence, the management of work is attempted through organisation. Different approaches to organisation may then be compared and contrasted in terms of the mechanisms which they use to try to manage work and the people who do it.

Chapters 1–3 build the managing through organisation (MTO) framework. Chapter 1 examines the nature of the management process and shows how it has become separated from the work process and dispersed through different managerial jobs. Consequently, management has become not simply the management of work, but the problematic and contested management of other people, a characteristic exhibited in the content and form of managerial work.

Chapter 2 examines the means for managing others – power – and the process of its deployment – influence – primarily from the point of view of the individual manager. The effectiveness of power and influence is shown to depend critically upon behavioural responses to them which are, in turn, shaped by perceptions and evaluations of power, in particular the extent to which it is seen as legitimate. The problematic nature of managerial authority is thus demonstrated. It is also argued that managerial power draws to a large extent upon organisational power resources and, hence, operates within the context of organisations as systems of power and influence.

This is the starting point for an analysis, in Chapter 3, of the institutionalisation of management: the translation of the processes of planning/decision-making, allocation, motivation, co-ordination and control into impersonal arrangements and mechanisms. These arrangements for attempting the management of work on a large scale constitute organisation, the key elements of which are considered in the remainder of the chapter.

The different elements of managing through organisation form the framework of analysis for examining and comparing different approaches to organisation in Chapters 4–8. Each of these chapters has a similar structure and sequence. Firstly, the basic principles and key features of an approach are examined in detail, drawing upon evidence from the literature. These are then summarised in terms of the MTO framework, and the key issue or debate surrounding the application of the particular approach is considered. Lastly, the approach is subjected to a critical evaluation of its strengths and weaknesses.

Chapters 4 and 5 examine the 'classical' approach to managing through organisation, with Chapter 4 addressing the rationalisation of operational work and Chapter 5 the bureaucratic organisation of administration. The basic weaknesses of these approaches – inflexibility of people and work systems, low levels of work satisfaction and lack of commitment to work goals – form the starting point for more recent, alternative approaches to organisation. Chapter 6 considers the alternative to rationalisation of operational work: despecialisation through job redesign, group working and participation, and the concern with quality of working life and flexibility. Chapter 7 looks at the alternatives to bureaucracy: decentralisation to divisional, professional or adhocratic organisation, and the concern with flexibility and adaptability. Lastly, Chapter 8 examines the holistic approach of Japanese and 'clan' organisation and their concern with mobilising commitment.

Chapter 9 switches the focus from managing through organisation to managing within organisation, by examining the impact of different forms of organisation upon, firstly, management divisions of labour, and secondly, managerial work.

Lastly, without wishing to pre-empt the judgements of the critical reader, Chapter 10 offers some conclusions about the most durable, effective and desirable forms of organisation.

Therefore, the basic structure and argument of the book may be represented diagrammatically thus:

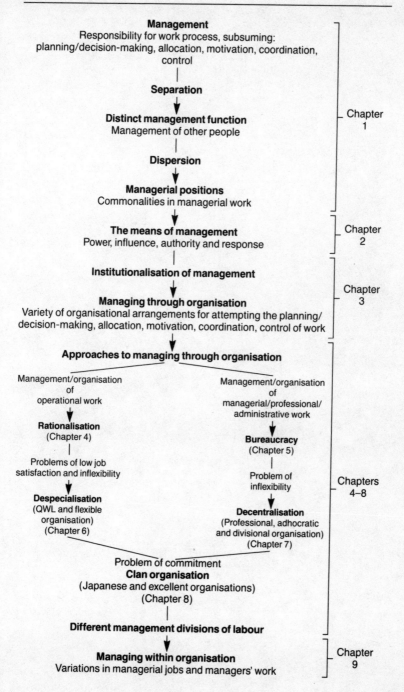

Management
Responsibility for work process, subsuming:
planning/decision-making, allocation, motivation, coordination,
control

Separation

Distinct management function
Management of other people

Dispersion

Managerial positions
Commonalities in managerial work

Chapter 1

The means of management
Power, influence, authority and response

Chapter 2

Institutionalisation of management

Managing through organisation
Variety of organisational arrangements for attempting the planning/
decision-making, allocation, motivation, coordination, control of work

Chapter 3

Approaches to managing through organisation

Management/organisation
of
operational work

Management/organisation
of
managerial/professional/
administrative work

Rationalisation
(Chapter 4)

Problems of low job
satisfaction and inflexibility

Bureaucracy
(Chapter 5)

Problem of
inflexibility

Despecialisation
(QWL and flexible
organisation)
(Chapter 6)

Decentralisation
(Professional, adhocratic
and divisional organisation)
(Chapter 7)

Problem of commitment
Clan organisation
(Japanese and excellent organisations)
(Chapter 8)

Different management divisions of labour

Chapters
4–8

Managing within organisation
Variations in managerial jobs and managers' work

Chapter 9

Chapter 1

Management, managing and managers

Few modern phenomena so patently pervasive and systematically scrutinised as 'management' have been so beset by ambiguity, confusion and, at times, obfuscation. In its English usage the term 'management' denotes, *inter alia*: an organisational function, an organisational stratum, an occupational group, an organisational process, an interpersonal process and an intrapersonal process (self management), each with their own associated body of knowledge and set of skills. The term is employed as both noun and verb, descriptively and normatively, approvingly and pejoratively. Moreover, all manner of edifices are constructed on these shifting sands. Management theory and management science encompass ideas which bear upon a wide diversity of topics. Management training and development are burgeoning activities, whilst management education is one of the few groves of academe still in full leaf, with ever more courses incorporating 'management', however incongruously, in the title. Fashionable obsessions with management effectiveness and, more recently, management competency (something of a retreat, to be sure) have spawned a great deal of research activity and 'training initiatives'. Above all, management is evoked as either panacea or scapegoat, the key determinant of the performance of business corporations, public institutions and, indeed, nation states. Yet all of these rest upon ambiguous, divergent or unexplicated conceptions of management.

The purpose of this chapter is to set the scene for the remainder of the book by addressing these ambiguities and setting out the particular conception of management being used here. We begin by considering the nature of the management process – what 'managing' work entails – and the different elements subsumed by that. We then trace, in a necessarily schematic fashion, the way in which management has become a distinct and separate function and the management process has become dispersed, and demonstrate how the content and form of the work of managers reflects this separation and dispersion. We show how managerial work reflects the fact that management is the problematic process of planning, allocating, motivating, coordinating and controlling the work of others.

THE GENERAL CONCEPT OF MANAGEMENT

Starting from first principles, we distinguish between management as a general, universal process and its specific social forms. In general, when human beings 'manage' their work, they take responsibility for its purpose, progress and outcome by exercising the quintessentially human capacity to stand back from experience and to regard it: prospectively, in terms of what will happen; reflectively, in terms of what is happening; and retrospectively, in terms of what has happened. Thus management is an expression of human agency, the capacity actively to shape and direct the world, rather than simply react to it.

The process of management, therefore, subsumes five conceptually distinct, if, in practice, intertwined elements. To manage work in general means:

1 Deciding/planning what is to be done, and how.
2 Allocating time and effort to what is to be done.
3 Motivating, or generating, the effort to do it.
4 Coordinating and combining disparate efforts.
5 Controlling what is done to ensure that it conforms with what was intended.

This formulation is very close to Fayol's 'classic' and oft-repeated conception of management as 'forecasting/planning', 'organising', 'commanding', 'coordinating' and 'controlling' (Fayol, 1949), but diverges in three respects. Firstly, it regards 'forecasting' as implicit in 'planning', but sees 'decision-making' as distinct. Secondly, 'motivating' is used to describe the general process for which 'commanding' is only one of a number of possible means. Thirdly, and crucially, 'allocating' is used to denote the process of dividing and distributing work. This reserves the term 'organising' to describe the ways in which all the elements of the management process are conducted on a large scale.

Fayol's basic formulation endures, despite claims that it is now dated and superseded. If all philosophy is a set of footnotes to Plato, management theory is, in large measure, a reply to Fayol's original memo. Some theorists more or less retain Fayol's categories as a framwork (Koontz *et al.*, 1984), whilst others use different terminology to restate Fayol, as in Barnard's elements of 'executive work' (Barnard, 1938) or Drucker's 'managerial work' (Drucker, 1974). Others focus upon one of Fayol's categories as the definitive management task and show in more detail either what it entails or how it may be done. Thus, management is treated, variously, as synonymous with planning/decision-making, organising/allocating, commanding/motivating, coordinating and controlling. Moreover, claims by researchers to have refuted Fayol by finding little or no evidence of his categories in studies of managerial work (Mintzberg, 1975; Stewart, 1983) are wide of the mark, since Fayol was concerned not to list observable features of managers' behaviour, but to set out the management functions required by an undertaking. As we show in this chapter and again in Chapter 9, the general process of management ramifies into the specific jobs and activities of managers in complex and variable ways: managers' activities cannot simply be 'read off' from the management process as a whole.

One important reason for this is that in shifting from a general conception of management as a process to the specifics of managerial work, we must recognise that management has become a separate function, or set of functions, undertaken primarily (but not exclusively) by a distinct group of agents, 'managers'. The central weaknesses in Fayol's formulation and subsequent developments of it are the assumptions that a distinct and separate management function is a logical necessity, rather than a product of historical development, and that 'management' is, unproblematically, the management of other people. Consequently, it is not always fully recognised that management in this particular form is a process which is social, in that it is conducted through interactions amoung individuals and groups; political, in that it entails attempts to modify others' behaviour in pursuit of possibly divergent outcomes;

and problematic in that reactions to attempts at management may not correspond with intended outcomes.

These particular characteristics of management are evident in everyday usage of the term. 'Management' and 'manager' are terms which are invariably qualified by some indication of what (and who) is being managed (hence 'works manager', 'product group manager', 'public sector management' and so on). A common definition of management sees it as 'achieving results through other people' (e.g. Heller, 1972) whilst managers are conventionally defined as those occupying positions with responsibility for the work of at least one subordinate. The dual derivation of the term – from *menager*, to use household resources efficiently, and *maneggiare*, to handle and train horses (Mant, 1977) – suggests responsibility for direction of both the material and animate (people, not horses) components of a work process.

THE SEPARATION, EXTENSION AND DISPERSION OF THE MANAGEMENT PROCESS

That 'management' has become the planning/decision-making, allocating, motivation, coordination and control of other people is the consequence of a complex series of developments, documented and theorised by a host of writers. Synthesising these accounts somewhat schematically, three key themes emerge: firstly, the management process has become separated into a distinct function; secondly, this function is extended by amalgamation with functions flowing from ownership; and thirdly, this combined function has become dispersed through different management specialisms and levels.

The separation of the management process occurs through a number of stages in two somewhat different contexts. The first is where an established work process, in which the management and execution of work are integrated, comes under the control of an external agency, whether private capital or the state. This external agency exercises control by virtue of owning and providing the financial and material resources necessary for the work process to take place, as in the case of the 'putting out' system, subcontracting, business acquisition or franchising. Initially, this means that the material inputs and outputs of the work process, but not the conduct of the work process itself, are controlled by the external agency, what is referred to by some as the formal subsumption of labour by capital (Marx, 1976; Burawoy, 1985). Owners of the work process exercise two functions by virtue of this. The first are ownership functions proper, which flow from the right to deploy monetary and material inputs and to dispose of the outputs of the work process. These functions, therefore, include: deployment of money, material and equipment; selling and marketing the product; maintaining relations with external interests such as financiers, shareholders, suppliers, customers or state agencies, together with the promulgation of ideologies to legitimate these functions. Owners also come to take responsibility for two management functions, previously integrated into the work process itself: deciding and planning what work is to be done, and controlling or monitoring outputs to ensure that work has been carried out appropriately. Initially, therefore, it is those parts of the management process which occur before and after the event which become separate from the execution of work itself and are conducted by owners or their agents. Management functions relating to how work is done – allocation to different individuals, motivation of effort and coordination – remain integrated into the work process.

The second stage in the separation of management occurs when direction of the work process itself, and not simply the deployment of its inputs and outputs, becomes the responsibility of owners and their agents. Often referred to as the real subsumption of labour by capital (Marx, 1976; Burawoy, 1985) this occurs with the concentration of the work activities of a private or state undertaking in a single organisation. Here, owners or their agents not only continue to exercise ownership functions and the management functions of planning/decision-making and control, but also assume responsibility for the other elements of the management process. As workers become employees, selling their capacity to labour, rather than the results of their labour, so motivation becomes the responsibility, and problem, of owners as employers. Consequently, they take increasing steps to determine how work is carried out by taking on the functions of allocating and coordinating work (Offe, 1976). Owners and their agents, therefore, assume responsibility for ownership functions and management functions combined, which become increasingly referred to as 'management'.

The second context in which separation of management functions occurs is where a work process grows and develops under owner/manager direction, typically where an individual or partnership starts an undertaking on the basis of their personal capital, skills, expertise or a combination of these. As long as the undertaking comprises a single individual or partnership, work, management and ownership functions are fused. The individuals decide on the work they will do, plan it, allocate their time and motivate, coordinate and control themselves, whilst also being responsible for deploying money and material inputs and selling/marketing the product. When, however, the undertaking expands and others are taken on as employees, although the allocation and coordination of work may continue to be carried out jointly, ownership functions and the management functions of planning/decision-making, motivation and control become the exclusive province of the owners or partners. Further growth invariably brings the appointment of a general operational manager responsible for all management functions, including allocation and coordination of work, whilst the original owner(s) concentrate on deployment of money and materials and disposal of the product. Therefore, at this stage in the growth of an undertaking, not only has management become separated, but once again, there are the beginnings of a dispersion of ownership and management functions.

This account of the separation of an extended management process from the execution of work should not imply that this process is inevitable or inexorable. There is considerable evidence to show that, historically, this process was contested and resisted and that for this and other reasons, the separation of management functions may be diverted, incomplete or, indeed, reversed. What this demonstrates is that once management starts to become a separate process, carried out by a distinct group, and therefore, becomes the management not only of work in general, but of other people's work, it becomes a contested and problematic process: the efficacy of the process of management critically depends upon the way those being managed respond to it.

Dispersion of this extended 'management' process in which ownership and management functions are fused is the consequence of increasing scale. These general functions become divided into different detailed elements which form the basis of different managerial specialisms at different levels. Thus, there is the development of an increasingly elaborate 'management division of labour' with each individual management position contributing a part of the total process. Management structures, therefore, replace market mechanisms as the principal means of allocating and coordinating the resources of business or organisational units (Chandler, 1977; Chandler and Daems, 1980).

Management structures and their associated management divisions of labour are shaped by the ways in which the management process is institutionalised in organisational arrangements. (This process of institutionalisation is examined in Chapter 3, and management divisions of labour are considered in more detail in Chapter 9.) For now, the important point is that the management process is the outcome of a complex web of interdependent activities carried out by a variety of different individuals whose common designation as 'manager' disguises their responsibility for distinctly different elements of the management process.

The above observations bear upon some important issues. The first is the debate surrounding the genesis of management as a distinct set of functions, and whether this is the ineveitable, technical consequence of an increasing scale of operations or the historically contingent consequence of inequalities in socio-economic power. On the one hand it is argued that the inevitable process of differentiation which accompanies increasing scale of operation also impinges upon the process of management, which becomes a specialised function like any other. In this view, management is seen primarily as a neutral, coordinating function and a concomitant of modernity and industrialism (Kerr *et al.*, 1973; Drucker, 1974). On the other hand are those who argue that management in its present form is the result of a desire on the part of those owning the means of production and purchasing labour power for operational direction of work, in ways that serve their material interests. In this view, management is seen as a class-based control function and a concomitant of capitalism in one guise or another (Braverman, 1974; Burawoy, 1985). We return to this debate in more detail in Chapters 4 and 5 where we consider the question of the inevitability of rationalisation and bureaucratisation. For now we must recognise that the political and technical origins of management are inextricable. Certainly, the initial separation of management is an outgrowth of disparities in socio-economic power, the acquisition or initiation of work processes by private capital or the state, and the desire for control which flows from that: hence the contested nature of that separation. However, once separate, the continued separation of the management function is reinforced by technical advantages of differentiation in increasingly large-scale undertakings and by the process of dispersion itself. Management as a separate function is a socially contingent phenomenon which has come to appear as a technically necessary one.

Many confusions and ambiguities in the terms 'management' and 'managers' are resolved by recognising that the management process is the outcome of a complex of interdependent activities. In particular, it becomes clear that 'management' is not synonymous with 'what managers do'. In the first place, those designated as managers are not necessarily responsible, even collectively, for every part of the management process. Since separation of this process is often incomplete or has been reversed, non-managers may engage in some form of management, if only of themselves. Management is not exclusive to managers. Secondly, individual managers do not perform management as a whole, but activities which form only part of the extended management process. Moreover, managers may also perform technical functions relating to the work process, and, like any other employees, may engage in various non-work activities whilst 'at' work. As a result, there are wide variations in the type of work and activities associated with managerial jobs.

Recognising that managerial work is part of the management process as a whole means recognising that it is part of a contested process of managing other people. Managerial work is inherently problematic because it is part of a management process which is itself problematic. This problematic character is reflected in the common features of managerial work. (The argument thus far is summarised in Figure 1.1.)

MANAGERS AND MANAGERIAL WORK

Research evidence points to both commonalities and variations in the content and form of managerial work.

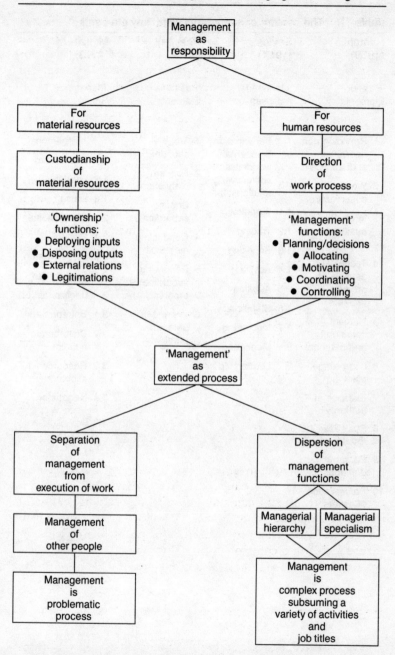

Figure 1.1 Developments in the management process

Table 1.1   The content of managerial work: key elements

Hemphill (1959)	Sayles (1964)	Pheysey (1972)	Mintzberg (1973)
'Position Elements'	'Managerial Activities'	'Position Elements'	'Managerial Roles'
1 Providing non-operational staff service	1 Participation in external workflows via following relationships:	1 Trouble-shooting	1 Interpersonal:
2 Work supervision		2 Forward planning	1.1 Figurehead
			1.2 Leader
3 Internal business control	1.1 Workflow	3 Briefing subordinates	1.3 Liaison
	1.2 Trading	4 Conducting meetings	2 Informational:
	1.3 Servicing		2.1 Monitor
4 Technical aspects of product markets	1.4 Advising	5 Reviewing subordinates' progress	2.2 Disseminator
	1.5 Auditing		2.3 Spokesman
	1.6 Stabilising	6 Interest in personal problems	3 Decisional:
5 Human, community and personal	1.7 Innovating		3.1 Entrepreneur
	2 Monitoring		3.2 Disturbance handler
6 Long-range planning	3 Leadership		3.3 Resource allocator
7 Exercise of authority			3.4 Negotiator
8 Business reputation			
9 Personal demands			
10 Preservation of assets			

Table 1.1 cont

Tornow and Pinto (1976)	Stewart (1967, 1976, 1980, 1982)	Kotter (1982)	Luthans *et al.* (1988)
'Management Position Descriptors'	'Recurrent Managerial Activities'	'Similarities in Managerial Behaviour'	'Categories of Managerial Activity'
1 Product, marketing, financial strategy	1 Liaison/ contacts	1 Setting agendas (planning)	1 Traditional management:
2 Coordination of organisational units and personnel	2 Maintenance of work	2 Network building (contacts)	1.1 Planning
3 Internal business control	3 Innovation/ risk taking	3 Network-using (persuading, getting things done)	1.2 Decisions
4 Product and service responsibility	4 Setting job boundaries	4 Implementing agendas (decision-making)	1.3 Controlling
5 Public and customer relations			2 Routine communication:
6 Advanced consulting			2.1 Exchanging information
7 Autonomy of action			2.2 Paperwork
8 Approval of financial commitments			3 Human resource management:
9 Staff service			3.1 Motivation
10 Supervision			3.2 Discipline
11 Complexity and stress			3.3 Managing conflict
12 Advanced financial responsibility			3.4 Staffing
13 Broad personnel responsibility			3.5 Training
			4 Networking:
			4.1 Interacting with outsiders
			4.2 Socialising/ politicking

The Content of Managerial Work

Eight researchers have identified elements which together form the content of managerial work, even if different managerial jobs display these in different combination (see Table 1.1.). Certainly, these lists display some discontinuity, even inconsistency, both internally and from one to another, an inconsistency which reflects different concerns and, to some extent, different research methods. However, amid this diversity, certain common findings recur. The first is that managers engage in specialist technical work, as well as general managerial or administrative work. Secondly, managerial work is sufficiently ill-defined that part of it is concerned with negotiating its own boundaries. Lastly, however, within these fluid boundaries, the following work elements are common, if not universal:

1 Acting as figurehead or nominal leader of a work unit, representing it and acting as point of contact.
2 Monitoring and disseminating information flowing into and out of the work unit.
3 Negotiating with subordinates, superiors, other managers, other work units and outsiders.
4 Monitoring workflow by handling disturbances, solving problems and dealing with disruptions.
5 Allocating resources in the form of money, materials and people.
6 Directing and controlling the work of subordinates.
7 Forming contacts and liaising with others.
8 Innovating, by looking for new objectives and methods to improve the work of the unit.
9 Planning what is to be done and when.

Two things are evident from this research evidence. Firstly, among the constituents of managerial work, there is an important distinction between tasks, which represent expected or intended outcomes, and observable activities which constitute performance of the job, even if in practice these are difficult to disentangle. Tasks, such as those evident in Mintzberg's (1973) 'interpersonal' and 'decisional' roles, Kotter's (1982) 'network building' and 'agenda setting', Stewart's (1982) 'demands' and 'constraints' and in Luthans *et al.*'s (1988) 'traditional management' and 'human resource management', are essentially those aspects of managerial work which flow from the individual manager's function in and contribution to the overall management process. Activities, on the other hand, reflect how managers undertake these tasks and are, as Stewart (1976; Stewart *et al.* 1980; 1982) clearly demonstrates, amenable to choices of both content and methods which are common to all managerial jobs. Thus although the manager's work is part of the management process, it is not a microcosm of that process.

Secondly, the common task elements of managerial work are the practical manifestations of the more abstract functions of planning/decision-making, allocating, motivating, coordinating and controlling. What the research evidence does is to fill in much of the fine detail about what those general functions entail and provides fresh insights and subtleties. None the less, the existence of these common task elements, and not others, is attributable to the functions which flow from the responsibility, shared by all managers, for some work process and, crucially, the efforts of the people who form part of it.

The Form of Managerial Work

Research evidence also sheds light on how managers work, in a number of respects. Stewart (1976) traces the duration, time span, recurrence, unexpectedness and sources of initiation of managerial work and detects four distinct patterns, or rhythms: 'system maintenance', 'system administration', 'project' and 'mixed'. More generally, there is a lot of evidence on how managers allocate their time. The central findings are that managers spend little time on strategic matters or reflective planning, focus on concrete day-to-day problems, are subject to constant interruptions, hold short face-to-face meetings, commute rapidly between activities and react to rather than initiate events. For some (Luthans and Davis, 1980) this implies inefficiency and superficiality. For others, however, this form of work reflects the 'juggling' necessary for dealing with complex information, ambiguous problems and a large network of contacts (Kotter, 1982).

Studies of managers' interactions with others show that a great deal of managers' time is spent imparting or receiving information, predominantly through face-to-face interaction, and that much of this communication is lateral, with other managers, involves responding to the requests of others, and is informal in character.

Some studies, often those employing participant observation, highlight the informal, unofficial character of managers' activites. In particular, they point to the pervasiveness of 'political activity': developing and maintaining networks, instrumental socialising and the formation of 'cliques' of 'cabals' to secure or defend resources. Linked to this is the interpretation and negotiation of corporate policy and rules, as well as the boundaries and responsibilities of the managerial job in order to shift the 'balance of initiatives' (Sayles, 1964), alter 'personal domain' (stewart, 1980) and off-load time-consuming, low status activities (Dalton, 1959). Others, indeed, point to the way in which managers actively define or 'enact' the nature of their work and its context by managing the meanings of 'problems', 'procedures' and 'tasks' (Silverman and Jones, 1976; Golding, 1980; Gowler and Legge, 1983).

Taken together, this evidence shows that managerial work is indeed 'frenetic' in that it is:

1   Fragmented, comprising short, interrupted activites.
2   Reactive, responding to, rather than initiating, events and requests.
3   Exigent, concerned with *ad hoc*, day-to-day matters.
4   Negotiated, involving bargaining over the boundaries, content and style of work.
5   Eclectic, with rapid commuting between activites.
6   Thinking-in action, with decisions and plans developed whilst engaged in other activities.
7   Interactive, involving a high level of face-to-face communication.
8   Concrete, concerned with practicalities rather than abstractions.

Again, these characteristics are not accidental but flow necessarily from the location of managerial work within the management function as a whole and from managers' common responsibility for the work process and the efforts of those who are part of it. Securing this effort is problematic: it has to be made to happen, in the face of unintended responses or resistance. The 'frenetic' character of managerial work reflects this, as does more direct evidence of pressure and conflict (Dalton, 1959;

Fletcher, 1973; Kotter, 1982).

Overall, therefore, the commonalities of content and form in managerial work reflect the separation and problematic character of management. Variations in managerial work reflect the dispersion of management functions across a diversity of managerial jobs. These variations have been extensively documented. Managerial jobs are shown to vary in terms of the balance between different elements of work content, types of contact patterns, the amount of interaction and the extent of choice. These variations are linked with managerial specialism, function, level in the hierarchy, organisational size and structure, industry, form of ownership and national culture. (We examine these variations again, particularly with reference to form of organisation, in Chapter 9.) The important point here is that this variation in managerial work indicates the dispersion of the management function as a whole, and its horizontal and vertical divisions. In other words there are management divisions of labour in which managers themselves are managed.

What we have seen in this chapter, therefore, is that, in general, management entails taking responsibility for a work process, from which flow the processes of planning/decision-making, allocation, motivation, coordination and control. This responsibility and its subsidiary processes have become separated from the execution of work and fused with ownership functions, such that an extended 'management' is carried out as a distinct function, dispersed among different managerial jobs. Consequently, management is the inherently problematic process of managing others, whether workers or other managers. In the next chapter, we consider power and influence, the means whereby this problematic process is attempted.

FURTHER READING

Texts which trace historical developments in management include: Pollard (1968), Braverman (1974), Chandler (1977), Edwards (1979), Chandler and Daems (1980), Hill (1981), Littler (1982), Storey (1983), Burawoy (1985), Anthony (1986), Reed (1989) and Clegg (1990). Good reviews are to be found in Clegg and Dunkerley (1980) and Thompson and McHugh (1990).

Critical reviews of the research evidence on managerial work are to be found in Mintzberg (1973) and, more recently, Hales (1986). In addition to the studies cited in the text of the chapter, there is a host of studies which bear upon specific aspects of managerial work. These include: Carlson (1951), Burns (1957), Dalton (1959), Copeman *et al.* (1963), Brewer and Tomlinson (1964), Dubin and Spray (1964), Kelly (1964), Horne and Lupton (1965), Child and Ellis (1973), Fletcher (1973), Silverman and Jones (1976), Golding (1979, 1980), Weick (1979), Luthans and Davis (1980), Gowler and Legge (1983), Lawrence (1984), Martinko and Gardner (1984), Whiteley (1985) and Hales (1987b).

Chapter 2

Power, authority and influence

Since management is, *inter alia*, the management of other people, so a critical, if not defining, management task is that of influencing or modifying the behaviour of others. Influence, in turn, presupposes some leverage or means for attempting to ensure that those being managed respond as intended. That leverage is power, and it is with types of power, the forms of influence to which they give rise and the kinds of responses which they typically evoke, that this chapter is concerned. We begin by offering definitions of power and influence and then go on to examine, in the context of management: firstly, characteristics, types and dimensions of power resources; secondly, the modes of influence corresponding to these; and thirdly, typical responses to different types of power and influence in terms of perceptions, evaluations and behaviour. This leads to discussion of the issue of legitimacy and the relationship between power and authority. These ideas are then synthesised into a model showing how particular combinations of power, influence, degrees of legitimacy and response typically cohere.

The model is employed to examine two sets of issues surrounding managerial power: firstly, technical questions relating to a manager's power over others, whether subordinates, peers or superordinates, and secondly, the political issue of how managerial authority may be established so that managers manage by consent. We consider the problematic nature of managerial power and authority and the attempts to resolve this through new forms of power and legitimacy and the increasing depersonalisation of power. This leads us to recognise that the management of work is now primarily attempted through organisation and that different organisational forms represent different configurations of institutionalised power and influence. Therefore, although we begin the analysis of power from the point of view of the individual manager, we conclude that an adequate analysis of management processes must consider institutionalised power.

THE CONCEPT OF POWER

Any attempt to distil a comprehensive and generally accepted conceptualisation, let alone definition, of power from existing writings on the topic is a difficult task. Diverse and often conflicting conceptualisations are offered by the major theorists. Most striking is the lack of agreement on how to distinguish among 'power', 'influence' and 'authority'. For some, power is essentially a resource or capacity, whilst for others it is something exercised and, therefore, indistinguishable from influence.

The view of power as a capacity is itself beset with debate about firstly, where that capacity may be located – in individual persons, social positions, social relationships or social structures – and, secondly, whether it is a generalised capacity or a specific capacity to prevail over others. Where power is seen as a process, there is debate about whether it is manifested only in positive actions or through negative/preventative action or non-action, and whether it must be recognised only when it is effective.

Influence is either seen as synonymous with power or as a process, flowing from power resources. As a process, it is viewed, variously, as generalised or specific, intended or unintended.

As for authority, this is variously defined as the formally constituted power of position, legitimate power in general, power which is inferred as legitimate, since commands are obeyed, or power legitimated by the pursuit of collective goals.

Our discussion here follows Bacharach and Lawler (1980) and Handy (1981) in distinguishing between power as a resource, and influence as the process of attempting to modify others' behaviour through the mobilisation of power resources. This permits the important distinction to be made, in the context of management, between the way in which people are managed (i.e. how behaviour is influenced) and what makes that 'management' possible.

A failure to maintain this distinction is characteristic of the classic 'A–B' models of power which Lukes (1974) has termed, respectively, 'one-', 'two-' and 'three-dimensional'. The one-dimensional model (Dahl, 1957) asserts that A has power over B to the extent that A is able to get B to behave in a way that B would otherwise not have done. That is to say, power exists where A actively and wittingly modifies B's behaviour, despite B's opposition. The two-dimensional model (e.g. Bacharach and Baratz, 1962) asserts that power additionally exists where A is able to prevent B from behaving in certain ways. Lukes' (1974) three-dimensional model asserts that A additionally has power over B to the extent that A can influence B's wants and, thereby, B's behaviour. A's power resides in B's failure to recognise that their actions are in accordance with A's wishes and would be very different if they were not influenced in this way. Much of the debate over the three models revolves around whether power is only activated in situations of conflict, the degree to which it must be manifest in tangible or observable actions and the degree to which it must have a direct impact upon others' behaviour. There are, however, problems common to all three models.

As well as conflating power and influence generally the three models conflate power with successful modification of others' behaviour. The circularity of this is clear. On the one hand, the power of A is inferred from B's response, yet on the other hand, B's response is explained by the existence of power. In this, the use of power is not seen as problematic and the relational aspect of power is ignored since B's response is defined by A's power. B's perceptions and evaluations of A's power are seen as irrelevant or non-existent. This critically ignores the crucial distinction between, on the one hand, power and influence perceived as legitimate and, hence, responded to willingly, and on the other, power and influence perceived as non-legitimate and, hence, responded to expediently and grudgingly. The second weakness of the A–B models of power is their use of the abstract entities, 'A' and 'B'. What is unclear is whether A and B are persons or occupants of particular positions. Thus, the models fail to clarify the distinction between positional power (the access to power resources enjoyed by A by virtue of holding a particular position) and personal power (A's personal possession of power resources). A third limitation of A–B models of power is that in focusing entirely upon power as 'power over', or the advantage of one party over another, they exclude other, and important senses of the term 'power'.

To summarise, there are important distinctions between power as a resource, influence as a process and behavioural response to these. Distinguishing between potential power and its actual exercise has implications for the manner in which influence is attempted. Furthermore, forms of power and influence and, crucially, the way in which they are perceived, are likely to induce different kinds of behavioural outcome.

POWER RESOURCES

One strength of the A–B model of power is that it draws attention to the fact that 'power over' is essentially relational and relative: A has power with respect to B. In that sense, power relations are always asymmetrical. A has 'more power' than B if A possesses or has access to more of certain kinds of resources than B. Moreover, these resources must be things which B wants. Therefore, a power relation is a dependency relationship, and it is this which affords A the leverage with which to influence B's behaviour. Power resources may be defined, therefore, as those things which bestow the means whereby the behaviour of others may be influenced and power relations arise out of the uneven distribution of these resources.

To create dependency through unequal possession, power resources must possess three key formal properties: scarcity, importance (or salience) and non-substitutability. Things become power resources when they are only available to some, when they are desired because they satisfy certain wants and when there are no alternatives available. Therefore, a power relationship exists where scarce and desired resources can only be obtained through the particular relationship. Furthermore, it is the perception of, rather than actual, scarcity, importance and non-substitutability of the resource, by the relatively powerless, which is important.

There are a number of well-known typologies of power resources. These, too, exhibit a number of confusions. This is particularly true of French and Raven's (1959) classic typology. They identify and describe the different bases of social power as:

1 Coercive power, where the individual conforms to avoid negative consequences or punishment.
2 Reward power, where the individual conforms to receive certain benefits.
3 Referent power, where the individual conforms because they are attracted to and identify with another.
4 Expert power, where the individual conforms because they believe the other to have superior knowledge or skill.
5 Legitimate power, where the individual conforms because they accept the right of another to have power over them.

To these they later added (Raven, 1965):

6 Informational power, where the individual conforms in order to receive desired information.

Five main criticisms can be levelled at this typology. Firstly, though it claims to identify types of power base, it focuses upon reasons for conformity; that is, why individuals respond to attempts to influence them. But, as we argue later, responses to attempted influence are not simply a function of the type of power held by the influencer, but also of the perceptions and evaluations of the influenced. Secondly, the typology confuses conformity for extrinsic reasons (i.e. to obtain, or avoid, what the power holder has – rewards, information, punishment) and conformity for intrinsic reasons (i.e. because of what the power-holder is – expert, legitimate or personally attractive). The distinction between 'expert' and 'informational' power is hard to sustain, since one of the things which an expert has to offer is information. Thirdly, punishment and benefit are better regarded as different ways of employing any power resource (i.e. by giving or taking away desirable or undesirable things) rather than as separate power resources in their own right. 'Coercion' and 'reward' are better seen as forms of influence corresponding to physical and economic power respectively. Fourthly, legitimacy is more appropriately regarded as a dimension of all forms of power, rather than as a distinct type. Lastly, French and Raven give no indication of where power resources reside, whether in persons or positions.

In contrast, we distinguish four basic kinds of power resources:

1 Physical power resources, or the capacity to harm or restrict the actions of another, which others desire to avoid.
2 Economic power resources, or scarce and desired objects or the means of acquiring them (i.e. money).
3 Knowledge power resources, or scarce and desired knowledge and skill in the context of work. This knowledge and skill may be either:
   (a) administrative, concerned with how an institution operates; or
   (b) technical, concerned with how tasks are performed.
4 Normative power resources, or scarce and desired ideas, beliefs, values or affects.

Each of these power resources are, to varying degrees, available to managers – either as personal possessions or, more especially, by virtue of their position as managers. This distinction, between the personal and positional dimensions of managerial power resources arises from the growth of work organisations and concomitant dispersion of management and ownership functions which we noted earlier. Thus, to a large extent, managerial power is a function of the access which managerial positions afford to the economic, knowledge and normative resources of an organisation.

Two further refinements to the personal and positional power of managers can be made. Firstly, there is the distinction between ascribed and achieved elements of personal power; that is, between those power resources with which the individual is endowed (such as physical strength, inherited wealth, innate talent) and those which the individual has learned or acquired (such as accumulated wealth, knowledge and skill). Secondly, there is the distinction between permanent and contingent positional power; that is, between access to power resources which a position permanently and routinely affords (e.g. control of a budget) and access to power resources which a position occasionally affords (e.g. *ad hoc* acquisition of information). With these distinctions in mind, the personal and positional forms of power resources available to a manager may be adumbrated.

Physical power resources are comparatively rare or little used in modern work organisations. For completeness, however, it may be noted that managers may possess physical power resources by virtue of their own physical strength, or 'presence', or have access to physical power resources (e.g. security personnel) by virtue of their position.

Economic resources are, perhaps, the definitive managerial power resource. In large organisations, personal economic resources, such as individual wealth or income, bestow relatively little power, except in the case of large individual shareholdings. More important are the organisational resources to which managers have access by virtue of their position and control of budgets and assets.

Another important power resource which managers may possess is knowledge, and this may, equally, be of either a personal or positional kind. 'Administrative' knowledge of how an organisation works may be personal, as with individual experience built up over time, or positional, in terms of access to or control over information about the operation and performance of an organisation which the manager's position affords. This information may be available through access to documents (reports, files) or to other people (experts). 'Technical' knowledge of particular work processes may, again, be either personal, in the form of individual expertise and skill acquired through education, training and experience, or positional, in terms of access to or control over technical information, the expertise of others or technology itself which the manager's position affords.

Lastly, normative power resources may be available to managers. On a personal level, managers may hold beliefs and values, espouse ideas or have qualities of character and personality which others find attractive and beguiling. Equally, managers may have access to and control over certain organisational values and ideas or acquire whatever 'aura of office' their position carries. (These forms of power resource, and their personal and positional forms are summarised in Table 2.1.)

MODES OF INFLUENCE

Here, influence is defined as the attempt to modify others' behaviour through either the mobilisation of or reference to power resources. Hence, for each type of power resource, there are corresponding modes of influence.

Influence has a number of alternative formal properties.

Table 2.1 Types of power resource and their personal and positional forms

Power resource	Personal	Positional
Physical	Individual strength/ possession of means of violence	Access to means of violence
Economic	Individual wealth/ income	Access to/disposal of organisational resources
Knowledge 1 Administrative	Individual experience	Access to/control over organisational information
2 Technical	Individual skill/ expertise	Access to/control over technical information and technology
Normative	Individual beliefs, values, ideas/ personal qualities	Access to/control over organisational values, ideas/'aura of office'

Influence may be either overt, where explicit use or reference to power resources is made, or covert, where the existence and possible use of power resources remain implicit. Overt influence divides into that which relies upon the actual mobilisation of power resources, and that which relies upon their provisional (i.e. promised or threatened) use. Thus, each type of power resource has, corresponding to it, an overt (actual), an overt (provisional) and a covert form of influence. It is possible to distinguish between the positive and negative use of power resources to influence, that is, between the provision, the with-drawal or the withholding of resources.

Thus, economic resources are amenable to the following modes of influence: actual provision of monetary rewards (e.g. bonuses, pay increases); actual withdrawal/withholding of monetary rewards (e.g. fines for lateness, dismissal); promised provision of rewards (e.g. future pay increases); threatened withdrawal of rewards (e.g. written warning of dismissal); implied possibility of rewards (e.g. the 'understanding' that pay increases will reflect company performance) and, finally, the implied possibility of withheld rewards (e.g. the 'understanding' that poor performance may bring dismissal).

Whereas economic resources are offered as rewards for being subject to influence, knowledge is used primarily as the justification for being influenced in particular ways. Thus knowledge resources are used to influence through: overt rational persuasion embodied in instructions or rules, which may be of an administrative/procedural kind (e.g. 'record all deliveries in goods received sheet') or a technical kind (e.g. 'drill to 3mm diameter'); provisional suggestion (e.g. 'try it this way'); covert 'persuasion' in the form of unwritten rules and accepted practices ('how things are done here') or negatively, through withholding information (e.g. an absence of instructions on how to complete a particular task).

Use of normative power resources to influence others' behaviour reflects their dual character. Normative power resources in the form of meanings, values or ideologies are used primarily as the justification, rather than reward, for being subject to influence. However, normative power resources in the form of attractiveness of personality or aura of office are offered as forms of affective reward for being subject to influence. Therefore, normative resources are used to influence through: overt moral persuasion in the form of ideologies (e.g. 'for the good of the company') or the offer of affects (e.g. 'to please me'); provisional ideological suggestions (e.g. 'maybe this is the right thing to do') or promises of affects (e.g. 'I may think more highly of you as a result of this') and covert moral persuasion in the form of taken-for-granted ideological assumptions (e.g. 'a free market') or personal obligations (e.g. loyalty to a colleague). Failure to employ normative resources, such as an absence of moral persuasion (e.g. lack of company values) or affects (e.g. an absence of interpersonal bonds at work), may also influence behaviour.

The above analysis of forms of influence is summarised in Table 2.2. Although somewhat convoluted, it does indicate the rich texture of possibilities in the process of influencing others' behaviour. Clearly, some are rare in practice. For example, whilst the positive provision of meanings, in the form of ideas, values, myths, vocabularies and symbolic legitimations of actions, has a clear, and increasingly well-documented place in the manager's armoury of influence, failure to provide such meanings is only a form of 'influence' by default.

Table 2.2 Types of power resource and corresponding modes of influence

	Physical power	Economic power	Knowledge power	Normative power
Overt influence				
Actual/positive	Apply force/restraint	Provision of material rewards	Instruction/persuasion/rules	Provision of meanings (ideologies) and affects/moral persuasion
Actual/negative	Withhold force/restraint	Withhold material rewards	Withhold instruction/absence of rules	Fail to provide ideology or affects
Provisional/positive	Threaten force/restraint	Promise material rewards	Suggestion	Suggest meanings/promise affects
Provisional/negative	(Promise absence of force/restraint)	Threaten to withhold material rewards	(Threaten to withhold information)	Threaten to withhold affects
Covert influence				
Positive	Implied threat of force (menace)	Implied promise of material rewards	Unwritten rules/accepted practices	Taken-for-granted values/moral obligation
Negative	Implied promise of absence of restraint	Implied threat to withhold material rewards	Absence of unwritten rules/accepted practices	Absence of taken-for-granted values or moral obligations

It is also possible to distinguish among the different objects of the process of influence: that is, who and what are influenced. Briefly, managers may seek to influence subordinates, peers/ other managers, senior managers and those outside the workplace. Furthermore, managers may attempt to induce positive behaviours (e.g. higher productivity), prevent certain behaviours (e.g. poor time-keeping), overcome resistance to their own actions (e.g. unwillingness to adopt new shift patterns), change attitudes and dispositions, hence influencing behaviour indirectly (e.g. instilling greater concern with product or service quality) or, lastly, alter the outcomes of others' behaviour, or exercise 'fate control' (e.g. manipulating the agenda of workers' consultative councils in order to lessen the impact of participation).

Thus, from a range of possible modes of influence, managers have, in fact, a more limited range of appropriate modes of influence. Influence is 'appropriate' in three respects. Firstly, it corresponds to the power resources available to managers. Influence without the leverage of power is unlikely to work: managers cannot promise pay increases if their companies are bankrupt or attempt, plausibly, to specify ways of working if they do not have the knowledge to do so. Secondly, a mode of influence is appropriate if it utilises a power resource in a way consistent with its nature. 'Promises' of non-restraint, or 'threats' of a withdrawal of affects are at odds with the nature of the power resource. Lastly, modes of influence must be appropriate to intended outcomes. What managers seek to bring about, in terms of the behaviour or disposition of others, determines how they seek to do so. This is because of the way different forms of power and influence are perceived and evaluated by those subject to them.

RESPONSES TO POWER AND INFLUENCE

Since power is relational, responses to the use of power and influence do not simply flow as predictable, inevitable consequences. Thus, force does not necessarily bring submission, rewards do not always entice, rationality may not persuade and moral exhortation may fail to inspire. Rather, the perceptions and evaluations of those subject to influence based on imbalances of power shape their behavioural responses to such attempts, responses which are underpinned by whatever countervailing power resources are available. Whether the attempt to use power in order to influence behaviour succeeds depends upon the reactions of those over whom it is being exerted.

As for perception, the key issue is whether power and influence are recognised by those subject to it, which in turn reflects the visibility of imbalances in power resources and how explicitly influence is exercised. The more obvious the attempt to influence and the more evident is the disparity in power resources underpinning it, the more a relationship is recognised as an unequal power relationship by those subject to it. This is important in two ways. Firstly, recognition is a prerequisite for any subsequent evaluation of power and influence. Secondly, where this recognition does not occur or is distorted, power and influence may, paradoxically, be at their most effective because they involve the unobtrusive manipulation of others. This is more likely with covert forms of influence such as implied force, agreed rewards, unwritten rules and accepted obligations.

Once power and influence are recognised as present, those subject to them evaluate, or form judgements, about them. Crucially, this entails judgement about the propriety, or legitimacy, of both the process of influence and the power resources upon which it is based. Those subject to power and influence ask, in effect, whether it is proper that others seek to influence their actions, whether they accept what they are required to do, whether it is proper that others possess or control more resources and whether they should use these to exert influence. The more these questions are answered in the affirmative, the more are power and influence deemed to be legitimate.

'Authority' may now be defined as the possession of power resources and attempts at influence which are deemed legitimate and, hence, acceptable by those subject to them. In contrast, 'naked power' is where power resources and influence are deemed non-legitimate. In principle, every type of power resource and corresponding mode of influence may be regarded as either legitimate or non-legitimate. In practice, however, physical power and influence by force or threats are almost always deemed non-legitimate by those subject to it (though not necessarily by third parties), whilst normative power and influence by moral persuasion are almost always deemed legitimate (except, perhaps, for a situation of helpless fatal attraction to a set of ideas or a person). In contrast, economic and knowledge power may be deemed either to be fairly held and acceptably used and, hence, legitimate, or the result of privileged possession or access, and hence regarded as non-legitimate.

What determines whether economic and knowledge power are judged as legitimate or not is a function of the attitudes, values and orientations of those subject to them, which are, in turn shaped by many social forces. What may be decisive, however, is the effect of competing ideologies of power. Diffuse attitudes are given sharper focus by the existence of coherent ideas offering either justification for or critique of the prevailing distribution of economic and knowledge resources. The extent to which economic and knowledge power are seen as legitimate, therefore, reflects the balance between competing sets of ideas. This balance in turn, reflects the distribution of normative power resources. The legitimacy of economic and knowledge power is underpinned (or undermined) by the balance of normative power. We return to this point later.

The importance of different evaluations of the legitimacy of power and influence lies in their impact upon behavioural responses. There is considerable debate about whether power and influence are 'real' only if they are accepted by those over whom they are exercised, or whether the hard reality of power is quite independent of its evaluation. The debate is made more complex by a tendency to focus upon different issues. Firstly, there are different conceptions of 'effective' influence, particularly in terms of what kinds of behaviour are intended and how long those behaviours endure. For example, against the view that physical coercion (or its threat) is effective regardless of what those subject to it think of it, it is often argued that coercion merely evokes contingent 'compliance', in the sense of carrying out no more than is nominally required only as long as the threat of coercion remains. Thus, the extent to which power 'must' be legitimate depends upon the nature and duration of its intended effects. Secondly, different kinds of 'power setting' are cited to argue the importance of legitimate power. Yet, clearly, the need for legitimacy in a high-security prison, where the aim is, predominantly, restraint, is very different from a religious order where nothing less than positive moral attachment will suffice. Between these two extremes, work organisations present a more complex and problematic setting.

The relationship between types of power and forms of

response in different settings is traced by a number of writers. Etzioni (1961) distinguishes among alienative, calculative and moral involvement as responses to coercive, remunerative and normative power, respectively; Handy (1981) discerns compliance, identification and internalisation as responses to power and influence, and Fox (1985) distinguishes between compliance and consent. A model of responses to power and influence may be pieced together by synthesising these analyses (see Figure 2.1).

In this model, responses to power and influence lie along a continuum from positive to negative. Positive responses are consistent with the intentions of those exercising influence, and may be regarded as degrees of compliance. Following Etzioni (1961), however, it is argued that such compliance is qualified by different degrees of cognitive involvement, or the extent to which the individual not only behaves compliantly, but also feels positively about doing so. At one end of the continuum is behavioural compliance coupled with a positive cognitive or emotional attachment to that behaviour. This response may be termed 'commitment', or behaviour imbued with feelings of attachment and self-identification and with the energy and persistence associated with that. At the other end of the continuum is what may be termed 'alienative compliance', where behaviour is broadly consistent with the intention of those exercising influence, but where there is negative involvement in that the individual neither believes in nor feels positively about their behaviour, makes no investment of the self in it and seizes any available opportunity not to comply.

In between is a more contingent form of response which may be termed 'calculation', where those subject to influence weigh up, according to a rational calculus, the costs and benefits of compliance. The response is contingent in that the outcome is indeterminate. It may be either cognitive commitment, where the individual is persuaded that compliance is correct and has, therefore, some cognitive commitment to it, or instrumental compliance, where the individual sees only external advantages in complying. Whilst there is cognitive commitment in the first of these, in the second there is not. In neither response is there any affective commitment.

All the above represent forms of compliance, differing in how compliance is offered, which, in turn, reflects the extent to

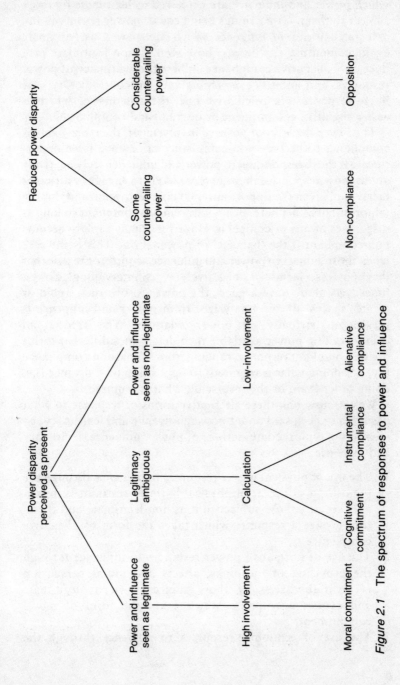

Figure 2.1 The spectrum of responses to power and influence

which power and influence are perceived as legitimate by those subject to them. Other things being equal, power resources and associated forms of influence which are viewed as legitimate evoke commitment, whereas those seen as non-legitimate produce only alienative compliance. Where the legitimacy of power resources and influence is ambiguous or contradictory, the likely response is a calculative one, the outcome of which is either cognitive commitment or instrumental compliance.

The lower the level of positive involvement, the more likely is compliance to become non-compliance at any available opportunity. If those responding to power and influence feel negatively about those responses, they are more likely to engage in different behaviour, given the opportunity. Of course, 'opportunity' is the important qualifier here. Behaviour remains compliant so long as disparities of power compel it. However, it may rapidly become non-compliant if the 'balance' of power shifts. This is the case when those subject to power and influence acquire, or realise that they possess, forms of 'negative' or 'countervailing' power. Indeed, as many have argued, the power to obstruct, avoid or create 'spaces' of autonomy free from power and influence is present in virtually all power relations. The amount of countervailing power available then determines different forms of non-compliant response, ranging from simple non-compliance (i.e. not doing what is required) to opposition or resistance (i.e. doing other than, or the reverse of, what is required).

We can now link these alternative forms of response to what has already been said about power, influence and legitimacy, by identifying typical combinations of power, influence, legitimacy and response.

1 The use of physical power resources to influence through the imposition or threat of physical harm or restraint is invariably seen by those subject to it as non-legitimate and therefore evokes a response which takes the form of alienative compliance.

2 The use of normative power resources to influence through the provision of meanings, affects and moral persuasion is invariably seen by those subject to it as legitimate and evokes a response which takes the form of moral commitment.

3 The use of economic resources to influence through the

provision or promise of material rewards (or the threat of their withdrawal) may be seen as either legitimate or non-legitimate. It evokes a calculative response, which produces instrumental compliance (i.e. compliant behaviour contingent upon the continued perception that the benefits of that behaviour outweigh the costs).

4   The use of knowledge resources to influence through rational persuasion, rules and procedures may also be seen as either legitimate or non-legitimate. This, too, evokes a calculative response which produces a response in terms of rational commitment (i.e. compliant behaviour contingent upon the continued perception that the required behaviour is reasonable).

These links between power, influence, legitimacy and response are summarised in the model in Table 2.3. As well as providing a synthesising theoretical framework, the model may be used to address some of the issues relating to managerial power and influence.

THE POWER AND INFLUENCE OF MANAGERS: TECHNICAL ISSUES

The main technical questions relating to managerial power and influence concern the way in which particular managers may influence their subordinates, peers (other managers) or superordinates and the issue of group or departmental power within an organisation.

An individual manager seeking to manage others by exercising influence over their actions, would need to consider:

1   the power resources available to them;
2   whether those resources are personal or positional and if positional, how access to them is secured;
3   the modes of influence available to them;
4   whether forms of influence must be made explicit or can remain implicit;
5   how these different forms of power and influence are likely to be perceived and, in particular, whether they will be seen as legitimate or non-legitimate;
6   and, therefore, what the responses to different attempts at influence are likely to be.

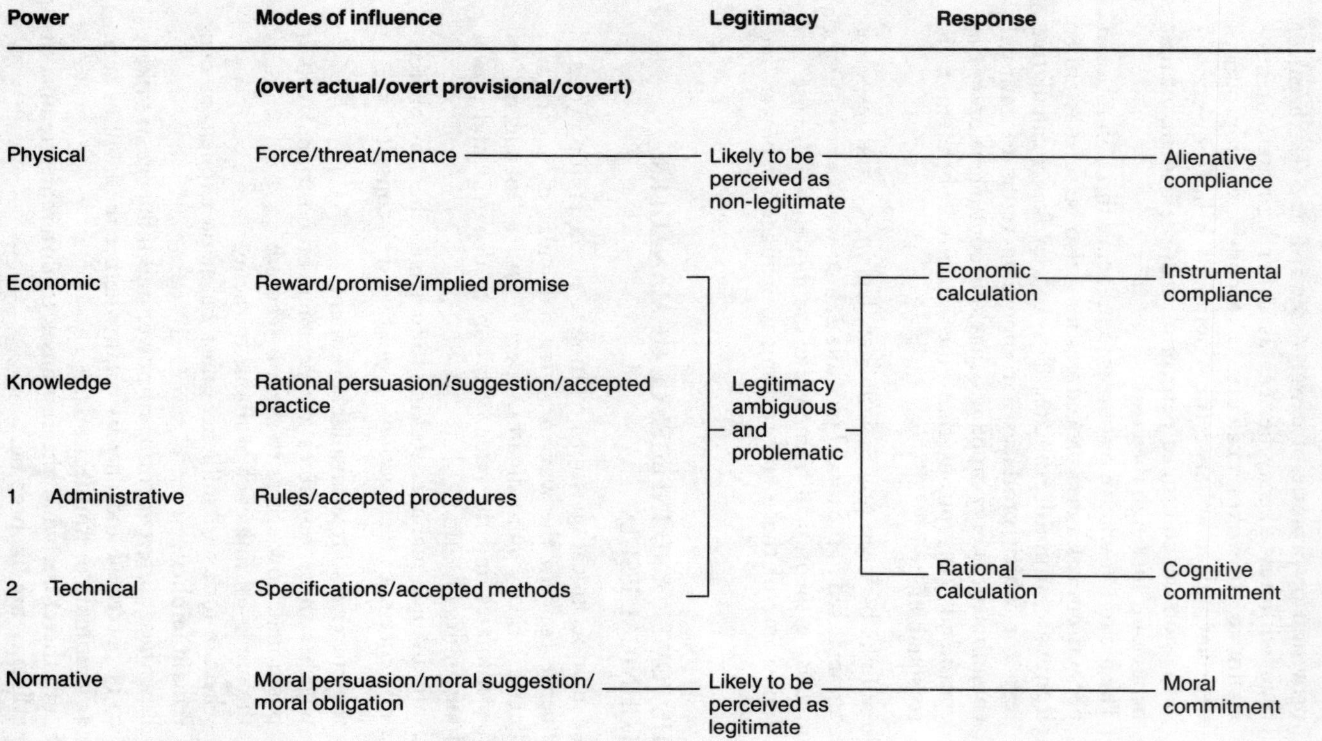

Power	Modes of influence	Legitimacy	Response
	(overt actual/overt provisional/covert)		
Physical	Force/threat/menace	Likely to be perceived as non-legitimate	Alienative compliance
Economic	Reward/promise/implied promise		Instrumental compliance
		Legitimacy ambiguous and problematic	Economic calculation
Knowledge			Rational calculation
1 Administrative	Rational persuasion/suggestion/accepted practice Rules/accepted procedures		Cognitive commitment
2 Technical	Specifications/accepted methods		
Normative	Moral persuasion/moral suggestion/ moral obligation	Likely to be perceived as legitimate	Moral commitment

Figure 2.2 Power, influence, legitimacy and response: a model

On the basis of answers to these questions, the manager may form a judgement about the most effective form of influence at their disposal, in terms of what is most likely to produce the intended effect.

Individual managers also need to consider their power in terms of its 'domain' or 'extensiveness', the number and nature of those over whom influence may be exercised; in terms of its 'scope' or 'comprehensiveness', the number of actions or issues over which influence may be exercised; and in terms of its 'weight' or 'intensiveness', the degree of power and influence exercised over a given domain and scope (Kaplan, 1964; Wrong, 1979).

To a large extent, answers to these questions are specific to individual circumstances. Research evidence shows that different managerial jobs provide access to different types of power resource and different modes of influence in different settings or over different issues. For example, different types of power are effective under different conditions (Shetty, 1978), the importance of personal and positional power varies by context (Peabody, 1970), different managerial jobs have access to different types of domain and scope of power and influence (Stewart, 1976; Kotter, 1982), the power and influence of similar managerial jobs may vary across different spheres of organisational activity and different issues (Henning and Moseley, 1980; Stewart et al., 1982) and disparities of power vary among organisations (Tannenbaum, 1968).

However, there is also evidence of some common features of managerial power, both vertical and horizontal. Firstly, evidence confirms our model of different power resources available to managers. Although physical force or threat is rarely used by managers, there is evidence of its use in earlier stages of industrialisation (Thompson, 1968; Burawoy, 1985), in 'peripheral' industries within advanced industrial societies (Roy, 1980) or in the work organisations of totalitarian societies (Etzioni, 1961). Access to and control over economic resources is, however, more typically the basis of managerial power. As the agents of the legal owners of business organisations, or part-owners themselves, managers are 'empowered' to manage by having delegated control over the economic resources of the organisation. This may be translated into influence in the form of the provision or promise of economic rewards, or the actual or threatened withdrawal of these rewards through dismissal or redundancy. Managers also possess knowledge power, either in the form of personal technical knowledge or skill acquired through education, training and experience, or through the access to information and technology afforded by their position. This gives them the means to influence behaviour by specifying, through commands, rules, technical procedures or suggestions, how something should be done or why certain actions are necessary. The 'monopolisation' of knowledge about work and organisational processes by managers is extensively, if controversially, documented (Braverman, 1974; Hales, 1980; Wood, 1983). Finally, some managers derive power from their personal charisma and charm or beliefs and values which others find attractive. Also, by virtue of their position and identification with their employing organisation, managers have access to organisational beliefs, values and ideologies (Peters and Waterman, 1982; Peters and Austin, 1986).

Evidence on the power of managers over other managers relates to situations where formal disparities of power do not, initially, exist and where, therefore, the power of particular managers or departments emerges informally out of interactions. A constant theme runs through the diversity of evidence: the creation of dependency relationships. Kotter (1977, 1985) suggests that managers may create dependency in others by building a reputation as an expert; by fostering others' identification with them; and by creating obligations by doing favours and fostering others' beliefs that they are dependent. In terms of our model, these represent, respectively: the creation of knowledge power; the development of personal normative power (in the form of charisma and moral obligation); and the opportunistic use of position to acquire knowledge or economic power resources. This emphasis on knowledge or expertise as the key to the creation of dependency relationships between managers is echoed in evidence which shows power and influence flowing to those with particular, scarce skills (Dalton, 1959; Crozier, 1964), those prepared to deal with risks, problems and indeterminacies (Kanter, 1977; Legge, 1978; McCall, 1979), those able to create a belief in their ability to deal with indeterminate problems (Johnson, 1977; Boreham, 1983) and those controlling information by virtue of their position (Pettigrew, 1973).

The creation of dependency is also cited as a basis for departmental power (Hickson *et al.*, 1971). Here, power reflects the extent to which departments control the 'strategic contingencies' of others by playing a central and non-substitutable role in reducing uncertainties (for example, by supplying important information, assistance or materials). Although different studies identify different departments as powerful – such as sales (Perrow, 1970) or production (Hinings *et al.*, 1974) – dealing with uncertainty and the creation of resource dependency are offered as key explanations of this.

To view managerial or departmental power as a purely technical question, however, is to ignore the important political dimension of that power. In particular, it implies that acquiring power and exercising influence by creating dependency is an unambiguous and uncontested process: unambiguous in the sense that there is agreement on what constitutes 'uncertainty' and 'scarce resources', and uncontested in the sense that the responses to power and influence are those of acceptance and compliance. Neither of these assumptions is necessarily correct.

THE POWER AND INFLUENCE OF MANAGERS: POLITICAL ISSUES

A key political issue surrounding managerial power is how managers may manage by consent. In terms of our earlier analysis the question resolves into: what forms of managerial power and influence may be established as legitimate and hence are more likely to evoke commitment, rather than compliance? That managers should seek to manage by consent rather than coercion reflects the central 'managerial problem' of not simply overcoming potential resistance to the direction of effort, but of securing positive commitment to certain kinds of actions. This implies that managerial authority is a critical prerequisite for effective management. Yet such authority is inherently problematic.

As we have seen, the power resources typically available to managers in large work organisations are threefold: firstly, positional economic power in terms of access to and control over organisational resources (in particular, budgets) which may be offered or promised as rewards, or whose withdrawal may be threatened; secondly, personal knowledge power, in terms of information and expertise acquired through training and experience; and thirdly, positional knowledge power in terms of access to organisational information and technology, which may form the basis of instructions and rules. In short, managers' ability to manage inheres in their capacity to reward, dismiss, regulate or suggest.

However, both economic and knowledge power resources, together with their corresponding modes of influence, are problematic in that both their perceived legitimacy and responses to them are unpredictable. This unpredictability arises because the response is mediated by calculation, or, put another way, cooperation is contingent upon the perceived balance between 'inducements' and 'sacrifices' (Barnard, 1938). Thus, those being offered rewards (or threats of their withdrawal) calculate whether the rewards are sufficiently desirable to warrant behaving in ways demanded by the manager. Similarly, those being 'persuaded' by instructions, rules and procedures consider whether what they are being asked to do is the most appropriate form of behaviour and whether the benefits of doing so are sufficiently great. One difficulty is that those making these calculations may come to the conclusion that the rewards and/ or risks are not sufficient to induce them to behave in the ways required. Hence, employees may fail to respond as intended to piece-rates and bonuses (Roy, 1969), fail to be overawed by the prospect of dismissal or challenge managerial rationality (Nichols and Beynon, 1973; Fox, 1985). Furthermore, the terms of the calculation may shift over time as the perceived 'value' of rewards, risks of dismissal or rationality of work procedures fluctuate with rates of inflation, economic expectations, the state of the labour market and the rate and effects of technical change. Rewards, threats or arguments which resonate under certain conditions do not do so under others.

The unpredictability of response to the use of economic and knowledge power resources also arises from their potentially contested legitimacy. Those who do not possess and are denied access to economic resources or knowledge may perceive the control of these resources by others as non-legitimate, 'monopolised' wealth and knowledge (Anthony, 1986; Storey, 1985; Fox, 1985). Where inequalities of status and condition between managers and employees are not only seen to exist but are seen as being unfair, managers are seen as exercising power and influence non-legitimately for the purpose of sustaining these inequalities. In such circumstances, employees define their interests and goals as being divergent from those of managers. Furthermore, managerial expertise is deemed non-legitimate if it is perceived as essentially manipulative; that is, employed for the attainment not of socially neutral goals, but of goals which serve the interests of managers and employers and which reinforce disparities of economic power and the inequalities of condition which flow from them. Hence, the 'rationality' embodied in managerial rules and directives may be called into question by asking 'rationality for whom?' and may be counter-posed by alternative 'modes of rationality' (Clegg, 1979).

Where the ability of managers to offer economic inducements or to persuade is called into question, the response to such inducements or persuasions shifts from rational commitment or calculative compliance towards alienative compliance. That is to say, employees feel themselves coerced, either by superior economic force or by the force of technology and ideas, and comply only insofar as they are unable to challenge these forces.

From a managerial point of view, this creates two serious difficulties. Firstly, grudging compliance with managerial instructions is an increasingly inadequate form of employee behaviour in many modern work organisations. The complexities of work processes, market pressures and, in service industries, the critical impact of employee behaviour on consumers' experience of the product, all combine to require that employees increasingly work 'responsibly' and with concern for, rather than indifference towards, what they are doing. Increasingly, work requires not compliance, but commitment (Fox, 1985; Storey, 1985).

The other serious difficulty is that alienative compliance is a precarious form of behavioural response, since any loss of managerial power relative to employees increases the probability of non-compliance. This probability is made actual by the existence of employees' countervailing power, which, since it is based upon economic and knowledge power resources, renders managerial power even more precarious. In other words, the bases of managerial power are, at the same time, sources of opposition to it; the 'dialectic of control' (Giddens, 1982) reflects the essential interdependence between managers and managed. Whatever power advantage managers may possess, they ultimately rely upon the effort and knowledge of employees to carry out the work.

To be sure, employees often possess only 'negative power', the power to prevent or obstruct rather than initiate (Rus, 1980). This makes it no less real. Economic countervailing power mainly resides in the collective capacity to withdraw labour (strike) or to decrease its intensity (withdrawing co-operation, go-slows, overtime bans), a capacity usually predicated upon the existence of trade union organisation. But even in the absence of collective action, individual acts of non-cooperation or sabotage can thwart managerial intentions. Employees also have countervailing knowledge power by virtue of firstly, their own skill or knowledge stemming from experience and proximity to actual work processes and secondly, the opportunity afforded by their requirement to apply and, therefore, interpret, instructions and rules (Mechanic, 1962).

The mere existence of these forms of countervailing power does not necessarily mean that employees engage in permanent, sustained opposition to managers whenever managerial legitimacy is questioned. Prevailing ideologies may be sufficiently strong or hegemonic as to make existing systems of economic power and related definitions of rationality appear natural, inevitable and immutable. The resulting 'broad acquiescence' to management by employees, stemming from an assumption that fundamental changes in the distribution of power are neither feasible nor desirable, may however be accompanied by 'detailed recalcitrance' on specific issues (Fox, 1985). Employees may not challenge the idea that work must be managed, nor that this is the manager's function, yet may challenge specific managerial attempts to direct work and behaviour.

Therefore, the types of power and influence to which managers have access do not automatically bestow authority. Yet the need for such authority in order to, at the least, prevent non-compliance and opposition and, at best, generate commitment, is evident. How, then, may managerial authority be established? In answering this question, it is important to distinguish between attempts that have been made to establish managerial authority, and arguments about how such authority should be established.

THE SEARCH FOR MANAGERIAL AUTHORITY: NEW SOURCES OF POWER AND LEGITIMACY

Historically, managers have sought to build authority in two ways: firstly, by looking for alternative sources of power, which are more likely to be perceived as legitimate, and secondly, by seeking to make power relationships and the process of influence more depersonalised and obscured. In particular, managers have sought to supplement economic and knowledge power with normative power and to augment influence through reward and persuasion by personal appeal or moral exhortation. This attempt takes a number of forms. Firstly, it is always open to individual managers to develop and exploit their personal charisma or beliefs. This, however, is not available to all, and because it is specific to particular individuals it cannot form the basis of a system of managerial authority. Secondly, attempts may be made to develop and exploit the 'aura' of the position of manager. To a large extent, however, this aura has become diluted precisely because of the dispersion of the management function and the proliferation of managerial jobs. Lastly, and more significantly, there is the attempt to articulate broader ideas and values which offer various moral justifications for why work is organised as it is, and which may be referred to as 'ideologies of management'.

Such ideologies usually incorporate two components: firstly, a depersonalisation of power and power relationships, and secondly, legitimations of the position and functions of managers. The depersonalisation of power involves shifting the perceived location of power away from particular individuals or social positions and towards a more distant third party outside the manager–subordinate relationship. Work is portrayed as subject not to the dictates of managers, but of broader imperatives which impinge upon managers and subordinates alike. The manager is, therefore, cast in the role of carrier or mouthpiece of these broader imperatives. It is possible to identify three such ideologies, each an attempt to depersonalise power resources and to offer a particular portrayal of the managerial role.

Firstly, economic power is depersonalised by reference to the imperatives of the market in terms of competition between companies (or, more recently, between nation states) and consumer requirements. Economic efficiency and effectiveness become the justification for particular ways of managing work and the manager is cast in the role of the bearer of market logic and economic rationality within the organisation. Secondly, knowledge power is depersonalised by reference to the imperatives of science and technology. Technical efficiency, not monopolised knowledge, is the justification for how work is managed, and the manager is cast in the role of 'scientist'. Lastly, normative power is depersonalised by reference to the moral value of organisational goals and to an organisational mission, transcending the interests of individuals. Here the manager is cast in an evangelical role. These ideologies, often interwoven, pervade managerial practices and taken-for-granted assumptions about organisational reality.

The depersonalisation of power at an ideological level would not be possible, or credible, however, were it not for the fact that the power to which managers have access has in reality become depersonalised. Implicit in the concept of positional power is a recognition that power is a structural phenomenon and that power relationships are impersonal and institutionalised. There has been a shift away from direct, overt influence, in the form of commands or regulations, towards less direct, covert forms, such as incentives, work methods embodied in technology, and the recruitment, indoctrination, training and appraisal of employees. These 'resistance-avoidance strategies' (Rus, 1980), rest on power resources which reside primarily with organisations and which are merely drawn upon by individuals. Interpersonal power relations are often merely a manifestation of 'structural domination' (Clegg, 1975). Indeed, the systemic character of power means that it does not always surface in visible relationships or issues, but, rather, underpins definitions of what is possible and influences behaviour covertly through taken-for-granted assumptions and understandings (Lukes, 1974; Clegg, 1979; Walsh et al., 1981).

Power as a structural or systemic phenomenon has a number of aspects. Firstly, economic, knowledge and normative power resources have an institutional form, with different individuals having differential access to them. Secondly, influence is attempted through institutional mechanisms or impersonal arrangements, rather than through face-to-face relationships. Thirdly, the responses typically invoked by particular modes of influence are collective responses. Structural economic power is exercised through reward systems, structural knowledge power through systems of rules and structural normative power resources through organisational rationales (or ideologies), each of which give rise to both intended and unintended responses.

Because of these unintended responses to institutional power and influence, the search for new forms of managerial power, legitimacy and authority has met with only partial success. Each new attempt to influence or manage employee behaviour brings in its train new forms of 'detailed recalcitrance' and non-compliance. The problem of managerial authority has yet to be resolved.

TOWARDS MANAGERIAL LEGITIMACY AND AUTHORITY: THE POWER OF COOPERATION

A number of writers have arrived at broadly similar conclusions about this failure by managers to establish legitimacy and authority. Essentially they argue that the future basis for managerial authority must lie in a recognition of the interdependent and cooperative character of work and, hence, focus upon power in the sense of collective 'power to' rather than personal 'power over'. Whatever the rhetoric, managers tend to assume that power is, and can only be, a zero sum game, and that their power is the inverse of the power of subordinates and their capacity to influence others' behaviour is a capacity to overcome potential resistance. Managerial actions are therefore focused entirely on the problem of resistance and possible 'solutions' to it. Managers may act 'coercively', using disparities of power resources to compel compliance (Knights and Roberts, 1982) or manipulatively, as 'raiders' (Mant, 1983), concerned only with defeating presumed adversaries, in this case subordinates. Managers may also seek to nullify the power of subordinates, by reducing their capacity to act at all, either by reducing their discretion at work or directing employee participation in work decisions towards matters where managers dictate the agenda (Fox, 1985; Storey, 1985). Managers may additionally seek to circumvent opposition through resistance-avoidance strategies and indirect controls (Rus, 1980). Lastly, managers may retreat altogether from the task of management, or the 'governance' of work, passing the problem on to others (Anthony, 1986).

Each of these 'solutions' brings its own attendant problems.

Coercion evokes mere compliance or, when the opportunity arises, 'counter-coercion' and so creates a vicious circle. Equally, manipulation creates an instrumentalism in social relationships which becomes embedded in individuals' orientations (Knights and Willmott, 1985). The curtailment of employee discretion brings a similar vicious circle in the form of 'institutionalised low trust' (Fox, 1985). Employees respond in kind to the limited trust placed upon them by regarding all interactions with managers as win-lose situations underpinned by a basic conflict of interests. The attempt to avoid resistance by imposing indirect controls reduces direct resistance to managerial influence, but at the same time increases indirect forms of resistance or lowers commitment. Lastly, managers' abdication of responsibility for management only shifts the problem elsewhere (e.g. to supervisors) and further undermines managerial legitimacy.

The solution to the problem of legitimacy may, therefore, lie in a recognition that power in the sense of 'transformative capacity' or 'power to' now resides in the interdependence which is characteristic of work organisation. If the effective achievement of goals is the outcome of cooperation, managerial legitimacy must, therefore, inhere in the manager's role within that cooperative effort and must rest upon shared goals and values. Although this argument is reminiscent of that advanced by a number of earlier writers (Barnard, 1938; Parsons, 1970) who conceived authority as a bestowed capacity to make decisions in furtherance of consensual collective goals, what is different here is the recognition that consensus cannot simply be assumed to exist, but must somehow be created out of disparities of power, conflicts of interest and potential dissensus.

The future basis of managerial legitimacy probably resides in greater social and work-place consensus, forged from wider participation in the processes of work organisation (i.e. management) and its outcomes (i.e. material rewards). This requires the development of work-places as 'communities' where relationships are imbued with a moral quality and are valued in themselves (Knight and Roberts, 1982; Anthony, 1986). In such a setting, the role of manager becomes one of creating and sustaining a sense of what work is for, either as a 'builder' of a moral framework which specifies both the processes and outputs of the system and to which work-place relationships are

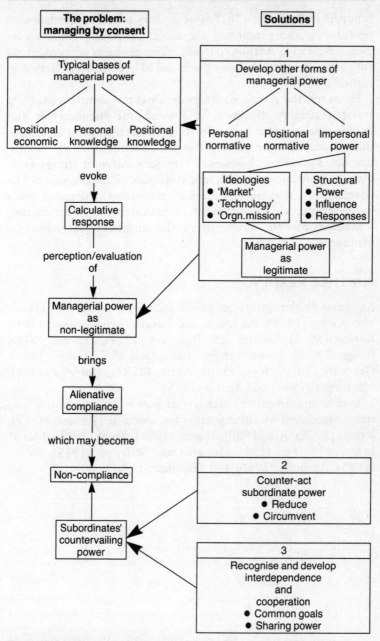

Figure 2.3 Managerial power and authority: the problem and solutions

subordinated (Mant, 1983) or as a 'story teller' concerned with articulating and promoting the moral purpose of institutions (Selznick, 1957; Anthony, 1986). (The problem of managerial authority and the solutions discussed above are summarised in Figure 2.3.)

However, the problem of legitimacy is not simply a problem facing managers. If power is a structural phenomenon and influence takes place primarily through the operation of institutional mechanisms, then different combinations of institutionalised power and influence represent different strategies of work organisation, or different strategies of management. The effectiveness of these strategies of management depends more upon the perceived legitimacy of management as an institutionalised process, rather than the authority of individual managers.

FURTHER READING

Key texts on the concept of power include: Dahl (1957), French and Raven (1959), Bachrach and Baratz (1962), Blau (1964), Kaplan (1964), Crozier (1973), Lukes (1974), Etzioni (1975), Clegg (1979), Wrong (1979), Bacharach and Lawler (1980), Graventa (1980), Rus (1980), Pfeffer (1981), Giddens (1982), Mintzberg (1983) and Kotter (1985).

Specific treatment of managerial power and authority and their associated problems may be found in Kanter (1977), Kotter (1977), Rus (1980), Handy (1981), Mant (1983), Mintzberg (1983), Fox (1985), Knights and Willmott (1985), Storey (1985), Anthony (1986) and Mangham (1986).

Chapter 3

Managing through organisation
A theoretical framework

We have seen how management as the broad responsibility for a work process, together with the management functions of planning, allocating, motivating, coordinating and controlling work, are separate from the execution of work itself and dispersed through different managerial positions. Because the common features and variations in managerial work offer important insights into the nature of management, we concentrated the analysis upon these and showed that most managerial work reflected a responsibility for planning, allocating, motivating, coordinating and controlling the work of others. We retained this focus upon the job of managing in Chapter 2, where we examined the means of managing, or influencing, the behaviour of other people, namely power.

The process of using power to influence others' behaviour corresponds to a pivotal element of the management process: motivation. Power resources, therefore, represent the basis for different forms of motivational inducement. However, much managerial power is positional, deriving not from personal characteristics and possessions, but from the access to resources afforded by a position in an organisation. Thus, power resources are organisational phenomena; organisations are systems of power. Equally, motivation is not simply a face-to-face process, based upon personal inducements. Organisations are also systems of influence, or motivation.

This observation is our starting point for this chapter and for the theoretical framework employed in subsequent chapters. We argue that not only motivation, but also the other management processes of planning/decision-making, allocation of work, coordination and control are, to a large extent, institutionalised; not confined to face-to-face relationships, but embodied in patterned arrangements applying to large numbers of people simultaneously. These institutionalised arrangements are the elements of work organisation, and 'organisation', therefore, may be regarded as management on a large scale and in its impersonal, institutionalised form.

In this chapter we trace, briefly, the institutionalisation of management in the development of large-scale organisation. From here, we show how different elements of the management process (or management functions) are incorporated into different aspects of work organisation. This is the starting point for the development of the 'managing through organisation' (here-after MTO) framework for comparing and contrasting different approaches to the organisation of work.

THE INSTITUTIONALISATION OF MANAGEMENT

Evidence on the institutionalisation of management, or the translation of management into organisation, is of two kinds: first, historical evidence on the growth of large organisations, and second, evidence on growth and associated internal change in individual undertakings. We confine ourselves to a brief summary of each of these.

The rise of large-scale organisations as actors on the socio-economic stage since the early nineteenth century is well documented and has raised a whole series of issues and engendered considerable debate. The most pertinent aspect of this for our purposes here, however, is that large-scale organisations are not simply the outcome of a burgeoning scale of operations, but of a more precise need for the management (or 'control', or 'domination') of large numbers of people. In short, organisations are not merely 'things' but instruments, defined as much by the means which they adopt to attain certain ends as by the ends themselves.

A second major theme in the growth of large-scale organisation has been the burgeoning of organisational power. As many commentators, from Weber (1949) onwards, have observed, it is organisations which own and control the resources which form the basis of power (Blau and Schoenherr, 1973; Clegg and Dunkerley, 1980). Thus, large state and private organisations control huge economic resources, are the repositories of vast amounts of information, knowledge and skill and develop their own pervasive norms and values. The corollary of these developments is a diminution in the power of the individual. Most individuals are employees, dependent upon large organisations for their livelihood; individual shareholders are dwarfed by institutional investors; individual skills are but a small part of the complex technical fabric of work processes; individual knowledge is increasingly confined to a small, specialised area; and individual attitudes and values must subsist within the context of state and corporate ideologies. Even though there are those who, by virtue of their position in state and private organisations, have disproportionate access to and control over organisational resources, their power is dependent upon organisations and, because of that, is constrained in particular ways.

The differential access of individuals to organisational power resources is part of a broader, third theme in the growth of large-scale organisation: differentiation and stratification. As a result of both the separation of management functions from work processes and the elaboration of the division of labour within both 'management' and the work process as a whole, large organisations are divided horizontally into distinct segments of work or functions, and vertically into distinct strata. Whilst, as we shall see in the remainder of the book, the basis and the extent of these horizontal and vertical divisions may vary, certain broad areas can be discerned. Horizontally, there is the basic division between 'core' work processes directly concerned with the organisation's central activity, product or service, and 'auxiliary' work processes, concerned with technical or support services. Within this basic division are different parts of the core process and different types of technical and support services. Vertically, there is the basic division between the managerial or administrative strata, concerned primarily with aspects of the management process as a whole, and the non-managerial or operational strata, concerned primarily with executing the work process, a basic division made more complex by divisions within the managerial strata (senior, middle and junior managers), the non-managerial (skilled, semi-skilled, unskilled) and by intermediate positions concerned with both management and operational functions. An important attempt to combine horizontal and vertical divisions is Mintzberg's model of the five basic parts of the organisation: strategic apex, middle line, operating core, technostructure and support staff (Mintzberg, 1979).

What is sometimes only implicit in organisational analysis, but will be insisted upon here, is that different parts of an organisation may be organised differently. Put another way, different types of work may be subjected to different forms of management. In particular, managerial, administrative and technical-professional work tends to be managed or organised in rather different ways from that of operational, routine, clerical and service work.

The growth and internal development of individual undertakings is characterised by a similar central theme: as the undertaking grows, so it spawns ever more elaborate and impersonal mechanisms for managing work. Briefly, the typical small owner-managed firm with a 'simple structure' (Mintzberg, 1979; Scase and Goffee, 1980) is characterised by a separation of some management functions, but not all. Planning and decision-making resides with the owner-manager, but relies heavily upon informal interaction with the workforce. Owner-managers draw heavily upon their own economic and knowledge resources to motivate employees through rewards and rules underpinned by personal relationships and loyalties. Control also relies considerably upon personal loyalty, direct, face-to-face supervision and the application of the proprietor's standards or perceptions of market requirements. The allocation of work is usually very fluid and informal, with individual flexibility and little specialisation. Equally, coordination is through informal face-to-face contacts.

When such an undertaking succeeds and grows, five developments ensue. Firstly, individuals and groups increasingly specialise: individuals concentrate on particular functions, specialists are hired for particular jobs, departments as functional groupings evolve and the owner-manager withdraws from day-to-day operational management into management of the business. Secondly, mechanisms for control and coordination develop as face-to-face contacts and personal supervision become infeasible: rules, procedures and standards evolve. Thirdly, activities become increasingly formalised and impersonal, less spontaneous and personal. Fourthly, there is an increasing distinction between formal work arrangements and rules, and informal relationships and norms of behaviour. Lastly, the organisational 'system' begins to acquire a life of its own, beyond and above that of the individual participants in it. In short, what was previously management through informal, *ad hoc* face-to-face relations becomes management through formal, recurrent impersonal routines, or management through organisation.

MANAGING THROUGH ORGANISATION

Whilst it is true that the organisation of work on a large scale has tended to develop in particular ways, this is an issue taken up in the analysis of rationalisation and bureaucratisation in Chapters 4 and 5. More important for now is the general observation of the link between the growth of undertakings and the translation of the management process into organisational arrangements. In general, this has meant the development of mechanisms or systems for decision-making, allocating work, motivation, coordination and control.

Planning/decision-making

Institutional arrangements for planning work and taking decisions about its purpose and content subsume, firstly, locating the responsibility for planning and decision-making in particular positions in the organisation and secondly, creating channels of communication for conveying information.

Locating responsibility for planning and decision-making essentially entails allocating different types of plans and decisions to different planners and decision-makers. Plans and decisions may be differentiated according to their scope, or the areas of work to which they apply (e.g. finance, personnel, work methods), and their level of generality, that is whether they apply to the organisation as a whole (strategic plans/decisions) or to particular activities within it (operational plans/decisions). The allocation of planning and decision-making is differentiated primarily by the extent to which plans and decisions of a particular type are dispersed among many people and positions, or concentrated in a few. Thus, different types of planning and decision-making exhibit different degrees of centralisation. Where plans and decisions are made by a few and applied to many, they are centralised; they are decentralised when they are taken by those to whom they apply. Thus, planning and decision-making may be dichotomous, with a clear divide between those who plan and take decisions and those who do not; hierarchical, with gradations of responsibility for different levels of planning and decision-making; democratic, with wide involvement in decision-making; or dispersed, with wide responsibility for plans and decisions.

Information or communication systems are characterised by both the forms of information and the direction in which communications flow. Stocks (records) or flows (communications) of information may be formal (e.g. written memos, reports, manuals) or informal (e.g. 'word of mouth' communications, custom and practice). The flow of information can be either vertical, between positions, individuals and groups differentiated in terms of their status and level of responsibility, or horizontal, between positions, individuals and groups of equal status but performing different functions or different types of work. The predominant direction of communications reflects the extent to which planning and decision-making are centralised: the more centralised they are, the greater the requirement for vertical communication – of information upwards, and decisions, in the form of policy or rules, downwards.

Taken together, arrangements for the location of decision-making and the form and direction of communication constitute a vertical division of labour, or a way of dividing up and allocating responsibility for, on the one hand, the 'conceptual' aspects of work (planning, decision-making) and on the other, the 'executional' aspects (carrying out plans and decisions).

Allocating work

Arrangements for allocating work to different sub-divisions, groups or individuals constitute the horizontal division of labour. The central element of this is specialisation: the way in which and the extent to which different sub-units are concerned with a particular aspect of the total work process. Where work is conducted on a large scale, some form of specialisation is inevitable: what varies are the form that it takes, the level at which it occurs and its extent at the level of the individual job.

Differences in the form of specialisation reflect the fact that there are different ways of dividing up the total work process, on the basis of:

1 Types of skill (the manual and mental capacities of different workers: what they can do).
2 Functions (the different elements or stages which contribute to the work process: what happens to work-in-progress at a given time).
3 Outputs (the products or services which are the outcome of work activity).
4 Types of clients/customers (the different recipients of the outputs of the work process).
5 Location (where work activities occur).

Each of these, or more than one in combination, can form the basis of differentiation between jobs, work groups, sections or departments.

Related to this is the level at which specialisation occurs. In some cases, specialisation may occur at the level of fairly large groupings such as departments or divisions, with a fluid allocation of work within them. In other cases, it is smaller work groups which specialise, with individual group members having fluid job boundaries. Finally, specialisation may be at the level of jobs, with individual employees restricted to particular tasks. Different forms of specialisation may occur at different levels. Thus, for example, divisions may be based on geographical markets, departments upon specific products, work groups on functions, whilst jobs are skill-based.

Further, combining the form and level of specialisation produces a particularly important emergent outcome: the degree of job specialisation. The jobs which individuals do may be broad, with a range of responsibilities and variety of associated tasks, or they may be narrow, at the extreme confined to a single task or operation. Individuals, therefore, may be specialised technically or professionally (confined to the application of particular skills and knowledge); by role (confined to having certain duties or responsibilities); or by task (confined to performing certain manual or mental operations).

Although the vertical and horizontal divisions of labour are separate, they are clearly related. Since they constitute the way in which 'work' in all its guises may be divided up, together they may be referred to as the 'task system'.

Motivation

The motivation of large numbers of employees is attempted through motivational mechanisms which mobilise organisational power resources and their corresponding forms of influence. Leaving aside physical power, power resources are embodied in three modes of 'institutionalised influence', or motivational mechanisms:

1 Rewards, which draw upon economic resources to induce particular forms of behaviour by granting, promising, withholding or threatening to withhold rewards.
2 Rules, which draw upon knowledge resources (information, skills) to induce particular behaviour by persuasion or demonstration. As organisational knowledge takes two distinct forms, so rules may be technical (relating to performance of particular work processes) or administrative (relating to behaviour towards people or events).
3 Rationales, or ideologies, which draw upon normative power resources (beliefs, values) to induce particular behaviour by moral force or inspiration.

Variations in these motivational mechanisms are twofold. Firstly, each mechanism can take different forms, depending upon the type of power resources available and assumptions about likely responses by employees to different kinds of inducement. Rewards may be offered for different kinds of behaviour (output, loyalty, skill), may be offered to individuals or groups, and may be immediate or deferred. Rules, equally, may refer to different kinds of behaviour and may be imposed or agreed or devised by those to whom they apply. Rationales, or ideologies, will refer to different kinds of values, or desirable outcomes, to justify certain kinds of behaviour.

Secondly, the mix and balance between these motivational mechanisms differs among different approaches to the organisation of work. Different 'motivation systems' as a whole place different emphases upon material inducements, persuasion and moral exhortation, hence combine rewards, rules and rationales in differing proportions.

Coordination

Arrangements for attempting to ensure that different aspects of the work process, allocated to different sub-units, are synchronised and compatible, represent the coordinating mechanisms. These vary in terms of the locus of responsibility for coordination, the method by which it is attempted and its degree of formality.

Responsibility for coordination of work activities may lie with those carrying out the work, who interact directly, or through a third party. This third party may either be a superior in the hierarchy, a specialist individual coordinator (such as a liaison officer or 'troubleshooter') or a coordinating body (such as a steering group or liaison committee).

The manner in which coordination is attempted varies. The principal methods are: adjustment, tailoring activities in accordance with what is known about the activities of others; consultation/communication, providing a flow of information and advice about the activities of different units to those affected by these activities; and direction, issuing orders and instructions to different units. Lastly, these methods of coordination may be formal, relying on written communications or formal meetings, or informal, relying on oral communications or unscheduled meetings.

Whilst the locus of responsibility, method and degree of formality of coordination are conceptually distinct and offer a wide range of possible permutations, in practice they tend to coalesce into distinct coordinating mechanisms:

1 'Mutual adjustment' (Mintzberg, 1979), involving informal, reciprocal adjustment among those carrying out the work to be coordinated.
2 Hierarchical coordination, involving the use of formal directives from a superior individual or group.
3 Specialist liaison, involving the use of specialist coordinators, individuals or groups, who rely principally upon consultation and communication.

Control

When attempts to ensure that work conforms with plans and intentions are conducted on a large scale, they take the form of control systems and specific control mechanisms. These vary in three major respects: firstly, in terms of the focus of control, secondly, in terms of the locus of responsibility for exercising control and thirdly, in terms of the degree of formality and impersonality with which controls operate.

The focus of control refers to those aspects of the work process over which controls are applied. Attempts may be made to control, *inter alia*:

1 Inputs, or the materials and, more importantly, the knowledge and skills of those carrying out the work. In effect, this is *ex-ante* control, operating before the event.
2 Processes, or the technical and behavioural methods used in carrying out the work. This represents concurrent control, operating during the event.
3 Outputs, or the material, informational or financial results of a work process. This is *ex-post* control, operating after the event.
4 Values, or notions of what is important and desirable held by those carrying out the work. This is, in effect, meta-control, operating above the event.

Although these forms of control are not mutually exclusive, they rest upon somewhat divergent assumptions and, to some extent, preclude the need for each other. Therefore, control over inputs places methods of working and results on trust; control over outputs implies relative indifference to who carries work out or how, whilst control over processes permits the use of any inputs for certain types of output. However, different forms of control may be used in conjunction; this is to provide some form of reinforcement.

The locus of responsibility for control may rest with the individual (self-control), the work or colleague group (mutual control) or with an individual or body separate from the work process (external control). Whilst self and mutual control are necessarily personal and informal, external control may be personal, exercised by one individual over others, or impersonal, in the form of rules and regulations. Further, personal forms of external control may be either formal, through procedures such as reports, appraisal or information returns, or informal, through interpersonal contacts.

Combining these dimensions:

1 Self control involves the application of internalised rules and norms of behaviour relating to processes (methods of work) and outputs (standards) and of internalised values relating to ethics by those carrying out work.

2 Mutual control involves the enforcement of norms relating to inputs (standards of recruitment to the group), processes (work methods) and outputs (performance standards) as well as values (ethical standards) by members of a work group, specialism or profession upon each other.

3 External control may involve, *inter alia*, formal and impersonal rules and procedures relating to inputs (rules about recruitment, qualifications and experience), processes (technical methods and procedures) and outputs (performance measures and standards); informally transmitted values (the organisational ethos or philosophy); or personal monitoring and surveillance by one individual over another (direct supervision).

Together, the different mechanisms of coordination and control constitute the ways in which divided work is recombined, and may be referred to as the 'control system'.

The different elements discussed above are summarised in Figure 3.1. What these elements amount to is what is conventionally defined as organisation. Here, therefore, organisation is defined as an assemblage of institutionalised mechanisms through which the management of work is attempted. Expressing it in this way suggests a number of distinctive ways in which 'organisation' is analysed in later chapters.

Firstly, the concern is primarily with organising as a process, rather than organisations as things. Therefore, the aim is to compare different approaches to the organisation of work, rather than to list different organisational forms.

Secondly, as argued earlier, organisations (as things) are not homogeneous entities but combine different work processes which can be organised in different ways. The advantage of the 'managing through organisation' (MTO) framework is that it may be used to compare and contrast different forms of management used for different areas of work and categories of employees.

Thirdly, all the different elements of managing through organisation are, both in principle and in practice, variable.

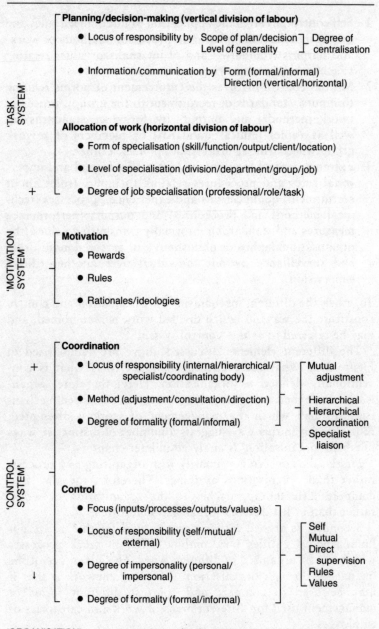

'ORGANISATION' as an assemblage of institutionalised mechanisms through which the management of work is attempted

Figure 3.1 Managing through organisation: an analytical framework

They represent different ways of going about the processes of planning/decision-making, allocating, motivating, coordinating and controlling work through different forms of task, motivational and control systems. Fourthly, and related to this, different approaches to organisation may be distinguished not only as combinations of different elements and mechanisms, but also, crucially, in terms of the relationship between the management process as a whole and the work process being managed. In some approaches to organisation, some or all elements of the management process are separated from the work process, thus responsibility for them rests with managers. In other approaches, some or all management functions are integrated into the work process itself so that, in some measure, non-managers manage themselves.

Finally, the organisational mechanisms which have been identified are merely attempts to manage work and bring about desired outcomes. Whether these attempts succeed depends upon the way in which those being managed respond to them. For many reasons, however, they may either fail to respond to the extent that is expected, or respond in quite unintended ways. Therefore, just as power and influence must be analysed in relation to the responses made to them, so approaches to management through organisation must be analysed in relation to their evoked responses and hence to their unintended, as well as intended, consequences.

Equipped with the MTO framework and bearing the above qualifications in mind, we may now turn to a substantive analysis of different approaches to organisation.

FURTHER READING

Analysis of the rise of large-scale organisations may be found in Weber (1949), Blau and Schoenherr (1973), Presthus (1979), Thompson (1980), Clegg and Dunkerley (1980) and Clegg (1990).

Alternative frameworks for the analysis of organisations are offered in Mintzberg (1979) and Dawson (1986).

Chapter 4

The search for efficiency
Rationalisation and scientific management

Having set the scene in the previous chapters and developed a set of conceptual tools for analysing different approaches to the management and organisation of work, we turn to a substantive examination of the first of these approaches: scientific management and work rationalisation. These ideas, taken together with those of bureaucracy, constitute what we shall call the 'classical' approach to organisation: an over-arching set of general principles which, despite detailed differences of emphasis and application, display broad agreement about how work is to be planned, allocated, motivated, coordinated and controlled. The ideas associated with the rationalisation of work represent the application of these principles to operational work which, at the same time, form the basis for completing the process of separating management from the execution of work. The rationalisation of work has the effect of transferring functions of planning, allocation and coordination to managers, whilst reinforcing the managerial monopoly of decision-making, motivation and control.

We begin by setting out the major contributory ideas to the approach which we have labelled 'work rationalisation', in particular the ideas of 'Scientific Management'. We describe the basic principles associated with this approach and the main features of work organised in this way and then summarise the approach in terms of the MTO framework. This enables an explicit comparison with 'craft' organisation of work and thus indicates the essential features of the process of rationalisation.

Two key issues surrounding the process of rationalisation are discussed. Firstly, we consider the debates about its starting

points, the logical and historical reasons for it and its different trajectories. Secondly, we evaluate the approach by
examining its strengths and weaknesses. In this evaluation a
central theme is the contradiction between the promise of
intended efficiency at the level of the system and the threat of
unintended inefficiency at the level of the individual. The gains,
in terms of technical efficiency and control, to be had from
making the work process as a whole more 'rational' are offset
by the losses in terms of human effectiveness and satisfactions
which flow from ignoring the experience of individuals and
groups within the work process. This reflects the potential
contradiction between management as planning, coordination
and control, and management as motivation, and the tension
between managers' desire for power over employees and the
need for employees collectively to have the power to perform
effectively. Consequently, the costs and benefits of rationalised
work look very different from the managerial and employee
points of view.

SCIENTIFIC MANAGEMENT AND RATIONALISATION

The approach to work organisation under consideration here is
difficult to label, since it is a composite of a number of different
strands. What is important to stress at the outset, however, is
that the focus of the analysis is neither simply 'Scientific
Management', nor 'Taylorism'. These ideas, although highly
influential, are both too narrow and, in other respects, too
broad for our purposes. The ideas of Scientific Management and
Taylorism, strictly defined, are too narrow. Not only have these
ideas been subject to a number of subsequent modifications or
additions which, while changing the details, have been consistent with their basic principles or terms, but they also had a
number of clearly identifiable theoretical antecedents. However,
these ideas are also too broad since some of the prescriptions of
Taylor and his followers never gained much acceptance and are
mainly objects of historiographical curiosity.

The approach here, as in subsequent chapters, is to distil the
common elements of this broad approach to organisation from
a number of both primary, prescriptive sources and secondary,
commentary texts.

RATIONALISATION: GENERAL PRINCIPLES

Five basic principles of rationalised work organisation may be discerned: systematic work methods; detailed division of labour; centralised planning and control; an instrumental, low-involvement employment relationship; and an ideology of neutral technical efficiency.

Systematic work methods are a general echo of Taylor's First Principle of Scientific Management: that work be subject to systematic observation, measurement, tabulation and analysis in order to generate scientific 'laws' of work. These set out the essential components of work tasks, their optimum sequence and pace, and form the basis of standard work methods, payment, workflow and the use (and design) of machinery. Systematic investigation and prescription of how work is to be performed also underpins the division of labour, managerial control, the employment relationship and the ethic of efficiency.

Detailed division of labour entails basing jobs on individual task elements of a work process. Employees are, therefore, allocated specific tasks for which they are selected, recruited and trained. This straddles Taylor's Second and Third Principles of Scientific Management: respectively, the scientific selection and training of workers and the 'bringing together' of scientifically analysed work and scientifically selected workers.

The first two principles of rationalised work concern how work may most effectively be divided and allocated. How it may then be coordinated and controlled is, partly, implicit in standardised work methods. However, it is also embodied in the principle of centralised planning and control. This is a more general version of Taylor's Fourth Principle of Scientific Management, that there should be a clear functional division between managers and workers, with the former exclusively carrying out management functions, whilst the latter are exclusively carrying out the work itself, and that this division represents a form of *de facto* functional cooperation. The principle is even better summarised by Braverman's (1974) felicitous phrase, 'the separation of conception from execution'. Responsibility for the systematic study of work and the use of this knowledge to plan and control work is to be the exclusive job of managers.

The fourth principle of rationalised work organisation flows almost as a negative implication of the first three. Since the management of work is to be attempted primarily through the rational ordering of the work system as a whole, all that is required of the individual employee is a disposition to carry out their allotted task. Hence, the employment relationship, the link between the employee and the employer, is an instrumental and low-involvement one. That is, the mutual obligations of the two parties are minimal: the employer expects employees to carry out their tasks as instructed, whilst employees expect a level of reward commensurate with their effort. Wider obligations are unnecessary. This is a more general version of an idea implicit in Taylor's Third Principle of 'bringing together work and the workmen', or translating potential to work into performance by firstly, the example of 'first class men' capable of sustained effort and willing to carry out instructions, and secondly, rates of pay tied to effort. The assumption, throughout, is that work effort is a disutility which employees will avoid unless threatened by economic sanction, or promised compensating rewards.

The fifth principle of rationalisation is largely ideological and refers to the pervasiveness of technical efficiency, as guiding principle and valued goal, in the way work is organised. The criterion of efficiency offers both an apparently unequivocal basis for the choice of particular methods of organisation and an unassailable legitimacy for this choice, since the pursuit of efficiency is held to be neutral, serving the interests of both employer and employee.

Application of these five principles of rationalisation results in a number of concrete features of work organisation, which we now consider in more detail.

RATIONALISED WORK IN PRACTICE: KEY FEATURES

Applying the principle of rationalised work methods results in modern forms of work study and industrial engineering, embracing techniques for deriving standard times, standard methods, job descriptions, planned workflow and mechanisation.

Work study has undergone considerable refinement since Taylor and Gilbreth's early promptings, but its essential purpose remains the same: to arrive at a technically best, or most efficient, way of performing a work task through objective scientific analysis. At its most basic it takes the form of time study of existing work methods. The search for different, and better, ways of working is the basic project of method study pioneered by Gilbreth and Gantt. Here the emphasis is on observation of work, systematic and standardised analysis and the production of activity and process charts. These, in turn, facilitate 'motion economy' through identifying and eliminating unnecessary movements and combining and synthesising those that remain, or replacing them by simpler ones. Motion study also entails the incorporation of rest periods and is most elaborately found in the Bedaux system and its variants (Littler, 1982) based on a unit of work measurement (the 'B') divided into work and rest periods and in the planning of shifts around 'circadian rhythms' (Folkard, 1987). Motion study also involves a recognition that improved work performance is a function of improved work layout and equipment design. These, however, are mainly developed in operational research which investigates problems of work allocation, sequencing and routing, and ergonomics, concerned with design of machine controls, displays and work stations. All of these, as Braverman (1974) notes, represent a shift from the contingent use of the insights of science in production, to the development of techniques expressly to solve production problems.

Application of these techniques produces the paraphernalia of rationalised work organisation: standard work times and methods. In the first of these, techniques such as 'methods-time-measurement' and 'predetermined motion time systems' are used to arrive at a standard time for performance of a task, through calculation of a basic time, to which 'relaxation' and 'contingency' allowances are added. These are then used to evaluate, retrospectively, individual work performance and form the basis of reward, discipline or training. However, they are also used, prospectively, to determine performance norms where these do not exist or are currently determined by custom and practice. Standard times presuppose standard methods. The 'best' way identified in work study becomes the way to perform a task, prescribed in job cards, manuals, Gantt charts and product specifications, and reinforced through training.

A key device for standardising work is mechanisation, replacing workers by machines, and rationalised work involves the constant search for mechanisation wherever it is technically feasible and economic. Machinery is used not simply as an aid to the work process but, crucially, as a key device for organisation and control. How work is carried out and at what pace is built into machines where the sequence of operations is controlled internally, increasingly by forms of programmed numerical control or microprocessors.

Centrally planned and controlled workflow and routing of materials takes many forms, but the most developed is the 'flow line' (or production line), which determines work pace and sequencing, effectively coordinating and controlling disparate work operations. Flow lines developed along with mass consumer goods industries, the archetype for which was automobile production, where the technique was developed by Ford from simple, progressive shop layout to a power-driven continuous line (Gartman, 1979). Even where flow lines are not employed, however, there may be regulated routing of materials as well as ordering, receiving and stock control systems, now often unified and computerised.

Work study also generates job descriptions which specify the content, context and standards of performance of a job and are used as a basis for recruitment/selection, training, job evaluation and remuneration. This formalisation of employee responsibilities also serves to codify the detailed division of labour.

Whether detailed division of labour is a necessary, or merely contingent, aspect of rationalised work is a matter of considerable debate (Braverman, 1974; Littler, 1982; Wood, 1983). This debate is reviewed below. For now, we consider the association between rationalised work and a high degree of horizontal specialisation, manifested in the separation of direct and indirect labour, fragmentation and deskilling of direct labour and specialised selection and training, all of which mean that employees are, essentially, managed as 'factors of production'.

In a detailed division of labour, functions form the basis of departments and work groups, whilst tasks form the basis of individual jobs. Further, the distinction between 'core' production or assembly activities and 'support' activities such as maintenance, set-up, packing and transport are the basis for the division between direct and indirect labour. This specialisation is intended to foster the dexterity of workers on core tasks, eliminate time lost in moving between tasks and permit the allocation of support tasks to less skilled, hence, cheaper, labour. This echoes the 'Babbage principle' (Babbage, 1832) of reserving expensive skilled workers for more complex tasks.

The jobs created by work study and detailed specialisation are, invariably, undemanding and repetitive, with the creation of the 'detail worker' (Braverman, 1974) reaching its apogee on the flow lines of Fordist work methods (Beynon, 1975; Littler, 1982). Here jobs are learnt in a matter of minutes, workers are fragmented functionally and spatially and the work group survives only informally, if at all. Recruitment/selection and training for these jobs are focused on the employee's physical and mental capacity to perform a given task, including, as graphically illustrated in Taylor's vignette of Schmidt the pig-iron handler (Taylor, 1912), a focus upon employee 'mentality' or disposition. Dexterity and obedience are key employee attributes. Detecting and enhancing these qualities are the function of a specialist personnel department.

The centralisation of planning and control has three aspects: the separation and increasing elaboration of the management function as a whole, the removal of planning and control from junior managers and supervisors to specialist departments and the increasing formalisation of planning and control. Again, work study is the cornerstone, since it is the basis of the managerial acquisition, development and monopolisation of knowledge of work processes. The result is a 'shadow' paper work process concerned with planning and control and embracing production engineering, organisation and methods, cost accounting and manpower planning. Many of these are relatively new functions spawning new managerial/professional specialisms (Esland, 1980), or 'think workers' concerned with the production of 'representational outputs' such as blueprints, charts, etc. (Hales, 1980). Specialist planning and control of labour means a diminution in the functions of supervisors and foremen to that of employees exercising direct supervision and enforcing work methods, work-place rules and quality standards set by others. The role of supervisor has also become fragmented with separate responsibilities for the work group, quality and maintenance, echoing Taylor's principle of 'functional foremanship'.

As personal direction and control of work by supervisors diminishes, so impersonal forms proliferate. Centralised planning and control of work rely upon formal, standardised feedback information, relating to production quota fulfilment, scrap rates, overtime and so on. Further, these controls operate through general and formalised mechanisms which focus primarily upon how work is carried out and take the form of job specifications, blueprints, manuals and the like. The role of foremen and supervisors is to monitor and enforce these prescriptions.

An instrumental, low-involvement employment relationship gives rise to a cluster of features, the most important of which are managerial assumptions about employee motivation. Perhaps Taylor's most enduring legacy is the absorption into managerial thinking of the belief that workers are an indolent rabble who must be coerced or bribed to carry out their work (Palmer, 1975), a view exemplified by Taylor's notion of 'systematic soldiering', where group-based work knowledge is used to subvert managerial intentions. This means that the atomisation of labour and the break up of the work group is a hidden agenda of rationalisation. Although their espoused views on motivation may have changed, managers' ideas in use have changed little (Hedberg and Mumford, 1979; Taylor, 1979).

A narrow employment relationship has, by definition, few characteristics since it is characterised by an absence of strands linking employer and employee other than money. This 'cash nexus' is predicated on limited expectations about effort and reward, the freedom of either party to terminate the contract, and hence the use of labour as a pliable factor of production. In principle, the employer offers no job security or career, and makes no claim to employee behaviour outside the confines of work. In practice, however, concern with employee obedience and attitudes formed outside the work-place, and the need for cooperation, mean that the employment relationship may exhibit paternalistic elements, as in Fordism with its emphasis upon high wage rates and a more intrusive managerial interest in employee behaviour.

A low-involvement employment relationship is also characterised by systems of evaluation and reward which focus primarily upon individual short-term performance. Again, the linchpin is work study and measurement, which attempt to determine a 'fair day's work for a fair day's pay' by specifying an objective performance–reward relationship. Appraisal and reward systems, therefore, focus on individual self-interest, with problems more likely to be seen as failures of competence or compliance, and dismissal used as a key disciplinary device.

The carrot to accompany this stick is usually some form of payment-by-results (PBR) system, in which individual output is rewarded directly and immediately. Whilst in general the assumptions of payment-by-results sit squarely with those of rationalised work organisation, PBR may take a variety of different forms. In practice PBR systems are usually hybrids, combining fixed day-rates with variable bonuses and thus imposing both a 'floor' and a 'ceiling' to actual pay, as in premium bonus systems or the Bedaux system. They are also usually 'proportional' and 'geared' (Warr and Wall, 1975; Webb, 1975). All these reward systems are not simply mechanisms for rewarding past effort, but represent attempts to elicit and control effort in the future, by specifying the effort–reward link, using rate setting to intensify effort and using diminishing bonuses to control labour costs.

The last set of features associated with rationalised work are its associated ideologies, which both express and seek to justify this approach to organisation. From the notion of neutral, technical efficiency flow a number of specific propositions, many of which own their provenance to the ideological force of Taylorism. In particular, the application of scientific work methods serves to justify both the way in which work is managed and, indeed, the fact that it *is* managed – by others.

The pursuit of technical efficiency is justified on the grounds of rationality and fairness. Efficiency is deemed 'rational' because it embodies the neutral logic of science, in the pursuit of 'more from less'. It is held to be 'fair', since increasing the output from a given level of inputs is in the interest of employers and employees, managers and workers alike. Scientific management, therefore, provides managers, the prosecutors of efficiency, an ideology not only for what they do, but for their very existence. It gives managers both the means to manage work and a rationale for doing so, since managerial instructions are based not on whim, but on the dictates of science (Bendix, 1963; Anthony, 1977). In short, it bequeaths to managers a form of technical knowledge power. Opposition to managerial control is defined as irrational.

We are now in a position to summarise rationalised work

organisation using the MTO framework. In brief, rationalised organisation represents the application of the 'classical' principles of centralisation, division of labour, external motivation, formal coordination and regulation of work methods to the management of operational work. It is where the separation of management functions is complete and where managers, alone, manage.

Work planning and decision-making are centralised in that they are the sole responsibility of managers and specialist professionals, hence there is a dichotomous vertical division of labour between managers as planners/decision-makers, and workers as those who carry out plans and decisions. The system rests upon vertical flows of formalised information: rules and instructions downwards, feedback information upwards.

The allocation of work rests on a detailed division of labour based upon the functional specialisation of departments and work groups and task specialisation by individuals. The degree of individual specialisation is therefore very high, with repetitive, deskilled and, often, mechanised, task-based jobs.

Motivation is largely external and is attempted through a particular combination of rewards, rules and rationales (or ideologies). Rewards are direct, immediate, primarily extrinsic and related to output or effort. Rules take the form of externally imposed technical work methods or specifications and workplace regulations. A rationale of technical efficiency seeks to direct effort towards the 'one best way' and instil obedience to managerial instructions.

The coordination of work is attempted through formal, external direction: in part, from the impersonal physical flow of the work process, but also from the direction of effort by managers and supervisors. Similarly, the control of work is external, focused upon the process or methods of work and relying upon both personal and impersonal mechanisms. Impersonal control is exerted by standardised work methods, embodied in technical specifications and the design of machinery. These standardised methods are enforced through personalised control in the form of direct supervision and surveillance by foremen. Internal control exists to the extent that employees respond to payment-by-results systems by pursuing economic self-interest. These features are summarised in Table 4.1.

Table 4.1 Managing through rationalised organisation

Management process	
Area of application	: Separation of management functions from work process.
	: Operational and some administrative work.
Planning/decision-making	
Degree of centralisation	: Highly decentralised and dichotemic: planning and decision-making exclusive to managers, workforce excluded
Information/communication flows	: Predominantly vertical and formal
Allocation of Work	
Form of specialisation	: By function or task
Level of specialisation	: Individual worker
Degree of job specialisation	: Very high: jobs based on narrow tasks
Motivation	
Rewards	: Immediate and extrinsic, based on individual output
Rules	: Technical work methods/specifications, workplace rules
Rationale	: Technical efficiency
Coordination	
Locus of responsibility	: Managers and supervisors; workflow
Method	: Direction
Degree of formality	: Formal
Control	
Focus	: Processes
Locus of responsibility	: External
Degree of impersonality	: Mainly impersonal
Degree of formality	: Formal

Hierarchical coordination

Rules and direct supervision

APPLICATION OF RATIONALISED ORGANISATION, THE CENTRAL ISSUE: ORIGINS AND TRAJECTORY OF THE RATIONALISATION PROCESS

So far, we have analysed rationalised organisation as something complete, distinct and unproblematic. We now focus upon the key issues surrounding the application of rationalised organisation by examining, firstly, the nature of the changes involved in the process of rationalisation, and secondly, the extent to which this process is an accurate representation of the changes which accompany increasingly large-scale organisation of operational work. Since the most systematic and celebrated account of the rationalisation process is offered by Braverman (1974), the issues surrounding it have come to be cast as the 'post-Braverman debate'. This debate resolves into three component issues, concerned respectively with the starting point, causes and consequences of rationalisation and, inevitably, has a historical as well as a current dimension.

On the question of a starting point, it has been contended that rationalisation in general, and scientific management in particular, are the practical and ideological instruments for the systematic destruction of craft organisation, through firstly, deskilling – the separation of conception from execution and the fragmentation of tasks – and secondly, concentration of control in the hands of managers (Marglin, 1976; Stone, 1974).

Using the MTO framework, we may conceptualise this process as follows. Under craft organisation, management is integrated into the work process, since craft workers manage themselves. Rationalisation, therefore, brings the separation of the management function. Thus, previously dispersed and informal planning and decision-making is concentrated in the hands of managers and formalised. Work is reallocated, with broad and varied occupations broken down into single-task jobs and replaced by machinery. The self-motivation of craft workers is replaced by external motivational mechanisms. Traditional, differential occupational rates of pay, reflecting skill and seniority, are superseded by homogeneous payments for time or output. Customary craft practices are replaced by 'scientific' work methods and an ideology of craft pride, obligation to the craft and deference to tradition are replaced by technical efficiency and diffuse obligations. Work is no longer coordinated by informal, face-to-face interaction (mutual adjustment) by workers, but by formal, external directives. Lastly, control shifts from the internal and mutual control exercised by craft workers on the basis of agreed craft practices, internalised through training and underpinned by craft pride, to external, impersonal controls. In sum, management becomes external to and imposed upon workers.

The accuracy of this description, albeit something of a caricature, is much disputed. It is argued, for example, that a 'golden age' of exclusively craft organisation never existed, and that far from constituting the archetype of small-scale work organisation, craft organisation is the exception. Historically it has been restricted to certain established, skilled occupations. Other employees have experienced very different forms of management, in which craft workers often played a key managerial role, hiring, firing and managing workers in their capacity as internal contractors, gang bosses or masters operating as agents of owners (Goffee, 1977; Littler, 1982).

Indeed, it is argued more generally that the precursors to rationalised organisation are not necessarily variations of worker management, but rather different forms of imposed management, varying in terms of where management functions reside and whether responsibility for management and employment of workers are separate or unified functions. Under 'entrepreneurial control', responsibility for both resides with the owner, whilst under 'traditional foremanship', the owner retains responsibility for employment matters but delegates day-to-day management to a foreman or chargehand. Lastly, under forms of 'internal contract', the owner abdicates the role of both employer and manager.

Therefore, the process of rationalisation involves either the transfer of management functions from workers to managers, as in the rationalisation of craft work, or the completion of this transfer, as in the rationalisation of work previously subject to entrepreneurial or 'delegated-entrepreneurial' control. Further, a number of different historical forms of organisation, such as paternalism, have intervened between entrepreneurial and rationalised organisation, whilst some industries (e.g. process industries) were, in effect, 'born rationalised' (Elger, 1983). Overall, therefore, it is clear that rationalisation does not proceed from a single point of origin.

Debate about the causes of rationalisation is between four types of explanatory account: the retrospective functional, the prospective functional, the historical and the action account. The retrospective functional account locates the cause of rationalisation in the need to overcome the limitations and contradiction of earlier forms of organisation. Whilst there is broad agreement that earlier systems required change, there is disagreement over which forms of organisation were failing. Some emphasise the limitations of craft organisation, in particular the way in which craft skills enable workers to resist attempts to impose external management by virtue of that knowledge. Thus, traditional ways of working and levels of effort were the targets of rationalisation. For others, rationalisation has sought to deal with the deficiencies of delegated management where lack of managerial control is attributed to negligence or pursuit of self-interest by foremen and contractors.

In this debate, a key issue concerns the criteria by which earlier forms of organisation are thought to be ineffective, in particular whether their deficiencies are technical (i.e. they are inefficient) or politico-economic (i.e. they poorly serve the material and control interests of owners). It is, however, implicit in most of these accounts that the deficiencies of earlier forms of work organisation are deficiencies from the point of view of owners and managers.

This issue also permeates the 'prospective functional' view, which accounts for rationalisation in terms of its capacity, or promise, to realise certain outcomes. Here the debate is about whether the potential benefits of rationalisation are those of improved technical efficiency, tighter managerial control or greater profitability.

The technical advantages are, not surprisingly, emphasised by the main advocates of Scientific Management and industrial engineering, who stress that rationalisation serves the interests of managers and workers alike. Even those who argue that rationalisation serves narrower purposes and interests concede that it promised, and delivered, real technical improvements in work organisation, such as more appropriate deployment of labour, increased dexterity and speed of work, improved work- and materials-flow and the systematic application of technology.

In contrast, others claim that the putative gains which most convincingly account for rationalised organisation are those of capitalist efficiency. They argue that, whatever the rhetoric of Scientific Management, the attractions of rationalisation lie in the deskilling of work which serves to make large elements of work susceptible to performance by unskilled and cheaper workers, facilitates replacement of workers by machines, and wrests control over the work process away from workers. In short, rationalisation reduces, weakens and cheapens the power of labour in the work process.

The issue then becomes whether greater managerial control is a necessary prerequisite of profitability, and this revolves around whether rationalisation is introduced primarily to cheapen or weaken labour. Those who see the weakening of labour as the prerequisite of profitability argue that managers must overcome generalised worker resistance to attempts at control and, thus, must reduce the leverage available to them by deskilling and division (Goldman and Van Houten, 1977; Zimbalist, 1979). A somewhat different twist to this argument is that rationalisation also serves to bequeath a role – that of coordinating a now divided workforce – to managers, thereby justifying their existence (Marglin, 1976).

Others caution against this view, arguing that profit may be pursued by a variety of means and that rationalisation is an attractive strategy only when the problem of profitability is a production problem (Kelly, 1982; Wood, 1983). Further, they argue that reducing labour costs by reducing the size, altering the composition and improving the utilisation of labour need not entail greater managerial control.

The different functional accounts have the merit of demonstrating how certain ideas chime with problems of work organisation on a large scale. Their weakness is in implying that these problems generated their own ready-made solutions. In contrast, the 'action' account examines rationalisation in terms of the force of ideas of its key protagonists. Whilst some writers deal with the influence of Gilbreth, Gantt and Bedaux, the majority focus upon Taylor, the peculiar conjunction of his biography and ideas and his role as ideologue and catalyst. The weakness of this account is that with its gaze fixed on the ideas of a single man, it loses sight of the general 'thrust for efficiency' movement (Palmer, 1975). Indeed, treatment of Taylor's writings as a paradigm case imposes an unnecessary restriction upon discussions of rationalisation.

A different kind of action account attributes the application of ideas associated with rationalisation not to their intrinsic persuasiveness, but to their promotion by professional groups whose interests they serve. For managers, Scientific Management provides both an ideology of management, a justification for particular forms of organisation and a managerial ideology – a justification for managers as a distinct profession (Perrow, 1979; Rose, 1988). Scientific Management also provides an analysis of work couched in engineering terms, thus rendering engineers those best equipped to solve them (Armstrong, 1986; Rose, 1988).

The merit of these arguments is that they identify some human agency in the process of rationalisation in the guise of groups who have the motive, in the form of collective interest, and the means, in the form of power resources, to introduce such changes. However, the explanation fails to show why the pursuit of certain interests is successful and also runs into the problem of whether rationalisation is a conscious, deliberately chosen, unified managerial strategy. Many doubt that managers possess a common collective interest which they pursue remorselessly (Salaman, 1982; Wood, 1983).

It is, therefore, probably prudent to regard the process of rationalisation as the outcome of a conjunction of forces. Within particular historical circumstances, recognition of the deficiencies of existing forms of work organisation and the promise of greater technical efficiency, managerial control and profitability is galvanised by the allure of certain ideas and their promotion by managers and industrial engineers.

The debate about the extent of rationalisation revolves around the degree to which it is applied fully and unopposed. Much of the debate is about how far Taylorism has become the basis for organising operational work. On this point, at least, the evidence is clear: orthodox Taylorism is more a prototype than an adopted blueprint. 'Full-blooded' Taylorism was limited historically to comparatively few organisations, principally in the USA (Nadworny, 1955; Littler, 1982; Burawoy, 1985). Elsewhere, watered down versions or other systems of work rationalisation, such as the Bedaux system, Fordism or generalised 'technical control' were introduced (Gartman, 1979; Littler, 1982).

However, Taylorism did play a crucial role as a set of vanguard ideas providing a basic philosophy on which more diffuse changes in organisation are based (Thompson, 1983) and which continues to underpin approaches to job design and to inform the practical activities, if not the values, of system designers.

However, at a practical level, rationalisation is not the exclusive model for organising operational work. Burawoy (1985) distinguishes between 'despotic' regimes, based on coercion, which subsume 'paternalistic' and 'patriarchal' varieties, and 'hegemonic' regimes, based on consent. He also notes the recent emergence of 'hegemonic despotism' where consent is mobilised in response to market coercion. Friedman (1977) distinguishes between 'direct control' involving task specification, minimal worker autonomy and close supervision and 'responsible autonomy' where workers are given broader job responsibilities, more discretion and relative freedom from supervision. We pick up on these and other variations in Chapter 6. The important point here is that these forms of organisation have, in certain instances, pre-empted as well as replaced rationalised organisation. Equally, craft forms of work organisation have endured in skilled areas of work in a number of industries such as construction, engineering and catering (More, 1983; Penn, 1983; Gabriel, 1988).

How far rationalisation is introduced smoothly and unopposed is also a matter of debate. Certainly, Taylorism evoked vehement and widespread opposition (Aitken, 1960). Worker resistance centred on the preservation of craft autonomy through segmentation and social exclusion (Stark, 1980; Thompson, 1983) or a refusal to operate new systems, enforced either by collective action or individual job mobility (Littler and Salaman, 1984). Opposition also came from foremen whose management role was much curtailed. More surprising, perhaps, was opposition from employers and managers, yet this proved decisive in many cases, particularly in the UK (Littler, 1982; Thompson, 1983). This opposition was partly in anticipation of likely worker resistance and a reluctance to provoke confrontation, partly the result of recognising the inherent problems of rationalised organisation and partly the result of a belief that economic conditions made such changes unnecessary. There is also evidence of general opposition to other forms of rationalisation, such as the Bedaux system or Fordism or to specific features such as piece-rates (Lamphere, 1979) or 'speed-up' (Beynon, 1975). However, this opposition has had limited success because some variant of rationalised work has become the dominant guiding principle for the organisation of operational work.

Whether the intended, or promised, effects of rationalisation ever materialised is also a matter of debate. Again, if the focus of the debate is kept to the narrow issue of deskilling and degradation of work, the evidence is clear. Because rational-isation creates, directly or indirectly, new areas of skill and autonomy (particularly in areas of technology and design), because there is both overt and covert opposition to and subversion of it, and because of the way in which changes in work organisation are mediated by changes in labour and product markets, deskilling is not the single, inexorable outcome of rationalisation. On the other hand, specific instances of delay, diversion or reversal of the process of deskilling do not necessarily mean that it is not a 'major tendential presence' (Thompson, 1983), particularly if new, skilled areas of work subsequently become deskilled themselves, as in the case of computer programming (Kraft, 1979).

The main components of the debate surrounding the process of rationalisation are summarised in Table 4.2. The broad conclusion to be drawn from this debate is that rationalised work organisation is not simply the destruction of craft organ-isation through the widespread, unopposed application of Scientific Management. Rather, it involves the gradual, negoti-ated and piecemeal supersession of earlier forms of organisation by the introduction of mechanisms which reflect the guiding principles of systematic work methods, detailed division of labour, centralised planning and control, an instrumental employment relationship and the cult of efficiency. It is this more equivocal process which has come to have a widespread, though not universal, application in the organisation of opera-tional work. Not only is operation work in most medium and large-scale manufacturing concerns still organised in this way, but many service industries, such as banking, insurance, catering, fast-food (Gabriel, 1988), budget hotels and retailing have only recently started to undergo the process of rational-isation. Although, as we see in Chapter 6, rationalised organ-isation is on the retreat in some quarters, elsewhere it endures and extends. If modern work organisation is not, and never

Table 4.2 The rationalisation of work: dimensions of the debate

Key issues

ORIGINS
What forms of work organisation are the starting point of rationalisation?

Main arguments:

Craft organisation *or* Simple/entrepreneurial organisation *or* Internal contract/delegated entrepreneurial organisation

CAUSES
Why does the process of rationalisation come about?

(Functional) (retrospective) — Response to 'crisis of control' in earlier forms of organisation:
- Craft
- Simple/entrepreneur
- Internal contract

or

(Historical) — Result of particular circumstances

or

(Action) — Result of ideas/actions of key actors:
- Force of ideas
- Occupational strategies

or

(Functional) (prospective) — Pursuit of outcomes:
- Technical / Control
- Politico-economic / Accumulation

CONSEQUENCES
How far has rationalisation proceeded?

Full implementation:
- Deskilling as inevitable
- Widespread application

or

Partial implementation:
- Opposition
- Alternative strategies

was, governed by Taylor's legendary stop-watch, much of it remains governed by the digital version.

RATIONALISED ORGANISATION: AN ASSESSMENT

Any assessment of rationalised organisation in terms of costs and benefits is complex, because of the absence of a single yardstick by which to judge it. Much depends on which benefits and costs are being considered and, critically, whom these affect. Very broadly, the potential benefits of rationalised work are those of system efficiency and hence accrue mainly to managers, whilst the costs are borne largely by the workforce. However, since these costs influence levels of motivation and effectiveness, their extent and severity determine the degree to which benefits are realised. Bearing this in mind, we examine the costs and benefits of each of the principles of rationalisation in turn.

Looking first at rationalised work methods, the principal organisational gains are those of improved productivity and closer managerial control. Productivity gains flow from more efficient expenditure of effort, use of machinery and better utilisation of materials and work-in-progress. Moreover, these are, in part, achieved independently of changes in physical effort since they stem from better ways of working. However, higher productivity also comes from faster work, brought on by the pace of machinery and flow-lines and changes in standard times ('speed-up'). Similarly, standard methods and mechanisation increase managerial control by facilitating the monitoring of use of materials, production costs, output quality and, crucially, worker performance, in terms of both output and methods of working.

Although there are grounds for deep scepticism of Taylor's messianic conviction that workers would enthusiastically embrace managerial directives and scientific methods (Taylor, 1947), rational methods bring some work satisfaction in the form of stability and predictability, a sense of performing a job well by developing a rhythm, or from being pulled along by the flow of work ('traction') (Baldamus, 1961) and from working with modern or high-tech equipment. Otherwise, the benefits of standard methods for workers are mainly the potential economic ones of higher pay and job security which may flow from efficient organisation.

The balance of evidence, however, suggests that intrinsic work satisfactions are minor, extrinsic benefits are problematic, and that both pale into insignificance against the detrimental effects which standard methods, output norms and machine-pacing can have on the experience of work. For the individual worker, rationalised work can bring four work deprivations: diminished job content, with loss of task and skill variety; reduced job control, with the loss of discretion over methods, tools, timing and pace of work; uncertain job context, with less sense of how work relates to that of others and fits into an overall process; and, lastly, possible job loss through redundancy.

How far rationalised work methods necessarily entail monotony, redundancy and deskilling is a matter of debate, to which there are four strands. Firstly, beyond a certain level of mechanisation, work may become 'reskilled' if automated equipment demands monitoring and trouble-shooting, rather than simple machine minding. However, the evidence for this is not strong, and there may be a skill 'hump' at relatively modest levels of mechanisation, beyond which skill requirements decline again (Bright, 1958; Nichols and Beynon, 1977). Secondly, workers may find elaborate ways of retaining variety and autonomy in the interstices of formally deskilled work through informal contrivances and interactions (Roy, 1973; Haraszti, 1977; Burawoy, 1979). However, whilst these may ameliorate workers' experience of work, they do not remove its causes and they may reduce levels of efficiency, safety or quality. Thirdly, mechanisation may create new jobs as it destroys others, either by creating new types of jobs, or extra jobs as production expands. However, the general displacement of labour from certain jobs or industries to others rarely involves the same workers: new jobs tend to be filled by new entrants to the labour market. Lastly, whilst anticipation of likely outcomes leads workers to resist standard methods and mechanisation, that is hardly a defence of the principle.

Resistance by workers to the imposition of standard methods and mechanisation not only leads to a failure fully to implement these, but also to their reduced efficacy once implemented. Reduced job content and control mean that the potential of the workforce in terms of the skills which they have acquired and their capacity for initiative and autonomy is under-utilised. Rigid adherence to standard methods may be adequate (if not especially desirable) for mass production and assembly of standard products, but not for complex products/services or sophisticated equipment. Low work satisfaction reduces morale and commitment, as well as encouraging absenteeism and labour turnover. Consequently, the individual human parts of an intentionally optimal system function sub-optimally.

The deficiencies of standard methods and mechanisation also spring from two inherent contradictions. Firstly, many forms of work are not amenable to performance in standard ways and there are fundamental difficulties with the assumptions of method study. There is serious doubt about whether, even for simple, physical tasks – such as shovelling (Taylor's favourite) or bricklaying (Gilbreth's obsession) – a hybrid 'best way' which is assembled from different tasks performed by different skilled workers is in any practical sense 'best' for everyone. In the case of production or interactive service jobs, where the nature of the work is complex and situationally contingent and where the end-product is tailored to specific customer wants, the notion of 'one best way' is even more difficult to sustain. Secondly, complex, interdependent work systems, because of their very complexity and tight coupling, are vulnerable to market changes which require rapid alteration in product specifications and to disruption in any single component of the system. One crucial 'component' is, of course, the workforce, who come to possess a source of countervailing power from their capacity to disrupt.

Many of the costs and benefits associated with standard methods and mechanisation apply to the application of detailed division of labour. Again, the central organisational benefits are those of efficiency and enhanced managerial control. Four aspects of detailed division of labour have the potential to increase economic efficiency. Firstly, fragmentation of tasks produces greater technical efficiency in that repeated tasks are performed more quickly. Secondly, using unskilled, hence cheaper, labour to carry out routine tasks lowers labour costs. Thirdly, fragmentation and simplification facilitate mechanisation or automation. Lastly, training is minimised and workers can be shifted easily between different jobs. A detailed division of labour may also make labour more easy to control as a result of labour substitutability and break-up of the work group. Physical separation of both tasks and workers reduces interaction, retards the development of common perceptions and attitudes and means that managers can deal with workers as relatively isolated individuals.

The extent to which workers are, in practice, more manageable depends upon how the detailed division of labour impinges upon their experience of work. Some may retain or acquire skilled jobs, and others may find routine, repetitive work congenial. But the evidence cited above suggests that detailed division of labour and the loss of job content, control, context and security, are sources of deprivation at work. Jobs are narrow, repetitive, pressured, spatially isolated, lacking purpose and offer little or no discretion or security. Consequently, there is resistance to fragmentation and deskilling, which, paradoxically, may be strengthened by the effects of fragmentation and deskilling in creating a homogeneous workforce, aware of its common deprivations and a vulnerable, interdependent work system. Worker reactions are, therefore, one of the principal reasons why the potential organisational benefits of division of labour fail to materialise and economic efficiency falls short of its potential.

Even where workers are relatively compliant, the obsession with system efficiency may blunt individual performance. Multifaceted individuals are strait-jacketed into one-dimensional jobs, and the potential of 'human resources', both as individuals and as groups, is wasted. In losing their power to resist management, individuals and groups also lose their power as a productive force. Further, a detailed division of labour is also beset by internal contradictions which echo those of standardised work. Interdependent work systems are vulnerable to disruption, dependent upon even workflow and slow to adapt. Notwithstanding its inroads into technical (Kraft, 1979) and clerical work (de Kadt, 1979; Crompton and Jones, 1984), the general applicability of fragmentation remains doubtful.

For advocates of rationalised work, the costs of centralised planning and control and of maintaining a paper process to monitor and direct work are outweighed by gains in efficiency and control. However, apart from the problem of the extent to which operational efficiency is enhanced by elaborate planning and controls, there is also the question of the efficiency of this administrative structure itself. Bureaucracy, as Chapter 5 shows, is also beset by contradictions and problems. Further, the removal of many management functions from first-line supervisors creates ambiguity and role-conflict in the position. Consequently, supervisors may fail to fulfil their function as enforcers of organisational rules and instead come to be a source of amendment, neglect and circumvention of these rules.

A low-involvement employment relationship is also a double-edged sword. Restricting the employer–employee relationship to a purely contractual one, with a straight exchange of effort for pay, has the advantage for the employer of being able to hire and fire as necessary, and for the employee of having a freedom from obligation, moral or economic, to a specific employer. However, employers do not always concern themselves solely with the economic performance of employees, but become involved in measures to promote employee conformity and loyalty, including welfare provision. The role of the personnel department can, therefore, become an ambiguous, even contradictory, one (Watson, 1986) in an attempt to counter the problems which result from the commodification of labour. If employees, like their labour, are dispensable and work is simply a means to an end, and an insecure one at that, workers may neither feel nor display much sense of loyalty or commitment to their employer. Their orientation to work is an 'instrumental' one (Fox, 1980) even if they are able to find 'expressive' satisfaction in informal activities and relationships at work (Roy, 1973; Burawoy, 1979).

More specifically, if employees seek primarily to maximise their earnings, payment by results is effective and workers motivate themselves. Further, rate setting provides a vehicle for intensification of work, whilst proportional rates stabilise effort and progressively reduce unit labour costs. For workers, there is the prospect of a high level of effort-related pay. However, the promise does not always materialise. To be sure, in certain circumstances (e.g. the Ford 'Five Dollar Day') rationalised work is linked to a high wage strategy. Elsewhere, higher earnings may be more the result of the bargaining power of labour than of piecework *per se*. The piecework form has no necessary implication for the level of pay. Moreover, workers may 'satisfice' rather than seek to maximise pay, either to stabilise their earnings, or from a suspicion that they may work themselves out of a job or find that jobs have been retimed and rates cut. This encourages output restriction, a practice embodied in informal group norms and enforced through informal sanctions and which includes attempts to have jobs generously timed, going slow on jobs where achieving quota is either too difficult ('gold bricking') or easy ('gravy jobs') or holding back completed work (Roy, 1952, 1973). Further, individual or group attempts to attain output targets may lead to practices such as hoarding work and equipment, ignoring specifications, breaking safety rules and ignoring quality (Haraszti, 1977). Consequently, even with payment by results, there is a need for costly supervision to enforce work rules and control quality. The high cost of securing the cooperation of the workforce in a low-involvement employment relationship may offset any benefits in terms of greater control.

Given workers' experience of rationalised work, it is not surprising that the ideology of efficiency does not find universal acceptance. Certainly it finds favour with managers, for whom it has provided both a managerial language and a legitimation of their function. For workers, however, the lure of efficiency is largely in terms of putative economic benefits. Even where those benefits materialise, there are a number of counters to managerial rationality. The first accepts efficient organisation as legitimate, but questions whether it is best achieved through a 'science of work'. Workers' own knowledge of organising work, acquired through direct experience of doing it, may be superior to that derived from observation and analysis. Yet rationalised work not only neglects this rich vein but often seeks to suppress it. Secondly, the benefits of rational efficiency may be seen as accruing predominantly, if not exclusively, to employers and managers, in the form of greater control, power and rewards. Although workers may not develop a coherent alternative view of how work may be organised, they may be suspicious of and reluctant to accept a managerial perspective (Nichols and Armstrong, 1976).

Lastly, the challenge to the ethic of efficiency and the cult of rationality may be on a wider social front. A general scepticism of science, rationalism and 'scientism' (Habermas, 1971), and a moral rejection of many of the outputs of rationalised work such as mass goods and services, morally repugnant products, and pollution, coupled with an emphasis upon emotionality, intuition and the quality of life, have surfaced on a number of occasions (e.g. the 1960s counter culture, the Green Movement).

One effect has been to engender a rejection or questioning, particularly by the young, of the core assumptions of rationalised work.

There are therefore clear limits to rationality as a set of guiding principles and concrete practices in the organisation of work. The potential of rationalised organisation is not always realised, partly because of its inherent contradictions, but predominantly because those subject to it have opposed it, actively or passively, through minimal levels of commitment and involvement. For rationalised organisation to remain as pervasive and enduring in the face of this indicates two things. Firstly, in the production of mass, standardised goods and services, the gains to economic efficiency prevail over the technical and human costs of using these methods. Secondly, and more importantly, however, rationalised organisation endures because it provides managers with a powerful weapon of control, and the status of the active agents in work. The desire to remain 'in charge' leads managers to overlook or underestimate the fundamental weakness of rationalised organisation, that the means employed for planning and controlling work in detail have the effect of reducing the commitment, responsibility and enthusiasm of those who have to do it. Rationalised organisation elaborately plans and controls what it does not always deliver.

FURTHER READING

The key discussions of rationalisation and Scientific Management may be found in Taylor (1947), Tillett *et al.* (1970), Braverman (1974), Mouzelis (1975), Edwards (1979), Perrow (1979), Hill (1981), Kelly (1982), Littler (1982), Thompson (1983), Wood (1983), Burawoy (1985), Rueschmeyer (1986) and Rose (1988).

On the debate surrounding the origins, trajectory and impact of work rationalisation see, especially, Aitken (1960), Braverman (1974), Stone (1974), Palmer (1975), Marglin (1976), Lazonick (1978), Edwards (1979), Zimbalist (1979), Stark (1980), Hill (1981), Littler (1982), Salaman (1982), Thompson (1983), Wood (1983), Littler and Salaman (1984), Burawoy (1985) and Rose (1988).

Chapter 5

The search for rationality
Bureaucracy and bureaucratisation

In earlier chapters, we noted that separation of the management functions of planning, allocation, motivation, coordination and control corresponds with increasing dispersion of these functions through a management structure: a separate *process* of administration gives rise to the growth of *an* administration. How an administration is organised, therefore, represents a way of managing the process of management and the managers who conduct it. In this chapter, we examine the most enduring and pervasive approach to the organisation of administrative or managerial work: bureaucracy. Having specified from among different variations what we mean by the term, we identify the basic principles upon which it rests, analyse the main features of bureaucratic organisations in practice and summarise bureaucracy in terms of the MTO framework. From here, we go on to examine the key issues surrounding bureaucratic organisation: firstly, whether there is a single homogeneous 'bureaucratic' form of organisation, and secondly, whether the process of bureaucratisation is inevitable.

From description and analysis of what bureaucracy and bureaucratisation entail, we turn in the latter part of the chapter to an evaluation of this approach to work organisation, and consider its strengths and weaknesses. In this evaluation, as in our earlier description, a central theme is the tension between the efficiency of bureaucracy as a technical work system and its effectiveness as a system of power and control. As with rationalised work, so with bureaucracy, we again confront the contradictions between management as planning and coordination, and management as direction and control and, relatedly, between organisation as a technical device, and organisation as

a political instrument. We argue that the durability of bureaucracy in the face of problems and inefficiencies testifies to a
preoccupation with direction and control on the part of those
who manage.

BUREAUCRATIC ORGANISATION: GENERAL PRINCIPLES

The concept of bureaucracy has dominated the field of organisation theory and, for many, 'large-scale organisation' and
'bureaucracy' are synonymous (Child, 1977; Presthus, 1979).
Equally, Weber's 'ideal type' bureaucracy (Weber, 1964) stands
as a kind of totem which many writers on organisation feel
obliged to dance around if their aim is ultimately to knock it
down. The ubiquity of the concept reflects reality, however, for
as we see below, bureaucracy forms the blueprint for the
organisation of managerial or administrative work in the same
way that rationalisation dominates the organisation of operational work. However, the ubiquity of the concept also reflects
its very different usages. Albrow (1970) discerns seven different
usages: 'rational organisation', 'organisational inefficiency',
'rule by officials', 'public administration', 'administration by
officials', 'the organisation' (*in toto*) and 'modern society',
whilst Beetham (1987) reduces these to three: a form of organisation in general; non-economic, grant-funded organisations;
and public administration. Our concern here is to consider
bureaucracy as an approach to the organisation of work,
recognising that parts of an organisation may be organised
bureaucratically, whilst other parts are not.

In identifying and setting out the general principles and key
features of bureaucracy, we draw upon writers whose names
inevitably read like a roll-call of the great and the good in
organisation theory. Two of these writers, Weber and Fayol,
deserve particular comment. Whilst it is true that Weber's
concern is with the wider issue of social forms of domination
and authority, and that his 'ideal type' bureaucracy is a way of
capturing conceptually the growth of rational-legal authority,
rather than a set of organisational prescriptions, none the less
his analysis of bureaucracy as a form of organisation has clear
practical implication. Fayol's writings are more evidently prescriptive, but are often regarded as 'formal theory', quite distinct

from analysis of bureaucracy. This distinction is largely arti-ficial, since both 'bureaucracy' and Fayol's 'formal adminis-tration' describe an essentially similar approach to the organ-isation of managerial work.

Three central principles of bureaucratic organisation, which subsume a number of more detailed characteristics, may be discerned: specialisation, hierarchy and impersonal rationality. In essence, bureaucratic organisation involves dividing adminis-trative work into specific functions and roles and then coordin-ating and controlling those diverse efforts through a combina-tion of detailed procedures and a vertical chain of reporting relationships.

Specialisation relates both to work and people: work is divided into detailed, interdependent functional areas and allocated to those with particular specialist skills and knowl-edge. Thus it subsumes departmentation by function, a role-based division of labour and the recruitment, selection, training and promotion of employees on the basis of technical or administrative expertise. Functional departmentation means that the overall work process is divided into its constituent elements or combinations of techniques which together shape the final 'product' (or service). These functional elements form the basis of departments, which are, in turn, divided into sections, offices and, at the lowest level, particular jobs. In addition, there are departments, and their respective sub-divisions, which provide technical or physical services to the core activities. Hence, there is the broad division between 'line' and 'staff' (Fayol, 1949). Within functions, jobs have designated bounded areas of responsibility and are limited to particular activities: there is role specialisation.

People, as well as jobs, are specialised in that recruitment and selection are on the basis of specialist expertise or potential to fulfil a particular work role, and rewards and promotion are on the basis of demonstrated competence. In fact, there are two distinct senses in which individuals may specialise: either as specialist administrators carrying out a detailed part of the administrative process, or as technical experts occupying staff positions.

The principle of hierarchy refers to a graded, vertical system of manager–subordinate relationships, or 'scalar chain' (Fayol, 1949), with each position having a defined area of responsibility and power in the form of access to organisational resources and reporting to the one above it. At the most extreme there is 'unity of command', where each employee receives orders from one superior only, and 'unity of direction', where there is only one head for any group of activities (Fayol, 1949). Orders and instructions flow downwards and control information flows upwards. Thus, hierarchy is a system of delegated power and responsibilities and graded rewards and status where the power attaching to a particular position is commensurate with responsibilities. There is some debate about whether bureaucracy is essentially 'centralised' or 'decentralised'. We address the details of this debate later. For now, we follow Rueschmeyer (1986) in viewing the principle of hierarchy as the delegation of power and responsibility within centralised control. Occupants of positions 'lower down' the chain of command are permitted, indeed obliged, to take certain decisions, but within the constraints of rules and policy decided centrally.

The extent to which hierarchy represents an authority system, rather than simply a distribution of power, flows from the principle of impersonal rationality. This means that decisions, actions and relationships are seen as means to particular ends, governed by considerations of what is both necessary and sufficient for the efficient achievement of these ends, and therefore immune from personal considerations. Impersonal rationality subsumes three other principles which pervade bureaucratic organisation: regulation, standardisation and formalisation.

Regulation means that behaviour is subject to detailed, comprehensive rules. What is to be done, by whom and how, are set out in detailed work procedures. The relationship between the individual and the organisation is specified by the terms of the employment contract and by rules relating to the rights and duties of the individual within the work-place. Lastly, relationships among employees are governed by regulations concerning the nature and scope of communications, instructions and mutual expectations. Insofar, therefore, as hierarchical relationships are seen as necessary for the fulfilment of certain ends and are governed by accepted regulations, a system of legitimate power, or authority, exists.

Standardisation describes the nature and purpose of rules, namely to impose conformity, regularity and predictability on relationships and work behaviour, through a process of categorisation (Merton, 1966). Classes of events or problems are handled in standard ways. Formalisation describes the form of rules which, in bureaucracy, has a reified and prescriptive quality. That is, rules specify what should be done, and have a concrete, usually written, form.

The principles of specialisation, hierarchy and impersonal rationality are closely linked in practice. Hierarchy is the principle of specialisation applied vertically and is itself rule-governed. Specialisation is the outcome of applying impersonal rationality to the division of labour. Regulation, standardisation and formalisation are only possible where work roles are specialised and controlled hierarchically.

BUREAUCRACY IN PRACTICE: KEY FEATURES

Each of the principles outlined above are manifested, to different degrees and in varying combinations, in six major features of bureaucratic organisation in practice: a formalised employment relationship; an elaborate division of labour; a centralised, yet delegated system of decision-making; a vertical coordination and control system; a proliferation of rules; and a focus on regularity, predictability and control.

The bureaucratic employment relationship is essentially contractual, in that the relationship between the individual and the organisation is specified in some detail in a formal contract. Thus, individuals are employees, recruited and selected on the basis of formal criteria relating to qualifications and experience. They occupy particular work roles, the duties and responsibilities of which are defined in formal job descriptions, whilst the relationship with other work roles is specified in reporting relationships and organisation charts. Employees are subject to formalised objective setting and regular performance review, appraisal and evaluation, all of which are themselves conducted on the basis of specified procedures. Thus the employment relationship is regularly monitored in routine ways.

Appropriate employee performance is encouraged by the use of a formalised reward and punishment system. Employees receive a regular, fixed salary, rising by periodic increments, together with a range of fringe benefits such as pensions, sick pay, welfare benefits, extramural facilities. An elaborate hierarchy of job grades, coupled with relatively secure employment, means that employees may look forward to career progression. Promotion takes place on the basis of regulated criteria, usually a combination of expertise (qualifications) and experience (seniority), operating within formal evaluation procedures undertaken by managers. Appropriate employee performance is also sought by the provision of regular and formalised training in technical and administrative skills and organisational procedures.

Inappropriate work performance is 'negatively' punished, i.e. by withholding rewards, by the provision of training or transfer. Disciplinary measures are reserved for infringements of workplace regulations and, again, follow routinised procedures such as verbal and written warnings, suspension and finally dismissal.

Thus, bureaucratic work organisation creates an internal labour market, with positions filled predominantly from within the organisation, except for certain posts acting as 'ports of entry' to which employees are recruited from outside (Doeringer and Piore, 1971). Considerable emphasis is placed upon the 'good employee' who internalises and willingly complies with organisational regulations. Thus the employment relationship is characterised by dependency, with employees increasingly 'locked into' the organisation because of the lure of career and promotion and the high opportunity costs of changing employment.

The elaborate division of labour has a number of aspects. Firstly, there is the broad division between line and staff (Fayol, 1949; Mintzberg, 1979), that is between those involved in the organisation's 'core' activity and those whose function is to service this activity, whether in a physical form (e.g. maintenance, catering), human form (e.g. personnel and training), conceptual form (e.g. planning and budgetary systems) or informational form (e.g. market research). In bureaucratic organisation, this division between core and subsidiary functions is sharp, reflected in the division between 'administrators' and 'technical specialists' (or 'experts'), not only in respect of work content, but also in terms and conditions of employment, power, status and orientations. This division gives rise to the distinction between 'administrative' and 'expert' authority (Albrow, 1970; Presthus, 1979), or between positional power based on administrative knowledge and personal power based on technical expertise. It also determines whether decision-making or advice/guidance are the central elements of an individual's work role and whether employees are 'locals', loyal to the organisation, or 'cosmopolitans', loyal to a profession (Gouldner, 1957). Indeed, staff may be subject to 'professional', rather than bureaucratic, organisation (see Chapter 7).

Within the broad line and staff functions are further, predominantly functional, divisions. Departments subsume sections, offices and specific jobs, each of which have bounded and interlocking areas of functional responsibility. There is a proliferation of job titles and grades (Edwards, 1979), with jobs differentiated both horizontally, by work content, and hierarchically by their breadth of responsibilities, by the amount of power which attaches to them, the degree of autonomy which they carry, as well as by salary and status.

This vertical division of labour also forms the backbone of a centralised, but delegated, decision-making system. Broad, strategic decisions are taken centrally, or at the 'top', whilst operating decisions of decreasing scope and constrained by broader policy are dispersed down the hierarchy. Thus, bureaucracy is 'decentralised' in the nominal sense that almost every employee takes some sort of decision (Pugh *et al.*, 1968; Perrow, 1972) but is 'centralised' in the substantive sense that key decisions which set the parameters for detailed operational decision-making are taken by a relatively small number of senior managers (Mintzberg, 1979; Rueschmeyer, 1986).

Following Mintzberg (1979) we can identify two categories of key decisions. The first is policy: broad statements about the objectives and *modus operandi* of the organisation. In bureaucracy, policy is decided by senior managers and is imposed 'top-down' through the hierarchy, where it is translated into increasingly specific operational activities. The second major type of decision is rule-making, concerned with how things are done. Rules take a variety of forms, but all seek to direct and channel the behaviour of employees by specifying what actions are (or are not) to be taken in specific circumstances. Rule-making in bureaucracy is undertaken mainly by central, specialist departments. Thus, for example, rules relating to the nature of the employment relationship or to general conduct at work will be developed by the personnel department. These rules are not so much filtered down as imposed as standard procedures upon appropriate operational areas. The function of the administrative hierarchy in this case is to identify and apply rules appropriate to their specific area. In short, rules and procedures *flow* down, whilst policy *filters* down.

Information and communication flows are predominantly vertical. Decisions and rules are communicated down whilst feedback information flows upwards. These communications are largely formal, with impersonal interaction between managers and subordinates through memoranda or reports. Hierarchy is also evident in a unified, vertical coordination and control system. Bureaucracy is 'imperatively coordinated' (Weber, 1964). This takes two different forms. First, coordination of activities comes from compliance with rules and procedures which carry indications of when activities are to be carried out, and from whom and to whom work is to flow. Secondly, coordination comes about through the flow of information passing between, and by decisions taken by, managers with hierarchical responsibility for different areas of work. Thus, coordination is through the force of either impersonal rules or commands issued from a particular hierarchical level.

In bureaucracy, coordination and control are inextricable, since control is effected through a combination of impersonal rules and the monitoring of subordinate behaviour by managers. Further, since detailed specifications of what is to be done, when, how and by whom, are formulated centrally, so control is, in effect, exercised centrally, even if its enforcement is delegated to lower-level managers. Hierarchy means that all but the lowest levels both control the work of others and are themselves controlled from above: every employee is, in a rudimentary sense, a 'manager' (Edwards, 1979). However, there is a wealth of difference between the control exercised by senior managers and that exercised by junior managers, in terms of numbers of subordinates, areas of control and degrees of discretion.

Although monitoring of performance involves the direct intervention of managers in the work of subordinates, this intervention is carried out impersonally. It takes place between office holders, not personalities, and with regard to the objective situation and the regulations, not personal preferences. Thus, bureaucracy is characterised by the infusion of control into the system of social relations itself. 'The system' stands as a reified entity over and above individual employees.

The practical embodiment of this reified system of control are rules, regulations and procedures. No form of work organisation, nor indeed any form of ordered human activity, operates without rules of some kind. What is distinctive about bureaucratic organisation is their number and formality. The hallmark of bureaucratic organisation is the attempt to direct work behaviour through formal regulations covering, if not every eventuality, then most. Within this 'proliferation of rules' (Perrow, 1972), we may distinguish three basic types. First, there are organisational regulations, designed to maintain discipline and thus specifying appropriate and inappropriate conduct at work. These are usually embodied in codes of conduct and company regulations, and relate to matters such as time-keeping, health and safety, and so on. The second category is the organisational 'constitution', which specifies employee rights. These are embodied in agreements and employee handbooks and cover matters such as industrial relations, grievance procedures, staff evaluation, promotion, pay and conditions.

Both types of rules are unremarkable and are likely to be found in any undertaking. The *differentia specifica* of bureaucracy, however, are administrative procedures which seek to specify how work is to be carried out, by indicating when and how events, people or materials are to be dealt with in the context of a particular work role. These procedures are embodied in job descriptions, manuals and work documentation such as goods received sheets, stock sheets, staff records, requisition orders, files and standard letters.

Written records and files are also characteristic of bureaucracy. As records of past actions they constitute a reference point by which present actions are guided, and thus conduce towards regularity, routine and continuity. Indeed, bureaucracy is the embodiment of an obsession with order: the attempt to regulate behaviour precisely so as to render it routine, predictable and easier to control. Whether bureaucracy is 'rational' or 'efficient' is considered below. For now, we may note that, whatever the outcome, the desire to standardise, routinise, regulate, predict and control is fundamental to the bureaucratic ethos. Whether or not it succeeds, bureaucracy attempts to legislate away all extraneous and unpredictable influences upon the conduct of work by reducing it to an impersonal, mechanistic process.

We can now summarise bureaucratic organisation in terms of the MTO framework. In bureaucracy, management functions are both separated from the work process and dispersed through a structure of managerial positions. Planning and decision-making is centralised and pyramidal, with policy and strategy formulated centrally by senior managers and implemented through tactical and operating decisions delegated down the hierarchy. The system rests upon a predominantly vertical flow of formal policy and procedures downwards and control information upwards. The allocation of work is on the basis of functional differentiation of departments and offices and role specialisation by individuals. The level of job specialisation is high, with job responsibilities closely circumscribed and autonomy constrained by policy and procedures. Overall, therefore, the task system exhibits a detailed vertical and horizontal division of labour.

Motivation relies upon channelling behaviour through rules which take the form of administrative procedures; deferred material and symbolic rewards in the form of salary, career, employment security and status trappings; and a rationale, or ideology, of 'administrative efficiency', emphasising the desirability of standard, predictable and 'proper' behaviours.

Coordination is hierarchical, relying upon the impersonal force of work procedures or formal directives from managers responsible for different functional areas. Control relies upon formal, external controls over processes, in the form of standard work procedures, and inputs, in the form of standard recruitment criteria and procedures, enforced through direct supervision, in the form of behaviour and output monitoring by line managers. Thus, bureaucracy is characterised by a formalised, prescriptive and multi-dimensional control system. These points are summarised in Table 5.1.

BUREAUCRACY IN PRACTICE, THE CENTRAL ISSUES: IS BUREAUCRACY A UNITARY FORM OF ORGANISATION? IS BUREAUCRATISATION INEVITABLE?

Thus far, our discussion appears to imply that bureaucracy represents a single, invariant form of organisation, within which differences of emphasis, but not differences of substance, are

Table 5.1 Managing through bureaucratic organisation

Management process	: Management functions separate from work process and dispersed
Area of application	: Managerial, administrative and some operational work
Planning/decision-making	
Degree of centralisation	: Centralised, but pyramidal: rules/policy decisions made centrally constrain lower-level operating decisions
Information/communication flows	: Predominantly vertical and formal
Allocation of work	
Form of specialisation	: By function
Level of specialisation	: Departments and work roles
Degree of job specialisation	: High: jobs based on prescribed roles
Motivation	
Rewards	: Deferred, extrinsic rewards for conformity and loyalty
Rules	: Administrative procedures
Rationale	: Administrative efficiency, conformity
Coordination	
Locus of responsibility	: Line managers; procedures } Hierarchical coordination
Method	: Direction
Degree of formality	: Formal
Control	
Focus	: Processes
Locus of responsibility	: External } Rules and direct supervision
Degree of impersonality	: Highly impersonal
Degree of formality	: Highly formalised

possible. Considerable evidence, however, questions the existence of one, unitary bureaucratic type and the validity of this
evidence needs to be assessed.

To some extent, the discovery of bureaucratic variation is a
function of the tendency to regard 'bureaucracy' and 'organisation' as synonymous, and hence to regard alternative forms
of organisation, even decentralised forms, as variations on
bureaucracy. We return to this in Chapter 7. Secondly, the
unitary form of bureaucracy which some attempt to 'disprove'
is something of an artificial construction. Weber's original
concept (Weber, 1964) admits of variation, in forms of authority, expertise and centralisation, and Fayol's fourteen 'principles of management' (Fayol, 1949) include a number of
contingent dimensions, such as centralisation, specialisation,
authority, the scalar chain, tenure and remuneration, which are
recognised as existing in various forms or to different degrees.

Research evidence points to variation in hierarchy, specialisation and rationality. Hierarchy varies in terms of the height
of the chain of command, hence bureaucratic organisations may
be 'tall' or 'flat' (Carzo and Yanouzas, 1969), and, corres-
pondingly, the span of control, or the number of subordinates
reporting to a manager, may be wide or narrow (Van Fleet and
Bedeian, 1977). This is confirmed by identification of different
'shapes' of bureaucratic organisation other than the traditional
pyramid (Kaufman and Seidman, 1970). However, whilst some
variation in hierarchy is possible within an organisation which
remains 'bureaucratic', beyond a certain point the absence of
hierarchy must connote not bureaucratic variation but a quali-
tatively different way of organising. This is confirmed by the
tendency of these different forms to be used for organising
professional employees, or 'staff'.

Bureaucratic organisation is also shown to be compatible
with specialisation, and in particular, departmentation, based
upon products, markets or geographical areas as well as functions (Koontz et al., 1984). At a more detailed level, specialisation varies in terms of the proportion of technical specialists
employed (Pugh and Hickson, 1973) and the degree to which
work roles are narrowly defined. 'Specialisation' may connote
routinisation, close definition or formalisation (Child, 1972).

The extent to which bureaucracy is uniformly 'rational' is
challenged in two ways. The first issue, whether bureaucracy is

'efficient', is considered below. The second focuses upon rules. Bureaucracy is shown to be compatible with different kinds of systems for drawing up rules. Gouldner (1964) distinguishes between 'representative' bureaucracy, where managers and subordinates jointly initiate and enforce rules, 'punishment-centred' bureaucracy, where managers impose rules, and 'mock' bureaucracy, where rules are imposed from outside. Littler (1982) notes a dichotomy in the guardianship of rules, between 'unilateral' and 'multilateral' systems. Again, however, how far organisations can shift to participative, multilateral rules, and remain bureaucratic is questionable.

Some studies suggest that features of bureaucracy represent dimensions or continua which correlate or 'configure' in different ways (Hall, 1963). The best documented, and most debated, relationship is between 'centralisation' and other features. A number of researchers (Pugh *et al.*, 1968; Blau, 1970; Child, 1972; Mansfield, 1973) suggest that 'centralisation' on the one hand, and 'specialisation', 'formalisation' and 'standardisation' on the other represent alternative bureaucratic strategies. Thus, work may be organised 'bureaucratically' either through having operating decisions taken centrally and transmitted as direct orders, or through the creation of standardised, formalised procedures by which decentralised operating decisions are guided. Thus, delegated operating decisions, albeit constrained by procedures, are regarded as 'decentralisation', and bureaucracy is deemed a 'decentralised' form of organisation. Pugh (1973) distinguishes between 'full' bureaucracy, where decisions are centralised and activities structured, and 'workflow' bureaucracy where highly structured activities mean that decision-making is decentralised. Similarly, Udy (1959) distinguishes between 'bureaucratic' (centralised) and 'rational' organisation.

Certainly, there is a difference of organisational approach being identified here, since managers can choose either to issue context-specific commands, or to codify generalised, impersonal commands into rules. However, it is clear that, in both cases, control is being exercised by those who issue the commands or make the rules, and the difference is largely tactical. Indirect control, through rules, is equally, if not more stringent, precisely because of its indirect, impersonal quality (Blau and Schoenherr, 1973). In short, bureaucratic organisation is, in essence, centralised, just as it is, in essence, hierarchical, functionally specialised and rule-governed.

Indeed, there is sufficient in common between the principles of rationalisation discussed in Chapter 4 and the principles of bureaucracy outlined here to regard both as variations on the same theme and, hence, collectively as the 'classical' approach to organisation. Where they differ is in terms of their areas of application and, related to this, their emphasis. Traditionally, operational work has been subject to rationalisation, whilst bureaucracy is a form of organisation reserved for managerial and administrative work. Linked to this is the sense in which rationalisation is the typification of a 'low-trust' organisational strategy (Fox, 1985), whereas bureaucracy, based on defined roles and procedural, rather than technical rules, rests upon somewhat less jaundiced assumptions about employees (Salaman, 1980). This distinction does not always hold, however. As Chapter 4 showed, clerical and administrative work is increasingly subject to rationalisation and, as we argue below, some areas of operational work have been organised along bureaucratic lines.

This links into the question of whether bureaucratisation, particularly of managerial and administrative work, is inevitable. The process of bureaucratisation is very much the combination of developments (described in Chapter 3) which occur when originally entrepreneurial organisations grow and management functions become, increasingly, dispersed and institutionalised, namely: managerial specialisation, coordination and control through hierarchy and impersonal regulations, a separation of formal and informal activities and the reification of organisation.

For many, these developments signify an inexorable pressure to bureaucratise administration, similar to the inexorable pressure to rationalise operational work, within large-scale organisation. They argue that management of work on an increasingly large scale necessitates differentiation and specialisation, which in turn necessitate vertical differentiation and delegation of responsibility to coordinate these diverse efforts and standardisation and formalisation to control them. Bureaucracy is seen as the inevitable consequence of size. A central debate is about whether this is a technical necessity – the only possible way of coordinating work on a large scale (Mintzberg, 1979; Presthus,

1979) – or a contingent outcome of inequalities of power and the needs of the powerful to control work (Thompson, 1980; Rueschmeyer, 1986). The position taken here is that bureaucracy becomes technically inevitable, given the separation of management and its exercise in the interests of owners and employers. Indeed, one concomitant of managerial power is a capacity to impose particular definitions of the imperatives of large scale.

The historical rise of bureaucracy is also unsurprising, if not necessarily inevitable, given the 'elective affinity' between bureaucratic organisation and wider socio-cultural change (Eisenstadt, 1959; Weber, 1964). Initially, bureaucracy was a form of state administration linked with the growth of rationality, the increasing application of means-ends orientation to social and economic life and a shift in the basis of authority from personal charisma or tradition to rational-legal forms. The adoption of bureaucratic principles of administration by other large organisations followed from the industrial-capitalist context in which they were operating and its prevailing ethos of means-ends rationality. With industrialism came the application of scientific principles to productive ends and the idea of technical rationality. With capitalism came economic calculation, the search for least-cost means of achieving particular ends and the idea of economic rationality. Both forms of rationality find expression in the principles of specialisation, expertise and planning and control systems.

At the same time, the growth of bureaucratic administration also depended upon the growth of literacy, urbanisation and an increase in formal political freedoms (Stinchcombe, 1965; 1969). Indeed, there is a close affinity between bureaucracy and 'modern' ways of thinking, characterised by mechanical understanding, measurement, analysis, abstraction, means-ends relationships and procedures (Berger, Berger and Kellner, 1974; Clegg, 1990).

On the other hand, there is historical and contemporary evidence that the bureaucratisation of business organisations which succeed and grow is neither instantaneous nor unstoppable. In essence, entrepreneurial forms of organisation, with a relative absence of managerial hierarchy, endure because proprietors do not trust managers to act in their interests and hence are reluctant to delegate decision-making. Even where such delegation does occur, it may be to family members who can be 'trusted', or to carefully groomed appointees whose loyalty is secured through long periods of managerial 'apprenticeship' and offers of partnership. In all of these cases, personalised and informal mechanisms of management are not replaced by impersonal, formal mechanisms. (The main dimensions of the debate on bureaucracy and bureaucratisation discussed above are summarised in Table 5.2.)

Further, 'bureaucratisation' is not synonymous with large-scale administration since bureaucratic principles may also be applied to operational work. Briefly, there may be the extension of the principles of hierarchical manager–subordinate relationships, specialisation based on role 'responsibilities' rather than detailed tasks, procedure-directed work-place behaviour and a formalised, career-based employment relationship for manual or blue-collar employees. These employees are usually highly unionised, with skills in short supply and/or are employees of large, monopolistic companies or state industries; such conditions both create the need and afford the opportunity for bureaucratisation. The attempt is to 'buy' the loyalty of unionised or skilled workers through the offer of employment security, fringe benefits, a 'constitutional' work-place where pay and grievances are negotiated and employee performance is assessed through agreed procedures, and 'managerial' responsibility. At the same time it attempts either to limit the oppositional power of established trade unions by involving them increasingly in the management process itself or to head off unionisation where it has not yet occurred (Goldman and Van Houten, 1977; Edwards, 1979; Burawoy, 1985).

BUREAUCRATIC ORGANISATION: AN ASSESSMENT

In our evaluation of bureaucratic organisation, its central elements – hierarchy, specialisation and impersonal rationality – are examined, firstly, individually, and secondly, in the way in which they configure overall. This approach not only permits a more systematic exposition but also makes the important point that the features of bureaucracy are double-edged, in that they have both intended and unintended consequences, and conduce to both efficiency and inefficiency.

The apparent impatience of many writers on bureaucracy to

Table 5.2 Bureaucracy and bureaucratisation: dimensions of the debate

Key issues	Main arguments		
IS BUREAUCRACY INEVITABLE?			
What were the internal pressures towards bureaucratisation?	Increased scale → Differentiation → Need for coordination → Hierarchy and rules ← Need for control ← Division ← Inequalities of power	or	
What was the context of bureaucratisation?	Modernity → Technical rationality	or	Capitalism → Economic rationality
IS BUREAUCRACY A UNITARY FORM?			
Is there one or many forms of bureaucratic organisation?	Bureaucracy as a single form (Hierarchy, Rationality, Specialisation)	or	Types of bureaucracy (Variation in forms of hierarchy, Variation in forms of rationality, Variation in forms of specialisation)
Is bureaucracy the predominant form of administration?	Predominant form → Universal pressure to bureaucratise	or	One of many (Survival of earlier forms (entrepreneurial, internal contract), New forms of administration (professional, adhocracy, divisionalised))

proceed to its detailed indictment means that its strengths often get little attention in the literature. Yet evident strengths and advantages there certainly are.

Hierarchy offers, at least potentially, the advantage of delegated decision-making within the context of centralised control and unity of direction. Further, centralised policy and rule-making affords two potential advantages. Firstly, since these decisions are taken by the same, relatively small, group of people, they can be taken consistently and swiftly. Secondly, decisions can be taken on the basis of wide feedback information and a close knowledge of policy. In short, policy decisions can reflect a broad overview of both ends and means.

At the same time, hierarchy permits coordination of specialised activities through systematic designation of both responsibility, or a sense of who is 'in charge' of a particular area, and accountability, in that those who are in charge are themselves answerable to others. Equally, responsibilities can correspond with different levels of decision-making, in terms of scope or 'time-spans of discretion', the length of time taken before the outcomes of decisions become known (Jacques, 1976).

Finally, the vertical differentiation of employees, combined with an internal labour market, facilitates both succession, the identification and advancement of successors to positions of responsibility and cooptation, the fostering of loyalty and compliance by providing security and rewards for seniority (Presthus, 1979).

The advantages of specialisation have, to some extent, been considered in Chapter 4 and need not be repeated here at length. The advantages of functional departmentation are, firstly, that it is a logical reflection of the different elements of the work process and of individual expertise, and secondly, that it facilitates centralised control since only at the centre do different functions 'come together' in a unified whole (Koontz *et al.*, 1984). Staff–line differentiation corresponds to different kinds of expertise and also maintains a clear distinction between primary and support activities. Lastly, role specialisation permits the appropriate use and development of specialist employees and clearly delineates individual responsibilities.

Impersonal rationality has advantages for organisational efficiency and control and for the experience of individual employees. As guides to conduct, rules and records make for greater predictability and thus reduce potential uncertainty, complexity and variability (Perrow, 1972; Walsh and Dewar, 1987). Since operations can proceed smoothly and consistently, without the delay or unpredictability of *ad hoc* decisions, there is continuity and durability. Formalisation of rules reduces communication time, by reducing complex instructions to simple formulae and offers standards against which particular actions may be checked or by which particular problems may be resolved. Formalised rules are also powerful ways of directing behaviour, precisely because they are impersonal. The *de facto* control exercised by those who formulate rules is masked by the appearance of rules as logical inevitabilities and by the illusion of freedom from overt control (Blau and Schoenherr, 1973; Edwards, 1979). This control is the stronger because rules also specify rights and make for fairness of treatment, which may serve to strengthen employee attachment.

Taken together, the principles of hierarchy, specialisation and impersonal rationality attempt to create a smooth-running administrative machine, with each part crafted precisely to carry out its allotted function and all the parts arranged in a logical structure, unified under central direction. Order, routine, predictability, precision, accountability and responsibility are the intended outcomes of this attempt, literally, to legislate away complexity, idiosyncrasy and unpredictability. The strengths of these principles and their apparent inevitability account for the pervasiveness of the bureaucratic form.

However, the features of bureaucracy which represent its potential strengths are also sources of weakness, either because of their intrinsic contradictions or because they produce consequences which are different from, even contrary to, those intended. Centralised decision-making can be remote from the operational levels at which rules and decisions apply (Crozier, 1964; Mintzberg, 1979). It may be based on information which, on its journey up the hierarchy, becomes out of date, over-processed, over-generalised and sanitised. Furthermore, policy and rules follow the same path downward through the hierarchical thicket, incurring delays, distortions, misinterpretations or failures to implement. Those to whom they apply may perceive rules as being inappropriate and out of touch with operational realities. Resentment of or lack of commitment to the content of centrally imposed rules may be exacerbated by a lack of involvement in the process of decision-making.

A hierarchical system may also become a device for abnegating responsibility, if decisions are referred upwards whenever there is the slightest ambiguity or doubt. Timidity and 'buck-passing' creates delays as decisions search for someone prepared to take them, and inevitably overloads senior managers.

The remoteness of the centre, combined with the control it is able to exert, creates the real possibility of centralisation becoming oligarchy (Michels, 1970; Presthus, 1979). Pressures of time, the need for increasingly specialised decisions and the tendency of those with power to retain and consolidate it mean that decision-making becomes increasingly unconstrained. Bureaucracy is, essentially, a way in which those who control organisations, the 'corporate group' (Beetham, 1987) or 'strategic apex' (Mintzberg, 1979), devolve the management process. There is, therefore, always a sense in which this group is 'above bureaucracy'. Oligarchic pressures mean that this group may also be 'beyond' bureaucracy, able to take decisions untrammelled by regulations and procedures. Bureaucracy then becomes solely an instrument of centralised power.

Hierarchy as a system of rewards and status also has its downside. Inequalities of status and condition create animosity between levels, exacerbated by the divide between policy and implementation. Thus hierarchy may create 'indifferents', who reject the rules of the bureaucratic game, and 'ambivalents', who accept the game but resent their inability to play it effectively (Presthus, 1979). Even those who accept and play the careerist game may develop status anxiety and a preoccupation with politicking, and hence do the things which are rewarded rather than what needs to be done. This may include avoidance of risk and initiative, rigid adherence to 'the rules' or bickering and battles for position (Crozier, 1964; Merton, 1966).

When we turn to the dysfunctions of specialisation we find evidence of routine work, boredom, low job satisfaction and alienation among clerical and technical workers (Aiken and Hage, 1970), administrative staff (Gouldner, 1964) and managers (Fletcher, 1973; Anthony, 1977, 1986; Thackray, 1988). The 'indifferent' response, where individuals regard work, not as a source of self-fulfilment or identity, but merely as a means of financing non-work activities, is clearly identifiable among managerial, administrative and professional staff managed bureaucratically. The consequence, in many cases, is managerial apathy, non-conformity and even militancy (Fletcher, 1973; Snape and Bamber, 1985; Goffee and Scase, 1989).

Instead of cooperating towards common goals, functional departments may become rivals, where conflict for organisational resources may result in the sub-optimal attainment of organisational goals. This 'goal-displacement' is reinforced by the tendency of specialist departments to pursue their own ends, to develop an insular outlook, to close ranks against outsiders and to engage in empire-building (Selznick, 1949; Crozier, 1964; Mintzberg, 1979).

Similar conflicts develop between line and staff functions (Dalton, 1959). Competition for resources is compounded by differences between the work background, knowledge and orientations of line managers and staff specialists. Reinforcing these differences is the clash between power based on formal position and that based on expertise. Thus, line managers feel threatened by staff expertise, whilst staff are frustrated by line managers' ability to reject advice.

Finally, expertise as the capacity to deal with uncertainty may become a source of power, used to further the parochial interests of particular departments or groups of employees. A key strategy which specialists deploy to further their interests or secure greater autonomy is the manipulation of rules.

Formalised rules and procedures, the cornerstones of bureaucracy, also represent major cracks in the fabric, particularly when they cease to be means to ends and become ends in themselves. The double-edged character of rules would not be so damaging were it not for the heavy reliance placed upon them. Attempting to guide work behaviour through detailed procedures is almost bound to fail, however, regardless of the response of those to whom they are applied. Firstly, the production of written procedures and records, 'putting everything in writing', absorbs a great deal of time and effort. Secondly, the greater the volume of rules, the greater the probability that different rules will be incompatible or contradictory. Thirdly, it is impossible to have rules to cover every possible eventuality. Attempting to do so proliferates rules to the extent that knowing the rules or devising new ones becomes more time-consuming than dealing with problems *ad hoc*. This would not matter if at this point strict compliance with the letter of the procedures gave way to actions consistent with their spirit. For this to happen, however, requires initiative and discretion, qualities which tend to atrophy when behaviour is hedged about by rules and non-conformity is punished.

The loss of employee initiative and willingness to exercise discretion in bureaucratic systems is well documented. Four interrelated tendencies are identified: over-conformity, minimal performance, lack of commitment and resistance to change. Over-conformity is the tendency to apply rules rigidly, regardless of the demands of the situation. This arises out of a combination of 'trained incapacity' in routine ways of working, and constant emphasis upon conformity and discipline. It is reinforced by rewards for conformity and not making mistakes, hence the operation of the 'Peter Principle', whereby individuals rise to their level of incompetence. The application of rules then becomes an end in itself and employees engage in the ritualistic behaviour which characterises bureaucratic 'red tape'. Indeed, over-conformity becomes a defence against the employee's increasing inability to deal with changed circumstances. Bureaucracy, therefore, gives rise to the 'bureaucratic personality' (Merton, 1966).

Minimal performance results from pressures upon employees to do only that which is required of them. Three things contribute to this. Firstly, performance may be defined purely in terms of compliance. Secondly, by specifying what must be done, rules imply that no more need be done: what is not in the job description or manual lies outside the employee's area of responsibility (Gouldner, 1955a/b; Crozier, 1964). Thirdly, the abstract, impersonal nature of rules detracts from feelings of personal responsibility. The results may either be the sclerotic effect of working to rule, or the danger of 'crimes of logic' (Presthus, 1979) as individuals simply 'obey orders'.

The impersonal character of work procedures and relationships contributes to a lack of employee commitment. Individuals feel they are insignificant cogs in a machine, and that their personal qualities count for little. Emphasis upon 'the system' and the apparent absence of human agency may engender the feeling that the system cannot be changed. Thus to over-conformity or ritualism is added 'retreatism', or a minimal personal involvement in the organisation (Crozier, 1964).

Bureaucracy has a tendency to breed either mindless conformity or mindful avoidance.

Rules and procedures are sources of resistance to change, especially if they become entrenched and immutable because those who formulate them have a stake in the status quo (Walsh and Dewar, 1987). Indeed, resistance to change is a central weakness of bureaucratic organisation as a whole. It results from the way in which the delays, timidity and inappropriate decisions spawned by hierarchy, the departmental rivalries and individual protectionism spawned by specialisation and the over-conformity and inflexibility spawned by over-regulated operations come together to produce a rigidly interlocked system.

There is a tendency for the negative effects of bureaucratic organisation to be dealt with by having more of the things which give rise to them: the bureaucratic 'vicious circle' (Crozier, 1964). The negative effects of centralisation and impersonality tend to be countered by greater centralisation of decisions and more rules. The unanticipated responses to hierarchy and rules bring forth more hierarchical control and more regulations (March and Simon, 1971).

This vicious circle reflects an over-arching emphasis upon formal organisational mechanisms for the achievement of ends. Bureaucracy leaves little to chance or invention. It is, therefore, not the specific rules of bureaucracy which are its undoing, but its faith in the power of rationality, the belief that the achievement of goals is guaranteed by formal planning, prescription and control. This ignores, treats as irrelevant or seeks to legislate away the human element of organisation. The identity of organisational members and the attitudes which they bring to work with them are ignored. So are the informal interpersonal relationships and groups which form in the work-place and which generate and enforce norms of behaviour. The impact of 'informal organisation' (Selznick, 1966) upon organisational processes is largely ignored. Yet the efficiency of bureaucratic organisation, far from being impaired, may be enhanced by informal, rule-bending activities by employees (Blau, 1970a). Indeed, as Chapter 7 will show, it is often the operation of the informal organisation which permits large bureaucratic organisations to cope with external change. This, however, merely serves to reinforce the point that the bureaucratic obsession with legislating for every eventuality can stand in the way of more appropriate, discretionary behaviour. The informal, un-official, unplanned relationships and activities which bureau-cracy treats as an enemy to be defeated may in fact be the allies of organisational effectiveness.

Given these deficiencies and inefficiencies, the persistence of bureaucracy as a form of organisation demands explanation. Two alternative explanations repeat our earlier observations. The first is that bureaucracy is inevitable because it represents the only feasible, if imperfect, way of organising administrative work on a large scale, and that hence, despite its inefficiencies, it is the best available. Bureaucracy is associated with the 'metaphysical pathos' of fatalism (Gouldner, 1955).

The other reason given for the durability of bureaucracy points to the primacy of considerations of control over con-siderations of efficiency, and to the way in which the desire to retain power over others prevails over the need to improve the collective organisational power to achieve particular ends. The power of bureaucratic organisation lies precisely in its imper-sonal, indirect character. Rules, which come to have a life and logic of their own, give considerable power to those who make them, a power which they are loath to relinquish.

Thus, although the inefficiencies of bureaucratic organisation are clearly recognised, their relevance to work organisation may be denied by equating 'bureaucracy' with 'state administration', or they may be perceived as regrettable but unavoidable. Of late, however, there has been a more determined search for ways of organising administrative work which, without re-linquishing control, might address the three central problems of inflexibility of employees and systems, employee dissatisfaction with work and lack of employee commitment. It is to attempts to deal with these problems that we turn in Chapters 7 and 8.

FURTHER READING

Writers on bureaucracy in its various guises include: Fayol (1949), Udy (1959), Hall (1963), Crozier (1964), Weber (1964), Merton (1966), Pugh *et al.* (1968), Albrow (1970), Blau (1970a), Perrow (1972), Mouzelis (1975), Jacques (1976), Child (1977), Edwards (1979), Mintzberg (1979), Presthus (1979), Salaman (1979), Thompson (1980), Rueschmeyer (1986) and Beetham (1987).

On variations in bureaucratic organisation see Udy (1959), Hall (1963), Gouldner (1964), Pugh *et al.* (1968), Child (1970), Mansfield (1973), Pugh (1973), Pugh and Hickson (1973), Pugh and Hinings (1976) and Mintzberg (1979).

On the tendency towards bureaucratisation, see Gouldner (1955), Weber (1964), Stinchcombe (1965, 1969), Perrow (1972), Jacques (1976), Child (1977), Mintzberg (1979), Presthus (1979), Thompson (1980) and Clegg (1990). The resilience of early forms of organisation in the face of bureaucratisation is documented by Pollard (1968), Littler (1982), Burawoy (1985), Goffee and Scase (1985) and Rueschmeyer (1986).

The problems of bureaucratic organisation are extensively documented in Gouldner (1955a/b), Crozier (1964), Merton (1966), Selznick (1966), Blau (1970a), Michels (1970), March and Simon (1971), Perrow (1971, 1972), Mintzberg (1979), Presthus (1979), Walsh and Dewar (1987), Peters and Waterman (1982), Kanter (1985) and Peters (1989).

Chapter 6

The search for quality of working life and flexibility
Job redesign, group working and employee participation

In Chapter 4 we considered the classical approach to the organisation of operational work in the form of rationalisation and Scientific Management. One of the central weaknesses of this approach is the tendency for detailed division of labour and imposed work methods to create, first, narrow, specialised jobs which both under-utilise and dissatisfy those performing them and, second, over-elaborate, inflexible work systems, prone to disruption and an inability to change. This chapter reviews forms of work redesign and employee participation which address these problems. The concept used as the peg upon which to hang discussion of a number of disparate ideas and practices is that of 'despecialisation' – the attempt to reverse the tendency of work rationalisation to specialise operational tasks and separate them from management.

We begin by examining the case for despecialisation, highlighting its dualistic and sometimes contradictory character, which is concerned at times with increasing employee satisfaction at work and the quality of working life (QWL) and at other times with organising work more flexibly and, hence, more efficiently. The basic principles of this approach are then set out, central to which is the distinction between horizontal despecialisation, the recombination of tasks and responsibilities, and vertical despecialisation, the recombination of conceptual work (decision-making) and operational work. Applying this distinction to different levels – the job, the work group and the organisation as a whole – provides a classifying framework for the different forms of despecialisation in practice: job redesign, group working and systems of employee participation. Each of these are considered in turn and they are summarised in terms of the MTO framework.

We then shift from description and analysis to evaluation, by considering whether and to what extent despecialisation represents a successful alternative to rationalisation. Firstly, we review the evidence on the success or otherwise of despecialisation in practice. Secondly, we attempt to explain the somewhat indifferent level of success of forms of despecialisation, focusing upon the validity of the assumptions which underpin them, the form which they take in practice and the methods used to implement them. This paves the way for an overall assessment of the benefits and costs of despecialisation which emphasises a central theme of the chapter: the constant tension between humanistic/QWL and instrumental/efficiency considerations and between the costs and benefits for employers and managers and for employees. Ambiguities in the criteria for judging the benefits of despecialisation flow, in large measure, from the question of 'benefits for *whom*?'

THE CASE FOR DESPECIALISATION

The case for reversing the process of detailed division of labour and separation of management functions from operational work set in train by rationalisation has changed somewhat over time. Initially, the focus of concern was the 'dehumanised' character of work organised in this way, and the need to improve the quality of working life of employees. However, there was always a pragmatic side to these concerns, which focused more upon the waste and inefficiency engendered by rationalised organisation, and this has come to the fore in a more recent concern with making work processes, and workers, more flexible (see Figure 6.1).

The humanisation/QWL case

At the level of ideas, humanistic reactions to rationalised organisation initially coalesced into the 'Human Relations' movement. However, this often amounted to little more than a demonstration of the existence of social relations at work and a plea for managers to recognise their importance. It rarely translated into concrete prescriptions for organisation, except

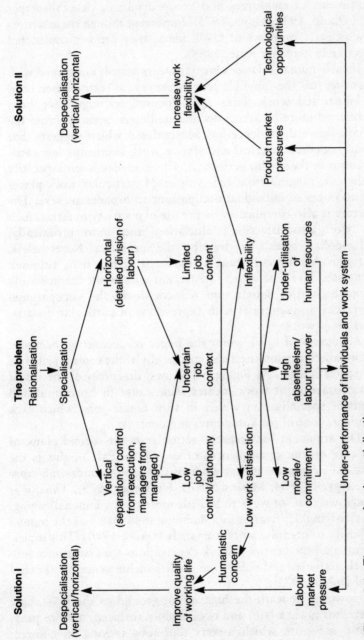

Figure 6.1 The case for despecialisation

to advocate a participative managerial 'style' sensitive to the sentiments of employees and group dynamics (Roethlisberger and Dixon, 1939; Mayo, 1975). Important though these writers are as early prophets of QWL ideas, they are not considered separately here (see Rose, 1988).

If early human relations writings were mainly concerned with warning of the possible consequences of rationalised and dehumanised work, later QWL-focused writings have been prompted more by actual documented consequences. From the 1950s onward, evidence has accumulated which suggests that routine manual, clerical and service work bequeaths few satisfactions to those who perform it. This evidence is not especially coherent, ranging from case studies of particular work-places or accounts of individual occupations to broader surveys. The picture is also complicated by the use of a variety of terms, such as 'work dissatisfaction', 'alienation' and, more prosaically, 'blue-collar blues' to describe the problem. Nevertheless, through this diversity runs a consistent theme: that, although expressed levels of broad satisfaction *with* work are generally quite high, this satisfaction reduces down the occupational hierarchy and contrasts with expressions of particular dissatisfaction *at* work.

Advocates of QWL point the finger of accusation firmly at rationalised organisation and specifically at the central principle of specialisation. As Figure 6.1 shows, diagnosis of the ills of dissatisfaction at work locates their cause in horizontal and vertical specialisation which in turn create jobs which lack content, control (or autonomy) and context.

The argument for despecialisation rests the second plank of its case on the consequences of such jobs. Part of this is the humanistic argument that work of this kind is undesirable *per se* (Argyris, 1964; Maslow, 1970; Hofstede, 1979). Thus, it is suggested that for work to be little more than an unchallenging, unsatisfying deprivation is a damning indictment of the human capacity to organise work humanely (Davis, 1980). This indictment is all the greater if work deprivations spill over into non-work activities and reduce the quality of life generally (Faunce and Dubin, 1975).

However, beneath the high moral ground of the QWL case there has always lain, and occasionally surfaced, a more pragmatic substrate which asserts that jobs lacking in content,

context and autonomy lead to sub-optimal employee performance and productivity (Herrick, 1981). The narrowness of
jobs is seen as diminishing employee performance, both directly
by under-utilising human resources and indirectly by creating
boredom and dissatisfaction at work which, in turn, bring low
employee morale and high levels of absenteeism, turnover and
stress (Hackman *et al.*, 1975). Thus employee deprivations and
organisational inefficiency have a common origin, and it is in
employers' interests to improve their employees' quality of
working life.

If excessive specialisation is the root cause of these difficulties, it follows that their removal requires a reversal, or
despecialisation, both horizontally and vertically. What is less
clear is whether forms of despecialisation designed to improve
QWL and those designed to improve efficiency are the same, or
different.

The flexibility case

A second wave of interest in despecialisation springs from
evidence that, far from receding after the initial flush of
enthusiasm for QWL ideas in the late 1960s and early 1970s,
the practice of work redesign and, to a lesser extent, employee
participation not only continued, but grew. Firstly, by the late
1970s, studies had identified the existence of forms of organisation of operational work based on 'responsible autonomy',
rather than 'direct control' (Friedman, 1977). Secondly, during
the 1980s, when organised labour became weaker, 'macho-
management' replaced participative management and having
work took precedence over the quality of working life, work
redesign continued. To be sure, much of this was, unashamedly,
an extension rather than a reversal of principles of rationalisation, involving tighter supervisory control, deskilling, speed-
up, mechanisation and greater use of hire-and-fire employment
practices. Other developments were different, however, and
observers argued that they arose less from a concern to humanise
work, more from the need to make work systems more flexible.
'Flexible specialisation' became, not altogether accurately, the
umbrella term to describe these changes (Piore and Sabel, 1984;
Atkinson, 1985).

Flexible specialisation as a form of work organisation arises as a result of both pressures and opportunities (Wood, 1989). The pressures come from the market place, in the form of more intense competition and shifts in consumer tastes away from mass, standardised products towards specialised, higher quality products. Stable mass markets are being replaced by volatile 'niche' markets, where competitive advantage goes to those able to adapt products rapidly to changes in consumer tastes. This means, inevitably, short production runs (or 'batch' production) and flexible operating systems, rather than flow lines (Kelly, 1982). Mass production methods become redundant because mass products have. The opportunities for introducing these changes are firstly, technological developments, notably in micro-processors, which facilitate the development of both information systems, for monitoring and controlling operations, and 'non-dedicated' production equipment (e.g. numerically controlled machines and robotics) and secondly, slack labour markets which mean that changes in job structures can be implemented without any significant union opposition.

The attainment of flexibility is not exclusively a result of changes in work organisation. Flexible specialisation may also entail changes in the relations between organisations, either through geographical dispersion or subcontracting of work operations. The two methods may be used in conjunction, to produce a 'diffused production network' (Murray, 1988). Flexibility may also entail numerical flexibility by either hiring/firing employees or buying/curtailing outside services. Flexibility in the amount of work required from certain employees is attained through temporary and part-time employment contracts, whilst flexibility in the level of services bought in is achieved by subcontracting and franchise arrangements.

In contrast, *functional* flexibility involves creating working arrangements in which employees move more freely between different work roles. Central to this is horizontal and vertical despecialisation.

DESPECIALISATION: GENERAL PRINCIPLES

The principles of despecialisation are, to a large extent, those discernible in the assumptions, often implicit, of more concrete discussions of, or proposals for, work redesign and participation. There are relatively few general expositions of despecialisation as a broad approach to work organisation. Moreover, it has been variously labelled as 'socio-technical design' (Trist, 1981), 'responsible autonomy' (Friedman, 1977), a 'new paradigm' (Van Assen and Webster, 1980), 'multi-form organisation' (Thorsrud, 1981) and 'post modernist de-differentiation' (Clegg, 1990). Atheoretical descriptions of changes in working arrangements are more numerous, however. What follows, therefore, is a synthesis of these general principles, together with the assumptions embedded in more concrete proposals.

To point up the contrast with rationalised organisation, the basic principles of despecialised organisation may be regarded as flexible work methods, the recombination of work tasks (horizontal despecialisation), the recombination of planning, control and execution (vertical despecialisation), a high-involvement employment relationship and a 'quality of working life' ideology.

Central to the idea of flexible work methods are two notions: firstly, that the work process is a variable 'socio-technical system' (rather than a determinant technical system) and secondly, that work methods should be the outcome of employee choice (rather than an imposed 'best' way). The concept of a socio-technical system, stated simply, suggests that any work system is a combination of both a material technology, representing tools, machinery, materials and techniques of operation, and a social organisation, comprising the psychological constitution of and social relations among individuals and groups who carry out the work. This social organisation, in turn, divides into a 'task system' of formal work roles, behaviours and relationships and a 'sentient system' of informal attitudes, behaviours and relationships (Miller and Rice, 1967). Central to this is the idea that the technical system is neither dominant nor determinant. Organising work, therefore, means designing both the social organisation and the technical system, and in this design there is a degree of choice. What is essential is that the technical system and the social organisation should harmonise. To achieve an optimal system overall, technology must be adapted to the circumstances, particularly the social circumstances, in which it is going to operate.

The principle of flexible work methods implies that there is no objectively 'best' way to perform a task which may be discovered by work analysts and imposed upon employees, but, rather, that employees themselves are best placed to discover and decide how to perform a task. Therefore, a diversity of methods is accepted, rather than being regarded as a problem to be eradicated. Despecialisation entails giving employees, either as individuals or groups, a degree of choice and discretion over aspects of their work, such as when it is done, where, in what sequence, how and by whom.

The general principle of despecialisation rests upon assumptions about employee motivation and organisational effectiveness. Employee motivation is seen as complex, in that people are assumed to fulfil a variety of needs at work, including social needs such as friendship and interaction, and psychological needs such as achievement, recognition, personal growth, responsibility and intrinsic enjoyment of the work itself (Herzberg, 1966; Schein, 1979). Work design, therefore, has to provide for this variety of needs. Moreover, from the point of view of organisational effectiveness, it is necessary to extend the scope of jobs, break down barriers between functions and remove divisions between managers and managed in order to tap hitherto under-utilised pools of skill and to render work systems more flexible.

Horizontal despecialisation is concerned with reducing the degree of specialisation of tasks and activities, whether at the level of the individual job, the work group or the organisation as a whole. At the level of the job, it means providing for more task variety, a greater use of skills and a closer fit between the job and a 'whole' task, or task sequence. This may involve either a different way of combining tasks, or a different way of assigning employee responsibilities. At the level of the work group, horizontal despecialisation entails giving a group responsibility for a discrete and substantial element of the work process, removing previous job demarcations and creating a multi-skilled group or 'matrix' (Thorsrud, 1981). Lastly, at the level of the organisation, horizontal despecialisation means moving away from a rigid system of functionally differentiated sub-units (departments, sections) and creating sub-units oriented towards products, markets or organisational problems. This utilises, in particular, the principle of bringing together individuals with different specialisms to work on a task as a team.

Vertical despecialisation is concerned with extending the

conceptual elements of work, such as planning, coordination and control, beyond managerial positions to employees generally. At the level of the job, it means offering a greater opportunity for employees to plan, monitor and control their own work and to coordinate their efforts with others – in short, to manage themselves. It also entails creating opportunities for employees to learn and develop. Similarly, more autonomy and opportunity for self-management may be given to a work group. Lastly, at the level of the organisation, vertical despecialisation means removing the rigid division between managers and managed by extending involvement in organisational decision-making and shifting the role of managers away from direction and control, towards technical advice and coordination.

The principle of a high-involvement employment relationship regards employment as a broadly-based, long-term commitment, based on loyalty and involvement by both employers and employees, rather than a purely contingent economic attachment. This implies not only fair pay, to reward commensurable contributions equally, but also good working conditions, in terms of both the physical setting and non-wage benefits, the provision of non-material, psychological rewards such as recognition and praise for contributions, and the provision of some form of security of employment together with opportunities for development and promotion. In short, employees are to be regarded not as factors of production to be used, but 'human resources' or 'human capital', to be conserved and developed.

Linked to this is the quality of working life ideology, or the conviction that work organisation must reconcile the interests and goals of both employers and employees and thus strike a balance between the pursuit of efficiency and economic performance on the one hand, and work which is fulfilling, satisfying and well-rewarded on the other. This rests on the assumption that such interests can and should be reconciled, if necessary by trading off some loss of technical efficiency for gains in employee satisfaction and effectiveness. Variations on the QWL theme also accompany forms of despecialisation more evidently concerned with promoting work flexibility.

These basic principles of despecialised organisation may now be summarised in terms of the MTO framework (see Table 6.1). Overall, there is an integration, or reintegration, of management functions into the work process and a 'demonopolisation'

Table 6.1 Managing through despecialised organisation: general principles

Management process	: Reintegration of management functions with work process
Area of application	: Operational work
Planning/decision-making	
Degree of centralisation	: Detailed operational decisions decentralised Strategic/policy decisions centralised, but more democratic
Information/communication flows	: Increased volume, vertically and horizontally
Allocation of Work	
Form of specialisation	: By skills or output
Level of specialisation	: Work group
Degree of job specialisation	: Low: wider job responsibilities
Motivation	
Rewards	: Intrinsic; group performance
Rules	: Employee/group-generated work methods; democratic work-place rules
Rationale	: 'Quality of working life'
Coordination	
Locus of responsibility	: Employees and team leaders $\Big\}$ Mutual adjustment and some specialist liaison
Method	: Adjustment and consultation/communication
Degree of formality	: More informal
Control	
Focus	: [Outputs] [Inputs and processes] = Self/mutual control of processes
Locus of responsibility	: [External] [Self/mutual] External control of outputs
Degree of impersonality	: [Impersonal] + [Personal]
Degree of formality	: [Formal] [Informal]

of management. Thus, aspects of planning and decision-making are devolved to employees or their representatives, and this is accompanied by an increase in the flow of information both vertically and laterally. The allocation of work is based on a reduced level of specialisation, with wider job and work group responsibilities, and on specialisation by skill or output, rather than functions. In many instances, specialisation is at the level of the work group, rather than the individual job.

There is greater reliance upon self-motivation by employees. They play a greater part in the formulation and enforcement of rules, whether as individuals and work groups responsible for their own working practices or as organisational members involved in drawing up work-place regulations. Intrinsic and non-material rewards connected with the nature of the work itself are given greater emphasis, as are rewards for group performance. 'Quality of working life' and its associated ideas (human resources management, industrial democracy) provide the rationale for changes in work organisation, and seek to create the normative force to generate commitment to these changes.

The coordination of work is increasingly undertaken by those carrying it out, on the basis of lateral communication, mutual adjustment and agreement, rather than by direction from above. Similarly, there is greater reliance upon internal controls, with individual employees and groups controlling themselves or each other. External controls shift away from the control of process and behaviour, to the control of outputs, in the form of performance targets (output, sales) and/or quality levels which may themselves be the result of negotiation. In short, employees are increasingly left to their own devices to plan, regulate, monitor and adjust the means by which they attain agreed performance and quality targets.

DESPECIALISATION IN PRACTICE: JOB REDESIGN, GROUP WORKING AND EMPLOYEE PARTICIPATION

Despecialisation is, to repeat, less a blueprint for wholesale changes in work organisation, more a theme running through experiments in job redesign, group working and employee participation. Work redesign tends to be reported as single case studies of a particular company or work-place, although there are also some broader comparative studies which are drawn upon here. Employee participation is reviewed more comprehensively, but only rarely linked to work redesign.

Our earlier distinction between horizontal and vertical despecialisation, operating at the level of the job or work group/ organisation produces a fourfold scheme for classifying the various and seemingly disparate types of work redesign and participation. Each of the different types are considered in terms of their characteristics, aims, associated changes and conditions under which they are introduced.

Horizontal despecialisation of jobs: job rotation and job enlargement

Job rotation is the most basic form of work redesign, since a structure of specialist jobs is retained, but employees become less specialised in that they rotate between different, if related, jobs at specified intervals. Thus, for example, workers may move between different stations on an assembly line, or different departmental duties. The QWL aim is to relieve monotony by offering some, albeit limited, work variety, whilst the efficiency/flexibility aims are to provide cover for absenteeism and to redeploy workers from slack to busy areas in response to workload fluctuations.

Some training in new skills or familiarisation with new tasks is a necessary concomitant of job rotation, as is a willingness on the part of employees to move between tasks or work areas, since this may disrupt routine or informal work group interaction. In practice, its limited nature means that job rotation is usually a component of wider changes in working arrangements (Birchall et al., 1982).

In contrast, job enlargement changes jobs themselves by extending them to include extra tasks or activities and bringing these closer to a complete work cycle. Since this often means replacing assembly lines by work stations at which a number of operations are performed, it is also known as 'flowline reorganisation' (Kelly, 1982). In production work, this often involves incorporating maintenance and set-up operations into jobs (Cotgrove et al., 1971). In clerical work, it typically involves making individual workers responsible for all stages, rather than just one, in a clerical process (e.g. processing orders or enquiries) relating to a group of clients, area or type of service (Hill, 1982).

The QWL aims of job enlargement extend beyond relief of monotony through greater task variety to creating the experience of completing a whole work sequence, of producing a tangible end result and of using a range of skills, all of which are regarded as conducive to more meaningful and satisfying work (Cooper, 1974; Hackman *et al.*, 1975). This, clearly, depends on the extent to which the new jobs span a work cycle and the nature of the component tasks. Moreover, job enlargement can sometimes amount to job 'loading': the employee simply does more work. Whilst scarcely consistent with QWL aims, this produces productivity gains. Other ways in which job enlargement improves efficiency are more subtle. Quality control improves without the need for separate, and costly, quality inspection if employees themselves monitor work quality, and the cost of handling materials is reduced by having a number of operations performed at a single work station. Flexibility is enhanced by the removal of external constraints on the work pace of the individual and by varying the number of employees working on a task by changing either the number of work stations or what is performed at each station (Biggane and Stewart, 1972).

An obvious concomitant of these changes is training in the skills required to carry out new additional tasks. Changes in rates and/or systems of pay may also be required, because there may be resistance to job enlargement if present jobs are linked to payment by results. Therefore, the willingness of employees to take on additional tasks is an important prerequisite.

Vertical despecialisation of jobs: job enrichment

Job enlargement may presage job enrichment since, in practice, it may be difficult to enlarge the scope of jobs in terms of tasks without adding extra responsibilities for planning, monitoring or control. Job enrichment occurs where a significant element of discretion and self-supervision is added to jobs, with the job incumbent given an opportunity to plan the work sequence, choose work methods and tools, allocate their time and monitor their output. Thus, for example, salespeople may be given discretion over passing on information, requesting technical

back-up, authorising minor refunds or replacements and negotiating prices (Paul and Robertson, 1976). In the well-documented experiment at Indiana Bell Telephones, clerks producing telephone directories were given whole directories to
prepare and check, encouraged to sell advertising space and
permitted to determine their own work pace and methods
(Ford, 1973).

Job enrichment is closely associated with the motivational
theories of Herzberg (1966) and hence its QWL aim is to add job
characteristics which, in Herzberg's terms, constitute 'Motiva-
tors', i.e. a sense of achievement and responsibility, recognition,
opportunities for personal growth and intrinsic work interest.
By adding 'autonomy' and 'feedback', employee responsibility
for work outcomes and knowledge of results are increased
(Hackman *et al.*, 1975). This requires that jobs can be redesigned such that how they are performed is a matter of real
employee choice, about tools or methods ('means discretion'),
knowledge and techniques ('skills discretion') or even the purpose of the job ('goal discretion') (Cooper, 1974). Further, jobs
must be redesigned such that the effectiveness of their performance is unambiguously attributable to the choices and actions of
the employee. This is not the case, clearly, where choices exist
only for trivial decisions or within tight constraints.

The efficiency gains of job enrichment flow from greater
application engendered by greater autonomy and higher levels
of commitment flowing from 'ownership' of the job, better
quality work expected from the application of employee experience to decisions, and more sustained work if higher work
satisfaction brings lower absenteeism and labour turnover.
Direct efficiency gains also result if 'enriched' jobs mean that
fewer employees are required for a given level of output.
'Labour elimination' also extends to foremen and supervisors,
many of whose roles pass to employees. Further, there is greater
flexibility if employees have a wider range of skills, more
responsibility and personal interest in work and a greater
capacity for problem-solving.

The introduction of job enrichment requires training in additional task and problem-solving skills, as well as, invariably,
new payment systems which reward performance and the
capacity to perform different kinds of work. It also requires a
reduction in levels of supervision and work regulation. Employee

willingness to take on extra responsibilities, high existing skill levels and a relatively homogeneous workforce are important preconditions.

The different forms of job redesign may be summarised in terms of the MTO framework (see Table 6.2). Whilst job rotation and job enlargement leave the management of work little changed, job enrichment entails some reintegration of management functions into the work process, with individual employees more responsible for managing themselves. Employees plan their own work and decide how it is to be carried out, although planning and decision-making are confined to immediate job matters. With all forms of job redesign, the allocation of work changes, with reduced individual specialisation and specialisation based on skill, output or client. Job enrichment in particular emphasises self-motivation, based on self-imposed rules, intrinsic and psychological rewards and a quality of working life ideology. Coordination relies on mutual adjustment between employees, supported by liaison, based on communication, between supervisors. Control relies more on employee self-control, with remaining external controls focusing on outputs in the form of performance levels and quality in the setting of which employees are more involved.

Horizontal despecialisation at the level of the group/organisation: task forces, project teams and autonomous work groups

A somewhat heterogeneous collection of group- or team-based changes in work design represent instances where despecialisation extends beyond individual jobs to encompass larger organisational sub-units. These are grouped together here because, in different ways, they represent a dismantling of departmental functional specialisation.

Task forces and project teams are more common in the context of managerial and professional work. However, they can also be applied to operational areas such as productivity, health and safety or product/service quality. Team members are drawn from different sections or groups, and in the team, roles and leadership are based on task-related knowledge rather than previous job titles.

One particular example of such a group is the quality circle,

Table 6.2 Managing through despecialised organisation: job redesign, group working and employee participation

	Job redesign	Group working	Employee participation
Planning/decision-making	Operational planning/decisions devolved to job holder	Operational planning/decisions devolved to group	Wider involvement in policy and work-place decisions
Allocation of work	Reduced job specialisation: inc. variety, integrity, responsibility. Skill/output specialisation	Group specialisation/job flexibility. Skill/output specialisation	
Motivation			
Rewards	Intrinsic rewards (variety, integrity, responsibility, control)	Intrinsic rewards (group work) Group performance rewards	Intrinsic rewards (involvement)
Rules	Self-imposed methods and rules	Group methods and rules	More democratic work-place rules
Rationales	Quality of working life/enrichment	Quality of working life	Participation/industrial democracy
Coordination	Mutual adjustment. Specialist liaison by supervisors	Mutual adjustment. Specialist liaison by team leaders	Communication/liaison through participative structures
Control	Self-control over processes. External control over outputs	Mutual control over processes and inputs. External control over outputs	Mutual control over outputs and processes
	(These are high for job enrichment, low for job rotation and job enlargement)		(These are high for codetermination, low for consultation and communication)

comprising six to ten members drawn from different jobs who meet voluntarily and regularly in company time to identify problems in product/service quality and to discuss, develop and recommend solutions. They may be managed either by an external steering committee, or internally by a group leader or 'facilitator' who assists group processes but does not impose a structure or agenda (Robson, 1984). Thus, for example, different departments of a motorway service area may contribute participants to a quality circle concerned with service quality in the facilities as a whole (Hales, 1987a).

In task forces and quality circles, efficiency rather than QWL aims predominate. However, they also provide vehicles for employee participation, contribution and involvement. To work effectively, they require a willingness and ability on the part of group members to cooperate in problem-solving, which necessitates voluntary membership and training in quality control techniques and group dynamics.

An autonomous work group usually entails merging a number of disparate individual jobs into a common group task. The group, collectively, agree performance targets, which they are responsible for meeting by deciding on the allocation of tasks to group members, working methods and scheduling. The group may also be responsible for liaison with other groups over materials or work-in-progress, equipment maintenance and training new group members. In practice, such groups vary considerably over the degree of autonomy which they are able to exercise (Warner, 1984).

Some autonomous work group experiments represent a return to pre-rationalised forms of work organisation (Trist and Bamforth, 1951). In other cases, assembly lines are replaced by group work stations where a whole sub-assembly operation is carried out, as in the Volvo and Saab-Scania experiments (Gyllenhammer, 1977; Blackler and Brown, 1980), experiments at Norsk Hydro and Texas Instruments (Herrick and Maccoby, 1975) and the recent introduction of team working in car and consumer durable manufacturing (Wood, 1989).

The QWL aim of autonomous work groups is to improve work content, context and autonomy, by giving group members a wider range of tasks, opportunity to use wider skills, involvement in a more complete work task, more say over their immediate work situation and the satisfaction of participation in a group. The efficiency aims are to generate better working practices, decisions and work quality by giving more discretion to those performing the work, whilst reducing the need for external supervision and quality control. Flexibility is increased by replacing job demarcations by broad group responsibilities within which work reflects the task in hand, and inspection and maintenance are integrated.

Autonomous work groups are usually accompanied by other changes such as group training in technical and social skills, introduction of flexible working arrangements (e.g. flexitime), pay based on skills and job capabilities, and a shift in the role of supervisor towards coordination and technical advice. The occasion for the introduction of autonomous work groups is often the introduction of new equipment or processes designed for group operation. This is made easier if the work process has discrete, bounded phases with distinct end-products, self-contained maintenance activity and clear performance feedback information (Susman, 1975) and if an informal social organisation with a high level of trust and cooperation already exists.

If we analyse group working in terms of the MTO framework (Table 6.2), we see that, in general, management functions are reintegrated into the work process, with groups to some extent managing themselves. Day-to-day work planning and operational decisions are devolved to the group, although broader, strategic organisational decisions remain in managerial hands. The allocation of work is on the basis of group specialisation, based on skills, outputs or clients. Job specialisation is relatively low. Group members to a large extent motivate themselves (and one another). Rules take the form of work methods evolved by the group. Rewards take an increasingly group form, both extrinsically in terms of group bonuses and performance related pay and intrinsically in terms of the satisfaction of group cohesion, interaction and autonomy. The group is also responsible for coordinating both the efforts of individual members and its work with that of other groups, through informal mutual adjustment or formal meetings between group leaders. Control over the immediate work situation is also exercised by the group. Mutual control over work processes and, to some extent, inputs by group members operates within external control over outputs, in the form of performance targets and quality standards.

Vertical despecialisation at the level of the organisation: forms of employee participation

Employee participation is, in effect, a partial dismantling of the division between the processes of 'conception' (decision-making) and 'execution' and between managers and managed, across the organisation as a whole rather than simply at the level of the job or work group. In general, participation schemes involve the creation of formal bodies composed of representatives from different levels in an organisation and concerned with broad work-place issues. Their broad remit and representative composition mean that they are often referred to as 'indirect participation' (as distinct from the direct participation in job matters offered to employees by job enrichment and group working). Although participation takes a wide variety of specific forms (IDE, 1981), four basic types may be distinguished: formal communication mechanisms, consultative bodies, structures of codetermination and financial participation. The first three of these form, in effect, a continuum of increasing levels of participation (Elliott, 1984).

Formal communication mechanisms

These take a variety of forms: annual company meetings, divisional or departmental briefings, presentations, newsletters and bulletins. In all cases, they offer 'participation' at its most basic: being informed of managerial decisions and organisational developments, often after the event, with involvement confined to reactions to the downward flow of information. Mechanisms for communicating information and opinions upwards are less common and, in the case of suggestion schemes, are limited to technical matters and are reliant on voluntary submissions.

Consultative bodies

These also take a variety of forms, with a wide range of titles, the most common being 'works council' or 'joint consultative committee'. Despite this variation, some common features are evident. Firstly, consultative bodies often have a tiered structure, with low-level 'plant' committees, intermediate 'works' or 'divisional' committees and higher-level 'company' committees.

Secondly, committees are usually composed of elected employee representatives and appointed managerial representatives. Thirdly, they usually stand apart from any system of formal collective bargaining or grievance procedures and hence their remit rarely extends to pay or conditions of employment. Rather, they operate as forums for discussion of general organisational or work-place matters, such as new work systems, training or work-place regulations, or matters of employee concern such as working arrangements or health and safety. Lastly, their functions are usually confined to discussion and advice, rather than decision-making (Marchington, 1988) and thus, they tend to have a largely passive role, reviewing, adjusting or legitimating managerial decisions (Teulings, 1987).

Codetermination

This too takes a wide variety of forms, both internationally and historically. Some are systems of 'worker directors', with employee (or trade union) representatives elected to the board of a company, as was the case in some limited experiments in the UK during the 1970s (Brannen, 1983). Others are systems of codetermination proper, where a board of directors reports to a higher 'supervisory' board to which worker representatives are elected, as in Germany and Scandinavia (Asplund and Von Otter, 1979). 'Worker management', as in the Yugoslavian experiments of the 1960s and 1970s, is where overall direction of an organisation is in the hands of a workers' council who then appoint the executive board and director (Kavcic, 1979).

The QWL aims of employee participation systems focus on the value of participation as an end in itself, on the assumption that employees feel greater involvement, commitment and satisfaction with work if they participate in decisions which influence their working lives (Robson, 1981). However, participation is also seen as a vehicle for improving the quality of decision-making, and hence enhancing organisational effectiveness by widening the basis of decision-making and securing wider acceptance. Decisions are based on more accurate and relevant information, and opinions which reflect operational realities. Wider 'ownership' of decisions leads to more enthusiastic and committed implementation. Further, bringing together representatives from different parts or levels of an organisation helps to break down departmental and status barriers.

Participation schemes can stand apart from other forms of despecialisation, although in practice they may be linked with work redesign (Birchall et al., 1982). Whether linked to other changes or not, participation schemes are more likely to develop under certain conditions. Broad social, political and legal conditions support or require management representation, and in many countries, such as Germany, and in Scandinavia, governments actively promote and assist the process (IDE, 1981). At the organisational level, employee and trade union attitudes are important. Employees generally are more willing to become involved if participative structures appear to offer some substantive role in decision-making, and this, in turn, is more likely where committees or councils can monitor and modify managerial decisions and less likely where they are merely 'talking shops' or rubber stamps for managerial decisions. Trade union reaction depends on how far consultation is seen as undermining the process of collective bargaining and the role of union officials in employee representation.

Introducing management participation requires a number of considerations. Firstly, there is the need to consider what participation is for in terms of the range and specificity of matters on which employees are consulted. Secondly, the relationship between participation and collective bargaining structures needs to be clarified. Thirdly, thought needs to be given to appropriate structures, such as the number and level of consultative bodies and the size and nature of employee representation. Lastly, the question of the way in which participation is introduced, whether as managerial initiative, response to employee pressure or bilateral process, and who is to be the change agent, must be addressed.

Financial participation

Employees may not have any influence over how an organisation is run, but have an entitlement to share in the fruits of its success. This participation also takes a variety of forms, from 'co-partnership', where employees own the business, to forms of 'gainsharing' (or profit-sharing) which may or may not entail some form of employee share ownership scheme (ESOP). In effect there are three variables here: firstly, the extent to which employees 'own' a business (or part of it); secondly, the criteria for financial reward, whether linked to reported company profitability (profit-sharing) or to improvements in productivity and value added (gainsharing, as in the Scanlon Plan in the USA); and thirdly, the form of reward, whether as a cash bonus, individual share bonus, share trust or pension/welfare fund. In all cases, the broad expectation is that greater employee commitment to the organisation flows from an economic stake in its performance.

Viewed in terms of the MTO framework, employee participation involves employees in management functions, unlike work redesign which devolves management functions. However limited in practice, there is some abandonment of managerial prerogative in planning and decision-making. More democratic decision-making may be confined to aspects of work-place regulation, or may extend to organisational policy. Although it has little impact on the allocation of work, participation also addresses the question of motivation, by making work-place rules more democratic and thereby generating greater commitment to them. The emphasis of rewards also shifts towards the intrinsic satisfactions of involvement and influence, bolstered by ideologies of industrial democracy and participation. Co-ordination shifts away from hierarchical direction to a greater emphasis on lateral communication through participative structures. Control also shifts towards mutual, democratic forms if participative bodies develop, agree and enforce quality, safety and performance standards or codes of conduct.

DESPECIALISATION IN PRACTICE, THE CENTRAL ISSUE: HOW SUCCESSFUL HAS IT BEEN AND WHY?

Criteria and evidence of success

Two criteria may be used to judge the success, or otherwise, of despecialisation. The more limited criterion is the extent to which forms of despecialisation have, in fact, been implemented and have endured over time. The extent to which despecialisation fulfils its aims is a more stringent measure, but also a more problematic one, given the dual aims of quality of working life and efficiency/flexibility.

Overall, evidence on despecialisation in practice is patchy and confined to mainly descriptive case studies of particular experiments in work redesign and participation. Not only is it the successes that tend to get reported in these case studies, but their general implications are not always considered. Nevertheless, the evidence is fairly clear that despecialisation, in whatever form, is limited to *ad hoc* changes to parts (particular departments, work groups or jobs) of a narrow range of organisations, affecting a small proportion of employees. If despecialisation is in principle the alternative to rationalised work, it has not replaced it in practice.

The spread of specific forms of despecialisation echoes this general message. Job redesign is confined to specific localised changes, although by the early 1980s some 500 companies in the UK had experimented with job enlargement or enrichment (Warner, 1984). Job enlargement is mainly applied to operative jobs as part of flow line reorganisation, whereas job enrichment is more common in the reorganisation of clerical or administrative work (Kelly, 1982). Experiments in group working, despite the high profile of the Scandinavian cases, have been limited in extent and have changed over time from development of autonomous work groups in process industries, to the incorporation of team-working in general work reorganisation in manufacturing and services. Quality circles were popular during the 1980s, and by 1984 between 500 and 700 UK companies had them (Robson, 1984). Only half the experiments survived, however, and those that did involved less than 10 per cent of their companies' workforce (Hill, 1986). Generally, the 'flexible specialisation' initiatives have been limited and piecemeal (Wood, 1989b).

Works councils and joint consultative committees are the most widespread forms of participation, having enjoyed a renaissance in the 1980s (Marchington, 1988). In the mid-1980s, about half of all UK companies, mainly larger ones, had some form of consultative machinery (although few had a formal policy of consultation) and about half had a system for communicating company decisions and information (BIM, 1984). Generalisation about other forms of participation is difficult because of wide international variations (IDE, 1981). In the UK, worker director schemes were rare and short-lived (Brannen, 1983). In Germany and Scandinavia, codetermination is well established, but worker management in Eastern Europe dwindles. Financial participation appears to be growing, albeit from a limited base.

Evidence on the success of despecialisation in meeting QWL or efficiency/flexibility objectives is also patchy and confused. However, two broad conclusions emerge from the reported case studies. Firstly, where QWL aims of improving work satisfaction and lowering absenteeism and labour turnover are sought, they are usually, though not always, forthcoming (Lawler and Ledford, 1981). Secondly, however, there is conflicting evidence and interpretation on the extent of efficiency gains (Locke *et al.*, 1980). Studies measuring efficiency do so on different criteria (productivity, costs, quality) and some studies report no gains, and even reductions, in efficiency. Further, there is disagreement about whether efficiency gains are the indirect result of increased work satisfaction and morale, or the direct result of a more intensive use of human resources (higher levels of individual output, greater use of skills) or more flexible work systems. However, there has been a clear shift in the criteria by which work redesign and participation are judged in their own terms. Despite some continuation of the QWL rhetoric, the aim of these measures is, more explicitly, that of greater flexibility and efficiency.

Of the different forms of despecialisation, job enlargement, enrichment and group working generally improve work satisfaction, sometimes reduce absenteeism and turnover, but only occasionally improve quality and efficiency (Kelly, 1982; Hales, 1987a). Employee participation, however, whilst improving morale, has little effect on efficiency (IDE, 1981; Robson, 1981; Hales, 1987a).

Therefore, what emerges from complex and conflicting evidence is that despecialisation has had limited application and, where it has been applied, enjoys limited and varying degrees of success in meeting either QWL or efficiency/flexibility aims. (This evidence is summarised in Figure 6.2.) There are three possible reasons for this: firstly, the arguments for and assumptions of despecialisation may be flawed; secondly, actual forms of despecialisation may be inconsistent with their aims; and thirdly, the way in which despecialisation is introduced may be inappropriate. We consider these in turn.

'Success' as implementation

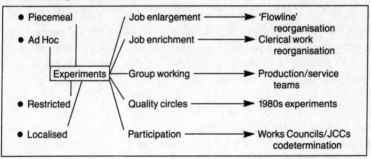

'Success' as meeting QWL aims

	Effect on work satisfaction	Effect on absenteeism/labour turnover
Job rotation	Small increase (reduced monotony)	Little effect
Job enlargement	Some increase (variety, skill use, whole task)	Some reduction
Job enrichment	Increase (variety, skill use, autonomy)	Some reduction
Group working	Increase (variety, skill use, autonomy)	Some reduction
Participation	Some increase (variety, autonomy)	Little effect

'Success' as meeting efficiency/flexibility aims

	Effect on flexibility	Effect on productivity	Effect on quality
Job rotation	Some increase	Some increase	Little effect
Job enlargement	Increase	Some increase	Some increase
Job enrichment	Increase	Some increase	Increase
Group working	Increase	Some increase	Increase
Participation	Little effect	Little effect	Some increase

Figure 6.2 Despecialisation in practice: the evidence

Despecialisation and work satisfaction

Somewhat confused evidence shows that a link between despecialisation and work satisfaction holds only in certain circumstances. Satisfaction appears most strongly linked with
involvement in decisions relating to the work situation (job
enrichment) or work-place (participation). Some, but not all,
employees show interest in greater autonomy (Wall and Lischeron, 1977; cf. Guest et al., 1980) and a lack of expressed interest
may simply reflect adaptation to unsatisfying work and lowered
aspirations. 'Autonomy', 'discretion' and 'control' recur as key
factors linked with work satisfaction in individual studies
(Goodale et al., 1975; Hackman et al., 1975) and in reviews
which show a stronger link between satisfaction and job
enrichment than with other, more limited forms of job redesign
(Filley and House, 1976). There is also evidence of approval,
albeit muted, and higher levels of expressed satisfaction where
participation exists (Warr and Wall, 1975; Wall and Lischeron,
1977). The link between other aspects of despecialisation, such
as job content (variety, skill, task identity) and context (task
significance, prestige, work group interaction) is less clear
(compare Hackman et al., 1975; Seashore, 1975; Warr, 1987,
with Filley and House, 1976).

Even autonomy at work does not necessarily lead to greater
work satisfaction if employees do not want it or if the reality
does not match the intention. Just as some employees may
harbour a real, or potential, desire for autonomy behind apparent apathy (Hofstede, 1979), others have little interest in, or
even an aversion to, more responsibility or participation in
decisions. These include those with 'low growth needs' (Hackman et al., 1975), an instrumental orientation to work (Goldthorpe et al., 1968), or who do not see work as a 'central life
interest' (Reif and Luthans, 1972). Further, greater personal
autonomy may come at the cost of reduced social interaction or
less security from being task proficient (Reif and Luthans, 1972;
Faunce and Dubin, 1975; Filley and House, 1976).

Where employees do welcome greater autonomy or involvement in decision-making, their satisfaction at work is not
enhanced if work redesign or participation schemes fail to
deliver these. 'Enrichment' and 'participation' in name are not
always enrichment and participation in substance. Changes in

the physical context of work do little to enhance work satisfaction (Lawler and Ledford, 1981). Job rotation and enlargement may not offer any greater autonomy, yet disrupt patterns of sociability, break up the rhythm of work or increase work load. Job enrichment or work group autonomy may offer employee discretion only on trivial matters, or within tight constraints (Knights et al., 1985).

Employee participation schemes may bring little substantive involvement in decision-making. Some, such as 'communication' schemes which require that employees are aware of what the company wishes to do, but without having any say in it, make little pretence of this. Others may fail to deliver greater promise. Works councils and consultative committees, even at corporate level, are restricted to safe, inconsequential issues and are constrained by agendas set by managers, inequalities of access to information and a remit which permits discussion but not decision-making. Consequently, they may simply become talking shops – places where employees let off steam, where grievances are diverted or contained and where approval and legitimation of managerial views and actions are sought (Ramsay, 1980, 1985). Equally, systems of worker directors or codetermination may fail to give employees much additional say in organisational decision-making if the power of boards per se is limited and real decisions are taken elsewhere; if senior managers set agendas and priorities and have greater access to information; and if worker directors become assimilated into informal managerial networks or a 'management' point of view (Robson, 1981; Brannen, 1983). Worker representatives may be compelled merely to respond to managerial initiatives, rather than developing their own agendas. Moreover, if they take an oppositional stance, decisions are made elsewhere, whereas if they accede to managerial point of view, they lose credibility with fellow employees. Either way, employees' sense of involvement and, hence, work satisfaction is much reduced if they are not listened to seriously, or are merely listened to but not given any power.

Work satisfaction, absenteeism, labour turnover, stress and productivity

Although the evidence is equivocal, general reviews confirm that high levels of work satisfaction are associated with lower levels of absenteeism, labour turnover and stress.

The link between work satisfaction and productivity is much less clear, however. Some interpret the evidence as indicating that employee well-being improves either individual performance (Warr and Wall, 1975) or organisational effectiveness through higher morale, lower turnover and better communication (Lawler and Ledford, 1981), whereas others doubt this (Locke, 1976). The problem is that a small positive correlation between work satisfaction and performance does not indicate causality. Thus, work satisfaction may be one of many causes or, indeed, an effect, of higher performance. Inferring causality means assuming that work satisfaction, rather than the incentive of material inducements or the opportunity afforded by better equipment, materials or organisation, is the key determinant of performance.

Further, there is evidence of improved work satisfaction without commensurate improvements in productivity (Locke, 1976) or improved productivity without improvements in work satisfaction (Kelly, 1982). Most decisive, perhaps, is the shift over time in the aims of despecialisation away from QWL and towards flexibility as means to higher performance. In effect, the QWL case proved too weak on its own to justify widespread work redesign and participation.

Despecialisation, efficiency and control

The case for despecialisation as a vehicle for improved efficiency rests upon its effect on both individual employees (who work better or harder) and the work system (which operates more flexibly), and therefore on greater technical efficiency, managerial control or both. Evidence from individual work experiments or reviews suggests that, in practice, certain forms of despecialisation, accompanied by other changes, produce tangible efficiency or productivity gains which explain both the survival of earlier experiments, and the resurgence of despecialisation.

Direct evidence on productivity gains from the 'flexibility initiative' is scant, but circumstantial evidence suggests that the resurgence of interest in work redesign is concerned with rationalisation rather than humanisation of work. Firstly, despecialisation occurs in industries where the need for more flexible work systems, in the face of labour and product market changes, is greater than the problems of low job satisfaction (Kelly, 1982) and it has been applied to jobs (mainly white-collar ones) where fragmentation and deskilling are limited (Paul *et al.*, 1969; Fein, 1970).

Secondly, forms of despecialisation have an obvious intrinsic potential for increasing productivity: job rotation/enlargement by switching workers between tasks and maximising the use of equipment; job enrichment by adding to these the advantages of self-motivation, accountability for quality and the use of accumulated 'tacit' skills (Wood and Mainwaring, 1985); group working by flexibility of work roles, improved workflow, reduced inventory, improved coordination, greater account-ability and, crucially, the elimination of supervisory staff; and participation, by offering better informed decisions, and greater commitment to them. Thirdly, work redesign is often accompanied by other changes such as retraining, new equipment and changes in employment conditions, pay levels and systems of pay which suggest the primacy of productivity considerations. Thus work redesign may represent an alternative 'value-added' (Capelli and McKersie, 1987) or 'flexibility' strategy for cost-cutting.

If despecialisation brings improvements in efficiency, these, in turn, may be spin-offs of a deeper purpose: greater managerial control. Measures which appear to involve a transfer of power to employees in reality lead to a strengthening of managerial power (Berg, 1979). Job enrichment and group working serve to make workers more 'responsible', more inclined to accept a managerial point of view and to identify with the enterprise as a whole rather than with their own interests (Ramsay, 1985). Given the opportunity to make small, operational decisions, employees may not aspire to bigger, strategic decisions, and given an exposure to 'company interests', employees may be less eager to pursue their own. Participation schemes, too, may strengthen, rather than weaken, the hand of managers by providing better and more sensitive information for managerial decisions; securing consent and legitimation for these decisions; offering safety valves for grievances; heading off or containing conflict by giving the impression of consultation; providing channels for the expression of a managerial point of view and, crucially, offering an alternative to trade union representation (Marchington, 1988).

How effectively despecialisation strengthens managerial control is debatable. Firstly, employees or their trade union representatives may see through the rhetoric of job redesign and participation, and may resist any changes. Certainly, there is evidence of employee opposition to and suspicion of any changes instigated by management. However, others argue that, even in opposition, employees, in effect, collude in their own subordination (Burawoy, 1979). Opposition which takes the form of increasingly instrumental behaviour merely serves to reinforce the view of labour as a commodity, hence as a factor of production to be manipulated (Knights and Collinson, 1985). Secondly, despecialisation may represent a kind of Trojan Horse: even if employees make only small and sometimes symbolic inroads into managerial prerogatives, such successes show what can be done, and thus stimulate and justify employee involvement in previously exclusive managerial concerns (Bosquet, 1977). Not surprisingly, there is frequent managerial opposition to employee participation.

Overall, therefore, despecialisation can and does enhance both technical efficiency and managerial control, even if it does not do so in all circumstances. (The above discussion of the evidence is summarised in Figure 6.3.) Despecialisation has the potential to both humanise work and make it more efficient. In practice, however, it is difficult to achieve both, and quite possible to achieve neither.

Implementing despecialisation

Irrespective of the substance of despecialisation, the way in which it is introduced also influences its chances of success. The complexities of the process mean that it is not possible to offer a simple 'check-list' for ensuring success. Rather, certain key issues need to be addressed, which resolve into questions of why change is carried out, what is involved, where change takes place and who is involved.

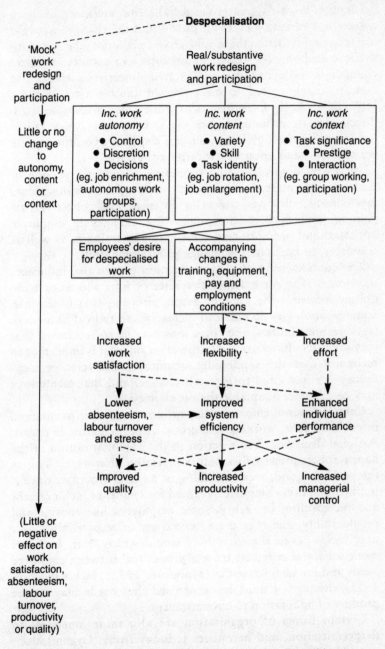

Figure 6.3 Despecialisation in practice: explaining the evidence

Changes towards greater despecialisation are more likely to endure if they have a clear purpose and if the changes wrought are consistent with these objectives. Because the aims of despecialisation are often ambiguous, acceptance requires changes to be consistent with stated objectives, whereas to endure, changes need to meet the substantive aims of those introducing them. Experiments in work redesign may be abandoned, despite bringing higher job satisfaction, if they fail to achieve efficiency objectives. Success depends upon the criteria for success – and upon whose criteria they are.

Successful despecialisation recognises that work redesign or participation must be integrated with other organisational mechanisms, such as systems of payment and collective bargaining, and may require supporting changes in employee appraisal and promotion systems, pay and training, as well as resources, to facilitate the change programme itself.

The context in which despecialisation occurs also influences its success. The pre-existing character of jobs and work technology influence the kind of despecialisation that is feasible. Some technologies do not lend themselves to radical changes in work responsibilities, and some jobs may be so routinised that they are difficult to enrich. On the other hand, it is important to recognise that the supposedly immutable character of technology is often cited to forestall change, and that technology may be far more adaptable than is claimed.

Certain types of employee may be more amenable to enlarged or enriched jobs, working in a group or participating in organisational decisions. The reaction to the Taylorist notion of the happy robot, prepared to endure privation at work so long as the pay was good, was something of an over-reaction, since it implied that every employee yearned for challenge, achievement and recognition. In reality, some employees like routine and predictability, and regard greater variety or responsibility as a deprivation, even though others would welcome it. In short, work satisfaction results from a proper 'fit' between employee needs and job characteristics (Mumford, 1972; Hackman et al., 1975) although it must be recognised that needs may be the product of adaptation to circumstances.

Certain forms of organisation are also more amenable to despecialisation, and here there is heavy irony. Organisations most able to introduce despecialisation are those where flexibility in working arrangements and a climate of consultation already exists and, hence, the need is less. Organisations which would benefit most from despecialisation are those least able to bring it about, precisely because of rigid horizontal and vertical differentiation. Further, organisations operating in stable markets with routine technology and homogeneous products have less need for flexibility than those operating in uncertain, volatile environments. In short, despecialisation occurs where environmental uncertainty creates the need and internal integration creates the possibility (Clegg and Wall, 1984).

The state of labour markets influences whether employers perceive a need to offer employees an enhanced quality of working life. Much of the interest in QWL during the late 1960s and early 1970s was in response to labour shortages and the problem of attracting young employees to routine factory and office employment. Indeed, economic aspirations, attitudes to work and the prevailing political culture are also important influences. Participation at work requires a minimum capacity for participation, in terms of level of education and engagement in wider political processes. Industrial democracy almost certainly presupposes political democracy.

The process of introducing despecialisation, and in particular the question of who is involved, influences its success. A number of alternative 'trajectories' are possible, such as 'top-down' planned or induced change, or 'bottom-up' evolved change (Keidel, 1982). Generally, the wider the involvement in change, the greater its chance of success. Change is less likely to succeed if it is associated with low status and/or specialist staff without support from senior line managers (Knight, 1979). The greater the depth (i.e. how many decisions) and scope (how many employees) of employee consultation, the more likely change is to be successful (Peterson et al., 1982). There is, to be sure, something distinctly paradoxical about introducing a system of employee consultation without consultation. Finally, consultants or independent change agents may be involved in change. Evidence on whether their involvement is essential is not clear, but it is clear that they do need the ability and integrity to act as 'honest brokers'.

Overall, therefore, the manner in which despecialisation is introduced influences, if not determines, its success or failure. Clear objectives, appropriate changes, a conducive social and organisational context, amenable jobs and employees and a wide consultation process do not ensure success. Their absence, however, guarantees failure.

DESPECIALISATION: AN OVERALL ASSESSMENT

Whether despecialisation is a successful alternative to the rationalisation of work is a moot point. When it is concerned with efficiency and flexibility rather than work satisfaction, it is more an extension of rationalisation, rather than an alternative to it. Further, the 'success' of despecialisation as a form of work organisation depends not only upon which criterion of success is used, but whose criterion, since work redesign and participation bring somewhat different consequences for employees, managers and employers. Lastly, despecialisation in practice takes the form of rather different kinds of work redesign and employee participation, each with their own strengths and weaknesses. Any assessment of despecialisation must take this variegation into account.

From the point of view of managers and employers, the potential benefits of work redesign are a more flexible and intensive use of labour and reduced labour costs, together with a more committed and 'responsible' workforce. Not all of these accrue from all forms of work redesign. Generally, job enrichment and group working are more likely to deliver flexibility and responsibility than simple job enlargement and job rotation. The problem for managers, however, is that job enrichment and group working also carry greater direct costs and greater risks. Potentially, the costs to managers of work redesign are the need for higher pay for remaining workers, training costs, possible loss of system efficiencies due to job changing, the possible elimination of lower-level manager/first-line supervisors and the political cost of a loss of managerial control over the work process. Managers, therefore, face a dilemma in work redesign: to maximise benefits through radical changes such as job enrichment and group working, or to minimise losses by opting for more limited changes.

From the point of view of employees, the costs and benefits of work redesign are, to some extent, a mirror image of those for employers. For employees, work redesign may bring more varied, complete, challenging and hence more satisfying work;

greater control over their immediate work situation and possible accompanying improvements in pay and conditions. These
benefits, too, are more likely to flow from job enrichment and
group working than from more limited forms of work redesign.
The potential costs to employees are job loss or displacement, a
loss of opportunities for informal interaction, and intensification
of effort. Once again, these costs are potentially higher with the
greater responsibilities of job enrichment or group working.

With participation, similar themes and considerations recur.
For managers, the potential benefits of employee participation
are promotion of a managerial point of view, improvements in
the quality of decision-making by increasing the input of
information and opinion, greater commitment to decisions,
containment of grievances and reinforcement of managerial
legitimacy. These are more likely to be forthcoming the greater
the number of decisions in which employees are involved, the
higher the level of participation and the more substantive the
employee involvement. This is more the case with codetermination or company-level consultation than with low-level works
councils or consultative committees. However, here too the
potential costs and risks for managers are greater. The costs are
those of time and resources spent organising and convening
meetings and processing information and opinions, whilst the
risk is that employees or their representatives will use participative machinery to challenge managerial prerogatives and
modify decisions in their favour. In short, managers face the
dilemma of having participation which is either consequential
but risky, or unchallenging but futile.

For employees, participation offers different degrees of
benefit. Higher-level and substantive participation is likely to
give employees a greater feeling of real involvement and control,
and to instil greater identification with the organisation. Low-
level, inconsequential or 'mock' systems of participation are
likely to induce only apathy or resentment.

Despecialisation in its various forms – job redesign, group
working and employee participation – is therefore ambiguous in
both aims and outcomes, reflecting a desire, on the one hand, to
present a humanistic alternative to the rationalisation of work
and, on the other, to offer a more efficient version of it. Even
when promoted under the banner of 'quality of working life',
despecialisation has usually also sought to enhance efficiency

through greater employee flexibility, responsibility, initiative, commitment and, more crudely, intensification of effort. Work redesign and participation tend to endure, therefore, only where flexibility and efficiency gains are forthcoming and sustained. Efficiency and flexibility have become, increasingly, the material reasons for despecialisation even if 'Quality of Working Life' remains the banner under which it is promoted.

FURTHER READING

Evidence on the low levels of work satisfaction associated with routine jobs may be found in Walker and Guest (1952), Blauner (1960, 1964), Friedman (1964), Fraser (1968), Beynon (1973), Terkel (1973), US Dept of Health, Education and Welfare (1973), Pfeffer (1979), Zimbalist (1979) and Cavendish (1982).

On the 'flexibility initiative', see Kelly (1982), Piore and Sabel (1984), Atkinson (1985), Buchanan (1987), Hyman and Streeck (1988), Wood (1989a), Thompson and McHugh (1990).

Reviews of work redesign practices and issues may be found in Davis and Cherns (1975a/b), Filley and House (1976), Weir (1976), Cooper and Mumford (1979), Duncan et al. (1980), Ondrack and Timperley (1982), Warner (1984), Knights et al. (1985), Hyman and Streeck (1985) and Wood (1989a).

Employee participation is reviewed in Wall and Lischeron (1977), IDE (1981), Robson (1982), Brannen (1983, 1984), Elliott (1984), Ramsay (1985), Poole (1986) and Marchington (1988).

Evidence on the effects of despecialisation is scattered and very confused, but see Warr and Wall (1975), Filley and House (1976), Locke (1976), Lawler and Ledford (1981), Kelly (1982), Reif and Luthans (1982) and Hales (1987a) for general reviews.

Chapter 7

The search for flexibility
Divisionalised, professional and adhocratic organisation

In Chapter 5 we saw how bureaucry, with its emphasis upon centralised planning and decision-making, detailed managerial division of labour, hierarchical coordination and control through rules and procedures, is prone to inflexibility and slow response to change. The principle of decentralisation and the different forms that it can take, which we examine in this chapter, are attempts to address these problems by making managerial, professional and administrative work more flexible and performance-oriented and making the organisation as a whole more responsive to the conditions under which it operates.

We begin by reviewing the research which documents decentralised alternatives to bureaucratic administration, and contingency theory which seeks to explain them. From here we go on to examine first, the central principles of decentralisation and second, decentralisation in practice, in its two basic forms: 'professional organisation' (partial decentralisation) and 'adhocracy' (full decentralisation).

The key issues relating to decentralisation, which we examine at some length, is whether environmental change and uncertainty brings an inexorable pressure on bureaucracies to decentralise. We show that, in practice, large organisations may deal with change by choosing alternative courses of action to that of radical decentralisation. They may alter their goals and objectives, adopt the limited decentralisation of the divisionalised form or attempt to control, or influence, the technological, socio-political and economic conditions in which they operate. We also show why they may choose to adopt these alternative courses of action by discussing the political and technical risks which attend decentralisation. This leads, lastly, to a more general evaluation of the strengths and weaknesses of decentralised organisation, in which we argue that whilst the greater individual autonomy facilitated by decentralisation is a prerequisite for flexibility and innovation, it poses technical and political problems of control and coordination. In a mirror-image of the analysis in Chapter 5, we see that, just as the inefficiencies of bureaucray may be tolerated, so the possibilities of decentralisation may be spurned, in order to maintain centralised control.

ORGANISATIONAL VARIATION AND CONTINGENCY THEORY

Since the 1950s, a growing literature has both documented and attempted to explain organisational variation. Its starting point was a series of research studies which called into question the basic, sometimes implicit, proposition of classical theories of organisation (Fayol, 1949; Urwick, 1952) that there was 'one best way' to organise, regardless of circumstances. They showed instead that organisational forms varied in different circumstances. This perspective, afforded by research showing that organisational forms vary, has led to contingency theory, which seeks to explain why this variation occurs by reference to contextual demands.

The key studies which provide the empirical foundation of contingency theory are summarised in Table 7.1. We will not reproduce the quantity and complexity of these, and other, findings here, but rather attempt to summarise the principal findings into a set of common, central propositions. This attempt at synthesis does, of course, face the problem that different studies use different terminologies and have different emphases and focuses. However, cutting through the complexity (and at risk of doing some violence to its subtleties), we can suggest that research studies have identified ten elements of organisation which, individually and in combination, vary with five contextual (or 'contingency') variables.

The ten variable elements of organisation have all been discussed in more detail in Chapter 3 and elsewhere, and so are presented in summary form here:

1 Degree of centralisation: management functions, particularly those of planning, decision-making and control, may be concentrated at the top, or dispersed through the administrative structure. (Since decentralisation forms the linchpin of this chapter, this element is discussed in more detail below.)

2 Number of levels in the hierarchy: some administrative structures are tall, with many managerial levels and narrow spans of control, whilst others are flat.

3 Basis of managerial power and authority: power may flow to managers with access to or control over resources, administrative knowledge, technical expertise or values and meanings.

4 Degree of standardisation: some administrative processes are routine, predictable and regulated by standard procedures, whilst others are *ad hoc* and discretionary.

5 Degree of specialisation: departments, groups or jobs may be restricted to specialised functions, or may have wide responsibilities.

6 Degree of formalisation: duties, responsibilities, reporting relationships and communications may be specified in detail and in writing, or be informal.

7 Number of integrating mechanisms: coordination may be tackled through many integrating mechanisms, or relatively few.

8 Direction of communications: information flows may be predominantly vertical or lateral.

9 Use of 'boundary roles': there may be many, or few, organisational roles or units concerned with monitoring, communicating or transacting with external parties across the organisation's boundary.

10 Ratio of managers to non-managers: the relative size of the administrative component may be large or small.

In summarising the contingency variables which define the context in which organisations operate, we again need to cut through some complexity and differences in emphasis given to these variables and to the linkages between them and elements of organisation. Broadly, the five contingency variables, together with the elements of organisation with which they are associated, are:

Table 7.1 The contingency perspective: principal studies and findings

Author/ researcher	Aspects of organisation emphasised	Forms of organisation	Contingency variables	Types of contingency
Woodward (1965)	Hierarchy: ratio of managers/clerical personnel; span of control; task specification; communications; specialisation; coordination; separation of administration		Production technology	Small batch/unit, large batch/mass, process
Lawrence and Lorsch (1967)	Differentiation: method of integration; conflict resolution	Differentiated/integrated, undifferentiated/loose	Environment (market) and technology	Homogeneous/heterogeneous, stable/dynamic
Thompson (1967)	Forms of coordination	Standardisation, planning, mutual adjustment	Technology/interdependence	Mediating (pooled), long linked (sequential), intensive (reciprocal)
Burns and Stalker (1968)	Differentiation; nature of tasks; responsibility hierarchy; expertise; authority; communication	Mechanistic, organic, pathological mechanistic	Market and technology	Stable/unstable
Morse and Lorsch (1970)	Rules; task specification	Supportive, structured	Goals and technology	Research, manufacturing
Perrow (1971)	Coordination; control; interdependence; authority; motivation	Rigid/centralised, flexible/decentralised	Technology (exceptions and search process)	Many/few exceptions, analysable/non-analysable

Pugh and Hickson (1976)	Specialisation; standardisation; formalisation; centralisation; general configuration	Full bureaucracy, workflow bureaucracy, personnel bureaucracy, implicitly structured, nascent full bureaucracy, nascent workflow bureaucracy, pre-workflow bureaucracy	Location, size, ownership, market, activities technology	Large/small, public/private, monopoly/competitive, manufacturing/services, workflow integration
Hage (1977)	Centralisation; hierarchy; no. specialists	Mechanical, organic	Technology Size market	Routine/non-routine, sophisticated/non-sophisticated, large/small, mass/segment
Mintzberg (1979)	Coordinating mechanisms (5) Design parameters (8) Key parts of organisation (5)	Simple structure, machine bureaucracy, professional bureaucracy, divisionalised form, adhocracy	Age, size, technical systems environment, power	Young/old, large/small, simple/sophisticated, regulating/non-regulating, simple/complex, stable/dynamic, locus of power
Handy (1981)	Power; decision-making; specialisation rules; task specification	Power task } cultures role person	Size technology, environment, goals	Large/small routine/changing, homogeneous/heterogeneous, steady state/breakdown
Donaldson (1985)	Basis of sub-units: formalisation/regulation	Functional } mechanistic product divisions matrix } organic project	number of products product mix change product life cycle	One/several related, several unrelated, slow/rapid, early/mature

1 Size and age Size is an internal contingency which is measured in different ways, although number of employees is the most common parameter. For many, size is the decisive contingency variable, with larger organisations characterised by greater specialisation, standardisation, formalisation and more elaborate administrative structures (Reeves and Woodward, 1970; Pugh and Hickson, 1973; Mintzberg, 1979). More contentious is the relationship between size and degree of centralisation, although much of this turns on whether operational decision-making in the context of centrally determined policy and rules constitutes a form of decentralisation. In Chapter 5, we argued that it does not.

Age is linked to size, since organisational survival and growth are linked. The repetition and codification of practices means that formalisation and standardisation increase with age. Further, organisation shows its age in the sense of reflecting both organisational fashions prevailing at the time of its inception (Stinchcombe, 1969; Meyer and Rowan, 1977) and the stage in the life cycle of its principal products (Nash, 1983; Donaldson, 1985).

2 Technology The link between technology and organisation is complicated by different conceptions of technology, how it varies, and with which organisational elements it is associated. Synthesising, technology subsumes, firstly, the *technical system*, varying by level of sophistication (how easy it is to understand) and regulation (to what extent it controls work methods) (Woodward, 1965; Thompson, 1967; Hage, 1977) and secondly, the *transformation process* of turning inputs into outputs, varying by uniformity of input and predictability of methods (Perrow, 1971; Hage and Aiken, 1972; Khandwalla, 1974). Further, there is the distinction between operational and administrative technology.

Taken together, the evidence suggests, first, that sophisticated technical systems are associated with differentiation/specialisation, decentralisation and extensive integrating mechanisms (Woodward, 1965; Lawrence and Lorsh, 1967; Hage, 1977) and second, that regulating technical systems and routine transformation processes are associated with specialisation, standardisation and formalisation of work (Woodward, 1965; Thompson, 1967; Perrow, 1971; Khandwalla, 1974). These effects impinge directly upon administration, because of the nature of administrative technology, or indirectly, because of the need to administer a particular operating technology. Further, the effect is curvilinear if technologies become more regulating and routine before becoming more sophisticated and non-routine (Woodward, 1965).

3 Environment Environment is an umbrella term to denote the external context in which organisation operates, including the economy, markets, society, culture, political and legal system. The decisive characteristics of environment for organisation, however, are degree of homogeneity (complexity/diversity), how rapidly it changes (stability) and to what extent change is foreseeable (uncertainty). Although these may vary independently, complexity, instability and uncertainty may combine to produce 'turbulent' environments, which are associated with decentralised decision-making, lack of standardisation or formalisation, and a profusion of integrating mechanisms (Lawrence and Lorsch, 1967; Burns and Stalker, 1968; Galbraith, 1973; Boseman and Jones, 1974).

4 Goals and activities These subsume different forms of ownership and performance criteria (e.g. profit versus not-for-profit) and the type and range of goods and services offered. Generally, public ownership or provision of uniform goods and services are associated with centralisation, standardisation and formalisation (Blau and Scott, 1963; Morse and Lorsch, 1970; Pugh, 1973).

5 Employees Differences in the skills, experience, attitudes and orientation of typical employees are associated with organisational variation. Employment of highly qualified, creative or 'knowledge' workers who place a high value on challenging work is associated with decentralisation, and with reduced levels of standardisation and formalisation (Morse and Lorsch, 1970; Handy, 1984; Drucker, 1988).

The existence of ten organisational variables contingent upon five contextual variables appears to suggest that organisation as a whole is infinitely variable. However, organisational elements co-vary in three important respects: first, specialisation, standardisation and formalisation are linked; second, centralisation, hierarchy and formalised vertical communications go together;

and third, unit differentiation, decentralisation and a variety of integrating mechanisms are linked. In practice, therefore, organisations are configured in a finite number of ways.

Indeed, two basic polar types of administrative organisation are often discerned. On the one hand there is bureaucratic or 'mechanistic' organisation (as discussed in Chapter 5) whilst on the other, there is decentralised or 'organic' organisation, characterised by decentralised decision-making, lateral communications, managerial power based on technical expertise, many integrating mechanisms and boundary roles and little standardisation, specialisation or formalisation. Further, organic organisation is associated with small and young undertakings, sophisticated but non-regulating technical systems, non-routine transformation processes, turbulent environments, heterogeneous activities and skilled or creative employees (Burns and Stalker, 1968; Hage, 1977; Mintzberg, 1979; Handy, 1984). It can, therefore, be both the precursor to bureaucratisation which comes with organisational growth and longevity (Stinchcombe, 1969; Goffee and Scase, 1985), and the successor to bureaucracy beset by technological, social, economic and political change (Burns and Stalker, 1968; Mintzberg, 1979; Donaldson, 1987).

This links into contingency theory proper, which explains organisational forms and changes to them by reference to the 'demands' of context. This takes two forms. Firstly, the substance of the link between contingency factors as causal, independent variables and elements of organisations as dependent variables is traced through the influence of intermediate variables, such as interdependence of work processes (Thompson, 1967), complexity of tasks (Collins and Hall, 1986), organisational strategy (Chandler, 1977; Donaldson, 1987), information-processing (Galbraith, 1977), work comprehensibility, predictability and diversity or speed of response (Mintzberg, 1979).

Secondly, contingency theory explains the necessity of certain organisational characteristics under certain conditions because of their impact on performance and survival. Thus undertakings which have forms of organisation consistent with the context in which they operate are successful and thrive; those which do not are unsuccessful and disappear (Lawrence and Lorsch, 1967; Khandwalla, 1974). This argument is most coherently stated in the Population Ecology thesis, which suggests that competition and selection produces populations of organisations which are structured in ways appropriate to their context (Hannan and Freeman, 1977; Aldrich, 1979). Others suggest that internal adaptation, rather than natural selection, is the major process at work (Nelson and Winter, 1982; Perrow, 1986). This, in turn, develops the idea that organisations are 'open systems', composed of interdependent parts, obtaining inputs (materials, people, ideas), exporting outputs (goods, services, information) and receiving feedback information from their environments across permeable boundaries (Emery and Trist, 1965; Katz and Kahn, 1970; Elliott, 1980).

If context determines organisation form, then changes in context necessitate change in organisation if an undertaking is to survive. Contingency theory argues, essentially, that as technology becomes more sophisticated and less routinised, environments more complex and uncertain, activities more heterogeneous and employees more skilled and sophisticated, undertakings must become more flexible and adaptable, and are compelled to move from bureaucratic to more decentralised forms of administration. In short, in the face of environmental turbulence, organisations 'decentralise or die'.

DECENTRALISATION: GENERAL PRINCIPLES

In common with many terms in the organisational lexicon, 'decentralisation' is used in diverse and sometimes ambiguous ways. One common usage refers to the geographical dispersion of an organisation's activities: retailers, hotel companies or banks are held to be 'decentralised' because they comprise a large number of units in different locations. This overlooks the question of whether the *management* of these organisations is decentralised or centralised.

Decentralisation can also be applied rather restrictively. For example, it is often regarded as synonymous with divisionalisation (Williamson, 1975; Chandler, 1977; Hill, 1984). However, as we argue later, divisionalisation is not only a very limited form of decentralisation but is often an alternative to wider decentralisation. In other analyses, decentralisation is seen as a characteristic of decision-making. Here, 'full centralisation' forms a limit case where all stages of all decisions are taken by a single individual and there is a continuum of degrees of decentralisaiton, with delegation of different stages in decision-making, different types of decisions (selective decentralisation) or all types (parallel decentralisation), either down the hierarchy (vertical decentralisation) or across, from managers to non-managers (horizontal decentralisation) (Mintzberg, 1979). Apart from the problem that horizontal decentralisation may rest more on job titles than any real shift in decision-making, the equation between decentralisation and the locus of decision-making ignores the possibility that other management functions may be decentralised.

'Decentralisation' is used here, therefore, as a shorthand term to denote changes in the organisation of managerial, professional and administrative work which entail the devolution of management functions to middle and junior managers who, to a greater extent than before, manage themselves. In what follows, therefore, we are concerned with the decentralisation of management.

From descriptions of specific forms of decentralisation, together with a limited number of more general analyses, certain common principles may be discerned which, to sharpen the contrast with bureaucracy, may be regarded as: devolution, reciprocal expertise and situational logic.

Devolution is the transfer of responsibility for and control over administrative and professional work to those performing it. Instead of a hierarchy, there is a flatter network of areas of activity with fluid responsibilities, lateral flows of information, horizontal and informal contacts, non-directive coordinating mechanisms and decisions taken closer to their level of application. Hence, junior managers are given greater discretion over how they perform their job and, to some extent, what they do, whilst teams are given greater opportunity for self-organisation. This, in turn, requires less external control over behaviour and more self- or mutual control over behaviour, reinforced by external control over outputs or performance.

Decentralisation requires more managers with generalist skills and orientations and a capacity for taking responsibility and, hence, requires a recruitment system to select for these qualities and a system of management training and development to augment them. Managers also require power in line with additional responsibilities, and this power is increasingly based on technical knowledge.

Performance control requires an appropriate system, including clear objectives which managers themselves are involved in setting (management by objectives), relatively simple and immediate performance measures and a related system of manager appraisal and reward.

Whilst even in the most decentralised form of organisation, policy and strategy formation are likely to remain centralised, they are more democratic and based upon information and opinion from a wider range of managers or specialists. Policy is therefore less the imposition of a grand design, more the emergent outcome of existing practices.

In large-scale administrative and professional work, specialisation is unavoidable. Reciprocal expertise, however, is a more organic way of coordinating specialists, by creating work units in which specialist skills and knowledge is pooled. Thus, decentralised organisation is based on teams, focused on particular tasks, projects or problems and incorporating a range of skills. Individuals, in different ways, have broader responsibilities. Professionals work within their specialism but work on a broad range of tasks. Middle and junior line managers have more generalist responsibilities. Thus, decentralised organisation has redundant functions, creating spare capacity by adding extra functions and skills to individuals and groups; requisite variety, creating flexibility through multi-skilling; and connectivity, by linking skills together. These offer the possibility of 'holographic' organisation where simultaneous specialisation and generalisation and self-organisation means that the activities of the whole are contained in each of the parts (Morgan, 1986). These characteristics, in turn, require systems for selecting, recruiting and training flexible specialists, together with appraisal and reward systems which focus on cooperation and team performance.

Lastly, decentralised organisation rests on situational rationality, an emphasis upon getting things done in ways dictated by and appropriate to specific situational demands. Rather than regular responses to predictable events, there is flexible response to the unpredictable and emphasis on *ad hoc* problem-solving. Thus, there is encouragement of openness, reflection, experimentation, risk-taking and learning. This is reflected in omnidirectional informal communications, the use of task forces to solve problems, institutionalisation of debate and conflict, individual autonomy, and appraisal and reward systems which focus on achievement and innovation.

The principles of decentralised organisation can now be summarised in terms of the MTO framework (see Table 7.2). The process of managing managers and professionals is devolved such that, to a greater degree, they manage themselves or each other. Operational planning and decision-making is undertaken by more junior managers or by teams with responsibility for a particular operational sphere, whilst strategic planning and policy decisions are more democratic. Consequently, there is a high level of informal, lateral communication.

The allocation of managerial work exhibits a reduced level of individual specialisation. Groups specialise in tasks or projects, but have a fluid internal division of labour. Individual jobs have wider professional or managerial responsibilities.

Motivation relies much more on self- or mutual regulation, intrinsic rewards and an achievement ethic. Thus, rules are formulated and enforced by managers themselves, rewards emphasise the intrinsic satisfaction of individual autonomy, team work and task accomplishment, and the prevailing rationale is that of 'getting things done'.

Since activities are dispersed and self-regulated, coordination is of critical importance, and there are a number of specialist coordinating mechanisms in addition to mutual adjustment. Lastly, control relies more on individual managers controlling themselves or each other, with external controls focusing more upon inputs in the form of managerial skills and attitudes, and/ or outputs in the form of performance.

DECENTRALISATION IN PRACTICE: PROFESSIONAL AND ADHOCRATIC ORGANISATION

Decentralisation refers not to a single state, but to a continuum, in that there can be different degrees to which management functions are devolved. Although in theory decentralised forms of organisation along this continuum are infinite, in practice two basic types can be discerned, representing, respectively, partial and full decentralisation.

Table 7.2 Managing through decentralised organisation: general principles

Management process	: Management functions remain separate but are devolved to middle and junior managers and professional staff.
Area of application	: Administrative, managerial and professional work.
Planning/decision-making	
Degree of centralisation	: Operational decisions decentralised. Strategic/policy decisions centralised, but democratic and emergent.
Information/communication flows	: Omnidirectional, formal and informal.
Allocation of Work	
Form of specialisation	: By skill, output or client.
Level of specialisation	: Group/team.
Degree of job specialisation	: Low: professional specialisation.
Motivation	
Rewards	: Greater emphasis to intrinsic satisfactions of autonomy and teamwork.
Rules	: Self/mutual regulation and enforcement.
Rationale	: Achievement ethic.
Coordination	
Locus of responsibility	: [Internal] and [Specialists] Mutual adjustment
Method	: [Adjustment] [Consultation]
Degree of formality	: [Informal] [Informal/formal] Specialist liaison
Control	
Focus	: [Process] and [Inputs] [Outputs] Self/mutual control
Locus of responsibility	: [Self/mutual] [External] [External] Performance control
Degree of impersonality	: [Personal] [Impersonal] [Impersonal]
Degree of formality	: [Informal [Formal [Formal]

Professional organisation (partial decentralisation)

Regarding professional organisation as an approach to management requires some justification, since professionalisation is often thought of as an occupational strategy, concerned with establishing or defending the immunity of an occupation from external management control (Esland, 1980; Johnson, 1980). The components of this strategy echo the characteristics of the oldest professions (even the very oldest), namely a set of esoteric skills and knowledge, surrounded by a raft of ethical constraints and considerations, acquired through lengthy, formalised training and practice, maintained by norms internalised by members of the profession and monitored by a professional body, all of which give the profession the capacity and a rationale to resist external managerial control.

With the growth of services previously rendered by autonomous professions, and the increasing provision of these services by large organisations, professionals as independent contractors, hired by and with obligations to clients, have increasingly been replaced by professionals as employees, hired by and with obligations to organisations. Whilst this may be accompanied by a diminution of professionals' exclusive claims to expertise and, hence, autonomy, some professions have sustained or established such claims. The central organisational issue relating to professions then becomes the problem of whether and to what extent professional autonomy is compatible with bureaucratic organisation (Wilensky, 1970; Hall, 1973).

Although questions raised by this issue surface in what follws, our concern here is somewhat different. We consider professional organisation as a form of management, arising either defensively, as a way of incorporating increasing numbers of professionally trained employees into bureaucratic organisations, or actively, as a way of obviating some of the deficiencies of bureaucracy in the face of more complex and turbulent environments, by organising managerial work more flexibly. Thus, professional organisation is either a way of balancing demands for autonomy with the need for control or of devolving management functions to those whose training equips them to manage themselves.

The essence of professional organisation is the selective recruitment of employees with technical and moral rules 'built in' (Perrow, 1979) through formalised training and experience, who are then left to manage themselves subject to meeting professional and organisational performance criteria. Hence, its key principles are: controlled recruitment, a professional division of labour, coordination and control based on professional standards and performance, and a 'career-for-loyalty' employment contract.

Professional organisation rests upon the employment of staff who have undergone a lengthy period of formal, standardised training, acquired accredited qualifications and experienced a period of professional practice. As a result, professionals are assumed to have internalised technical knowledge and skills, behavioural norms and ethical standards. Thus, recruitment policy is tightly and centrally controlled, and focuses on desired levels of qualification and experience, preferred sources of qualification, professional manpower planning and selection procedures. These seek to ensure that professional employees are both technically competent and potentially trustworthy, as well as loyal and committed to organisational goals.

Employees thus recruited are left, to a large extent, to work in their own way. The division of work reflects professional expertise in a number of senses. Firstly, the work role which individuals perform and the boundaries of their responsibilities are determined by professional identity and competence. Secondly, how these responsibilities are undertaken is a matter of individual choice based on internalised expertise. Thus, individuals are confined to the areas of jurisdiction of professional specialism, but undertake work which is varied and concerned with complex problem-solving. Internalised knowledge, reinforced by the advice or criticism of colleagues, means that professionals handle specific problems as examples of known 'types', dealt with in standard ways: the process of 'typification' (Mintzberg, 1979).

Coordination between professionals relies, in part, on these standard areas and forms of operation which enable some mutual anticipation of areas of concern and ways of defining problems. Similarly, professional self-control and autonomy are underpinned by technical skills and ethical standards acquired through training and experience. Freedom from external managerial control both arises from and is justified by the fact that professionals know more about their work than those who would manage them and, hence, it is the profession which influences the conduct of work.

Although professional employees are not entirely free agents, they are usually subject to indirect and non-intrusive forms of coordination and control. Firstly, the work of specialists is fused together in multidisciplinary project teams or task forces, where mutual adjustment or the demands of the work itself act as coordinating devices. Secondly, professional managers may be employed to mediate between professional groups or professionals and clients. However, in the 'dual hierarchy' of specialists and administrators, the power and influence of professional specialists is greater. Lastly, specialised coordinating mechanisms, such as steering committees, liaison officers or 'trouble shooters' may be used.

External controls over professionals focus upon inputs and outputs, rather than behaviour. Control over inputs, in the form of the skills of those carrying out the work, is attempted through centralised control over recruitment. In addition, professional specialists or managers are subject, individually or as teams, to performance control. For specialists, this means being judged on the quality or success of their work, which, given competing criteria of quality – in particular, whether it is professionals', their clients' or the employer's criteria which prevails – is difficult. For professional managers, it means being subjected to financial management control systems, based on cost or profit centres, or production control systems focusing on output levels, quality or effective use of materials or equipment (Kinnie, 1989). Thus, professional managers or specialists are free to run their own show, but not free to fail.

Because professional expertise is both relatively scarce and broadly applicable, professionals are potentially mobile, marketable individuals with a contingent loyalty to particular organisations. Establishing their loyalty may require, therefore, the offer of employment security, career and salary progression. In return, professionals are expected not only to remain with the organisation but also to place their skills at its disposal and to pursue organisational, rather than professional, goals.

We can now summarise professional organisation in terms of the MTO framework (see Table 7.3). Planning and decision-making are partly centralised, partly decentralised. Operating plans and decisions are decentralised, with professional

Table 7.3 Managing through professional organisation

Management process		
Area of application	:	Management functions devolved to middle/junior managers and professional staff.
	:	Administrative, managerial and professional work.
Planning/decision-making		
Degree of centralisation	:	Operational decisions decentralised to professionals, strategy/policy centralised, but may be consultative. } Partial decentralisation
Information/communication flows	:	Omnidirectional, formal and informal.
Allocation of work		
Form of specialisation	:	By skill/professional expertise.
Level of specialisation	:	Professional group, plus individual specialisms.
Degree of job specialisation	:	Moderate: individuals confined to professional area, but undertake complex and varied work.
Motivation		
Rewards	:	Intrinsic and deferred material rewards } Self-motivation
Rules	:	Internalised professional practices and norms
Rationales	:	'Professionalism', 'vocation'
Coordination		
Locus of responsibility	:	[Internal] [Specialists/coord. bodies] } Mutual adjustment and specialist liaison
Method	:	[Adjustment] and [Consultation]
Degree of formality	:	[Informal] [Formal/informal]
Control		
Focus	:	[Process] [Inputs/outputs] } Self/mutual control, Recruitment control, Performance control
Locus of responsibility	:	[Self/mutual] and [External]
Degree of impersonality	:	[Personal] [Impersonal]
Degree of formality	:	[Informal] [Formal]

managers and specialists exercising discretion over their areas of responsibility. Policy decisions, relating to business strategy or recruitment policy, remain centralised, however, the former because they override specialist interests, and the latter because they are crucial in securing those to whom operating decisions can safely be delegated. However, to varying degrees, professionals may influence policy through consultative decision-making, especially in 'single profession' organisations (e.g. a legal practice or university).

Work is allocated on the basis of professional specialisation, with individuals confined to areas of competence but, within those, undertaking complex, varied and open-ended work. Teams may specialise in particular tasks or projects but have a fluid internal division of labour.

Motivation of professionals emphasises self-motivation. Rules take the form of internalised practices and norms, inducing professionals to work in certain ways; rewards emphasise the intrinsic work satisfaction of variety, challenge and autonomy, as well as deferred material rewards of career progression; the inducement to adhere to particular standards of conduct and vocational commitment is provided by a rationale, or ideology, of 'professionalism'.

Because of the strong centrifugal forces of professional autonomy, coordination is a vital component of the management process. In addition to mutual adjustment through inter-personal contact and shared professional expectations, there is the use of multidisciplinary teams, professional managers as team leaders or coordinators, and specialist coordinating mechanisms such as liaison officers or steering committees.

Control over professional work relies a great deal on self-control by professionals over their behaviour, arising from internalised professional practices or standards, and mutual control by colleagues or members of the professional body. External controls are more indirect, focusing on inputs, in the form of employee qualifications or skills, and outputs, in the form of performance standards.

Whilst this approach to organisation is, in principle, applicable to all forms of work, in practice it is mainly used to manage either middle and junior managers/administrators or specialist 'knowledge workers'. These knowledge workers may produce work outputs directly for an employer (as in the case of research scientists, accountants, marketing specialists or legal advisers) or external clients (as in the case of lawyers, doctors, social workers or teachers). It is, therefore, either a way of managing those with professional qualifications, or of managing managers as professionals. In the former case, professional organisation often predates bureaucratisation. This is especially true in the case of professions which are unable to sustain a claim to exclusive expertise, or to resist rationalisation and deskilling. Where managers are managed as professionals, professional organisation represents an attempt to overcome some of the rigidities of bureaucracy through devolved responsibilities and individual flexibility. A more radical attempt to do this, however, is to be found in adhocratic organisation.

Adhocratic organisation (full decentralisation)

In essence, adhocratic organisation (Toffler, 1970; 1985; Mintzberg, 1979) involves the pursuit of innovation, problem solving and responsiveness to situational demands through the creation of a loose federation of temporary work units, or teams, in which technical expertise and creativity are given free rein. The system rests upon five central principles: a fluid division of labour, based on situational expertise; an absence of standardisation, formalisation and regulation; an absence of hierarchy; complex and sophisticated coordination; and a strong achievement ethic. Thus, adhocracy is defined as much by what is not present as by what is, and may be seen as a kind of anti-structure (or deliberate disorganisation), not readily amenable to normal forms of organisational representation, such as organisation charts, rule-books/manuals and job descriptions. In contrast to the bureaucratic pyramid, it is more like a molecular sphere, or 'constellation of stars' (Handy, 1981).

A fluid division of labour, based on situational expertise, is a way of deploying experts which reconciles the particular, bounded nature of technical expertise with complex, unpredictable and open-ended work. The basic work unit is the task force or project team, constituted on an *ad hoc*, fluid and temporary basis. Teams form to deal with a particular task. They comprise those whose expertise is pertinent to the task, so their composition may change over time, and they exist only for the duration of the task or project. Individuals, recruited for their expertise, are allocated not so much to rigid jobs as to membership of one or more teams, as the nature of the work demands. Within teams, individual responsibilities extend beyond performance of a fixed role, to the broader expectation of applying their expertise when required. Teams, in turn, may be part of wider groupings, in the form of fluid 'work constellations' (Mintzberg, 1979) rather than functional departments.

Fluid responsibilities are matched by variable, *ad hoc* work methods, in which problems and tasks are dealt with as they arise and according to their particular requirements. Thus, there is little standardisation, formalisation or regulation. Fluid responsibilities mean that formal job descriptions and reporting relationships are inappropriate, and the need for *ad hoc* work methods and problem-solving means that past practices cannot safely be codified into rigid rules and procedures. Instead, 'rules' take the form of generalised problem-solving routines internalised by specialists, and there is considerable reliance upon their continuing capacity to apply this knowledge and skill as required.

This requires, firstly, that specialists retain and develop their expertise through personal development and maintenance of external affiliations with professional bodies and other specialists. This 'cosmopolitan', rather than 'local' (Gouldner, 1957) orientation of specialists means that ways have to be found to encourage affiliation to the organisation and its goals. These include development of commitment to task achievement, through organisationally focused training and socialisation, and the offer of intrinsically rewarding work with high levels of personal autonomy, attractive salaries and opportunities for 'lateral careers', offering experience across different geographical work areas.

More conventional, vertical careers are precluded by the absence of hierarchy, the two central justifications for which wither away in adhocratic organisation. Firstly, a system for translating and transmitting detailed directives from broad policy becomes unnecessary if operating decisions are taken by specialists involved in the work itself. Secondly, referral upwards for managerial decision and direction is inappropriate for coordinating specialist work, since managers lack the necessary technical expertise. Thus, instead of segmented departments and hierarchical levels, teams are linked together in a loose federation. Decisions relating to the work of the team, which are often custom-made for a particular problem or task, are taken by team members individually or collectively. Power and influence flow to those with the pertinent technical knowledge, and leadership is fluid and situational.

Control over day-to-day activities also resides with team members, with control from the centre mainly focused upon outputs, or the extent to which individuals and teams complete projects in ways appropriate to organisational needs. Policy and strategy decisions may be taken centrally, but are arrived at through 'bottom up' processes of participation or consultation. Thus, policy and strategy formation is largely a process of discovery and consolidation of existing practices. This requires non-conventional policy-making systems, with greater emphasis upon qualitative data, 'feel', experimentation, iteration, conflict and negotiation. These, in turn, necessitate a high level of often informal vertical and horizontal communication.

A copious flow of information is also crucial for coordination which, given shifting work responsibilities, the free pursuit of specialist instincts for innovation and problem-solving, and a high level of individual or team autonomy, takes on a critical importance. Consequently, coordinating mechanisms are many and complex. Within teams, dovetailing the work of divers specialists requires a high level of communication and consultation, focused by the demands of joint work tasks. However, the need to reconcile possibly divergent specialist interests and perspectives, and to ensure that progress on projects adheres to organisational considerations and deadlines, may also necessitate a project manager or team leader offering guidance or advice, rather than managerial control. Project managers may also form the points of contact through which coordination among teams takes place. Additionally, there may be a variety of 'integrating devices' (Lawrence and Lorsch, 1967; Galbraith, 1977) over and above informal communications between members of different project teams. These include specialist liaison or integration roles, individuals or groups charged with facilitating lateral communications or resolving conflicts. A more elaborate approach is the use of the matrix principle. Here, groupings based on expertise interlock with those based on project, product, business or geographical areas to produce a network of multi-specialist teams in which individuals have a dual location (their specialist group and their project team) and a dual reporting relationship (to their specialist and project managers). As we shall see below, matrixes take a number of forms, including those which are little more than bureaucratic hybrids. The form most consistent with adhocratic organisation is the 'heuristic matrix' (Schull *et al.*, 1970) where the division of labour is fluid, group/team autonomy is high and hierarchy largely absent.

The most subtle, yet potentially most powerful, coordination and control mechanism in adhocracy is the achievement ethic, or a shared commitment by experts to 'get things done'. This is encouraged in two ways. Commitment to technical quality is encouraged by the nature of the work itself, opportunities to interact with other experts and emphasis upon personal development. Commitment to organisational goals is encouraged by fostering a task orientation, or desire to see a project through to successful completion, in the nature of the work itself and the dynamics of team working. This 'can do' approach may coalesce into a distinct organisational philosophy, or culture, articulated by the actions of key individuals and embedded in organisational processes. (We consider this point in more detail in Chapter 8.)

Summarising adhocratic organisation in terms of the MTO framework (see Table 7.4), we can see that, although the management process may remain separate from operational work, there is a comprehensive devolution of management functions to teams of experts who manage themselves. Planning and decision-making are either decentralised, in the case of operating plans and decisions, or consultative, in the case of policy and strategy. This necessitates a high level of lateral communication of informal and 'live' information.

The allocation of work is based on fluid specialisation at the level of the team. Although focused on particular projects or tasks, teams have a shifting, multidisciplinary composition and a temporary status. Job specialisation is low, with individuals applying their expertise in various *ad hoc* ways to different projects in the context of different teams.

Motivation relies heavily upon self-motivation. Internalised problem-solving skills, rather than formal rules, serve to direct efforts. Rewards, or inducements to effort, emphasise the intrinsic rewards of interesting and challenging work and

Table 7.4 Managing through adhocratic organisation

Management process	: Management functions devolved to teams of experts.
Area of application	: Managerial, professional and technical work.
Planning/decision-making	
Degree of centralisation	: Operational plans and decisions decentralised. } Full
	Strategy/policy emergent or consultative. } decentralisation
Information/communication flows	: Omnidirectional flows of informal 'live' information.
Allocation of Work	
Form of specialisation	: Outputs/projects (teams); skills (individuals).
Level of specialisation	: Team, fluid internal division of labour.
Degree of job specialisation	: Low: individuals apply expertise *ad hoc* to different projects in different teams.
Motivation	
Rewards	: Intrinsic rewards and team-based performance rewards. } Self/
Rules	: Internalised problem-solving skills; absence of formal rules. } mutual
Rationales	: Achievement ethic/'getting things done'. } motivation
Coordination	
Locus of responsibility	: [Internal] and [Specialists/coord.bodies] } Mutual
Method	: [Adjustment] and [Consultation] } adjustment
Degree of formality	: [Informal] [Formal/informal] } and specialist liaison
Control	
Focus	: [Processes/values] and [*Ad hoc* performance] } Self/mutual control.
Locus of responsibility	: [Self/mutual] and [External] } *Ad hoc* performance.
Degree of impersonality	: [Personal] [Impersonal/personal] } Control.
Degree of formality	: [Informal] [Formal/informal]

performance-related extrinsic rewards, often group-based, which are linked to successful completion of a project. Normative motivational force is provided by an ideology of 'achievement' or getting things done.

Coordination is a critical element in the management process and takes a variety of forms. In addition to mutual adjustment and informal liaison, there are team leaders, liaison officers and specialist coordinators (or coordinating groups) and, more elaborately, dual reporting relationships. In every case, coordination relies more on information and advice than upon instruction.

Control relies primarily upon team members to control themselves or each other, with a commitment to technical standards and task achievement enforced by team members forming the central control mechanisms. External controls are unobtrusive and focus mainly on performance. Much of this is *ad hoc*, however, since the absence of standard routines and predictable outcomes means that team or individual performance can only be judged by the eventual success of a project.

Although this form of organisation is, in principle, applicable to different kinds of work, in practice its application is limited in two ways. Firstly, adhocratic organisation is often confined to particular organisational sub-units, invariably those where experts are engaged in creative or technically complex work or 'newstream' (cf. mainstream) activities (Kanter, 1990). Thus, research and development laboratories, advertising, marketing and new product development, systems analysis and design groups may be pockets of adhocratic turbulence in otherwise bureaucratic organisations. Secondly, full adhocracy is restricted to organisations where the core activity is the provision of expertise, information or knowledge, such as consultancies, research and advertising agencies, project management groups, public relations firms and design houses. Here there is no distinction between operational, technical and managerial work, and the whole organisation can be regarded as an 'Operating Adhocracy' (Mintzberg, 1979). These organisations are small and relatively young, operating in volatile environments in which consumer tastes and technology are sophisticated and rapidly changing, and employing a high proportion of technical and creative specialists. Elsewhere, adhocratic organisation is confined to administrative and technical work or to senior, head office managers. This 'Administrative Adhocracy' (Mintzberg, 1979) is where administration of an undertaking as a business unit, or the development and marketing of products, are quite separate activities from operating processes which are routinised, automated or contracted out.

Clearly, however, in whatever form, adhocracy is rare and has not supplanted bureaucracy in the way that some predicted (Toffler, 1970; 1985). Neither, indeed, has more limited decentralisation, in the form of professional organisation. Since this flies in the face of the logic and predictions of contingency theory, it is the central issue surrounding decentralisation.

DECENTRALISATION IN PRACTICE, THE CENTRAL ISSUE: HOW AND WHY HAS PRESSURE TO DECENTRALISE BEEN RESISTED?

Is there an inexorable pressure to decentralise?

Combining the logic of contingency theory with frequently observed changes in the circumstances in which organisations operate suggests that, everywhere, bureaucracy must be under threat and that organisations are being compelled to decentralise. Contingency theory suggests that decentralised forms of organisation are necessary for the pursuit of diverse goals, using complex technology and skilled, sophisticated employees, in turbulent environments. If conditions under which organisations operate come increasingly to resemble this state, the organisation of work must become more flexible and adaptable and, hence, more decentralised. In fact, there is strong evidence that technologies are more sophisticated and rapidly changing, employees better educated and with higher expectations of work, and environments increasingly turbulent, with consumer tastes more sophisticated and labile, raw material supplies more unpredictable, competition more intense and the social, legal and political climate also more unpredictable and threatening to organisational interests (Handy, 1984; 1989). Given these changes, large organisations should have shifted to more decentralised forms, and bureaucracy should be in retreat.

This logic is echoed by commentators prophesying 'the end of bureaucracy'. To be sure, these prophecies take different forms, but most allude to the imminent, or recent, arrival of 'post-industrialism' (Bell, 1973) and to the affinity between its characteristics and adhocratic organisation. In the late 1960s and early 1970s, the increasing threat of governmental and legal constraints upon business, coupled with the demands of more educated employees, imbued with post-materialist values, for greater autonomy at work, were seen as the main forces acting in favour of decentralised organisation (Bennis, 1966). This argument had much in common with the quality of working life movement identified in Chapter 6. In the late 1970s and the 1980s, the need for decentralised administration was linked more to the rapidity of technological change, increased competition and the increasing complexity and sophistication of products, services and market structures (Peters and Waterman, 1984; Toffler, 1985; Peters, 1989). Most recently, decentralisation has been heralded as the organisational virtue arising out of a necessity to reduce managerial overheads in times of recession, by utilising much of the hitherto latent potential of information technology to replace the information processing functions of, and hence remove the need for, layers of middle management (Drucker, 1988; Kaye, 1989; Kanter, 1990). In short, adhocracy has swung from being a panic response to the anti-materialist counter-culture, to the scabbard concealing the sword about to be wielded against middle management.

Evidence on organisational change, however, gives little support to the logic of contingency theory or the prophets of adhocracy. Certainly, some organisations have experimented with limited forms of decentralisation, such as varieties of professional organisation, as managers and technical specialists who have undergone professional education and training are increasingly given wider responsibilities and more autonomy. Moreover, some organisations – usually with much trumpeting to drown out the noise of internal conflict – have adopted project team-based or adhocratic organisation at head office or corporate level (Ferguson, 1990). In both cases, the saving on overheads is of more than tangential importance.

Against this, however, must be set contrary evidence. Firstly, as we have already noted, adhocracy remains a rarity outside small, new, high-technology service firms. Few large, old-established manufacturing companies have shifted from bureaucratic to adhocratic administration.

Secondly, one bureaucratic response to increasing uncertainty, turbulence and the need for greater flexibility is to spawn hybrid versions of bureaucracy, rather than to decentralise. Thus, the basic features which define bureaucracy – functional division of labour, regulation and, above all, hierarchical control and coordination – are retained, but there is an attempt to 'open up' the system and improve lateral communications and the quality of decision-making by building in additional elements. Indeed, a first response is often to tighten bureaucratic controls and centralise yet further, with increasing information processing and decision-making burdens placed on senior managers. Thereafter, the development of 'pathological forms of the mechanistic system' (Burns, 1984) usually entails the creation of more intermediaries, 'assistants to' and a jungle of committees and working parties, all of which overlay, rather than replace, the bureaucratic structure. This is equally true of attempts to build a 'parallel organisation' (Stein and Kanter, 1980) of project groups, pilot groups and steering committees alongside conventional bureaucratic forms.

A related development is the creation of the hybrid 'matrix organisation' (Galbraith, 1977; Knight, 1977) in an attempt to break the rigidities of functional groupings by overlaying product, area or task groupings with their own hierarchical relationships. A 'routine' matrix (Schull et al., 1970) seeks to add a product or project focus to existing functionally based activities. It remains a bureaucratic hybrid, rather than a genuine form of decentralisation, however, because it retains the principle of hierarchy and simply increases the number of levels.

To some extent, the predictions of contingency theory are inaccurate because of weaknesses in the theory itself. One central weakness is its focus upon too few variables and the search for single independent determinate relationships between contingency factors and organisational characteristics (Schreyogg, 1980; Miller, 1981). This, crucially, ignores interactive or contradictory effects among different contingency factors (e.g. stable, routine technology but a turbulent environment). Further, contingency theory is based on the comparison between different organisational forms in different circumstances at one point in time. The process of organisational change in response to changed circumstances is rarely theorised, yet the implication, even in more sophisticated versions of contingency theory which consider intervening variables, is of a largely deterministic process, with contingency factors exerting an objective and irresistible force for change. A forceful and consistent criticism of contingency theory is that it is blind to the possibility that, as a result of human agency rather than abstract forces, contingency factors are not only susceptible to varying interpretation but are also, in many instances, the chosen constraints or deliberate creations of organisations themselves.

The implication of this last criticism is that by selectively interpreting and choosing or actively creating the contingencies which appear to impinge upon them, organisations and, in particular, large bureaucratic organisations with the necessary resources, are able to avoid decentralisation.

Alternatives to decentralisation

We can identify three separate, but not mutually exclusive strategies whereby organisations may avoid substantial decentralisation: the control of internal contingency factors, the control of external contingencies and the development of and reliance upon informal, rather than formal, organisation. We consider each of these in turn.

Control over internal contingencies

Two contingency factors, size and organisational goals/activities, are most evidently internal to, and hence under the control of, organisations which can to some extent choose how big they want to be and what kind of business they want to be in.

Perhaps the most favoured alternative to decentralising organisations which have become too large is, essentially, to turn them into a collection of small ones, through divisionalisation.

Divisionalisation entails arranging the organisation's broad activities into major product-based units, or divisions. With functions (e.g. personnel, marketing) duplicated across divisions, each operates as a semi-autonomous profit centre, or mini-company, responsible for its own operating and market decisions. The divisions are linked together by a head office or 'corporate' apex which controls the divisions, firstly through performance controls, and secondly through the controlled recruitment, development and appointment of divisional managers. Thus, whilst divisional general managers are free to run their divisions as they see fit, they are appointed by head office and are answerable for the financial and market performance of their division. In principle at least, underperformance means replacement of the divisional management team; persistent underperformance can result in the organisation divesting itself of the entire division. Whilst day-to-day management is devolved to divisional heads, head office retains five strategic functions. These are: design and operation of the management information system for communicating performance standards and results; appointment and development of divisional managers; provision of support services which relate to corporate activities (e.g. public relations) or which would be inefficient if duplicated across divisions (e.g. finance, legal, personnel); allocation of financial resources between divisions; and strategic corporate decisions, in particular those relating to the composition of the product portfolio. Thus, the divisionalised form injects a form of quasi-market discipline into the organisation, with head office acting as both market 'surrogate' (allocating resources) and a supra-market arbitrator (making decisions about overall corporate interests).

Adoption of the divisional form has been widespread among large commercial organisations and some state enterprises. It is, however, a very limited form of decentralisation and, as such, represents an alternative to radical decentralisation, for a number of important reasons. Firstly, divisionalisation only entails a devolution of day-to-day management from senior head office managers to divisional heads, i.e. to the next managerial layer down. There is no necessary devolution of management functions within individual divisions and, indeed, given the tight performance controls to which they are subject, divisions have a strong tendency to be centralised (Mintzberg, 1979). Divisionalisation thus replaces one large bureaucracy by a conglomeration of small ones. Further, there is a constant tendency for the relationship between head office and the divisions to become more bureaucratic, with more formal controls, more direct interference in divisional operations and centralisation of previously devolved functions, since senior head office managers are reluctant to give market logic a free rein.

Indeed, divisionalisation is a form of *centralisation* when large conglomerates are 'born divisionalised' through the amalgamation of previously independent companies and the replacement of markets by hierarchies (Williamson, 1975; Hill, 1984). Further, divisionalisation is, typically, the response to diversification by previously functional, bureaucratic organisations (Chandler, 1977) where diverse products require separate divisions and divisional structures reinforce diversification (Mintzberg, 1979). Lastly, divisionalisation only applies to the organisation of senior managerial work and, in particular, the division of labour, reporting relationships and distribution of power between senior head office managers and divisional heads.

Changes in activities, goals and objectives can also represent corporate-level attempts to avoid decentralisation (even though they may be undertaken for other reasons). A detailed discussion of corporate strategy is beyond the scope of this book, but we may note that where an organisation finds its major activities increasingly under threat (from competition, supply problems, legislation, etc.) it may opt to change those activities rather than seeking more adaptable and, hence, decentralised ways of pursuing them. Financial restructuring carries no necessary organisational implications, yet may give threatened organisations the financial means to weather a storm. Furthermore, where an organisation's portfolio of interests is under threat, it may choose to diversify into new, more stable, products or markets or, alternatively, to retrench by divesting itself of threatened activities. In short, organisations may prefer the merry-go-round of acquisitions and sell-offs to the plunge of decentralisation.

Organisations may also choose to redefine their activities or goals. Such redefinition is not difficult, given the many ways of measuring financial and market performance. What is necessary, of course, is for senior managers to effect this redefinition.

Control over external contingencies

Large organisations take an active rather than a passive stance towards their environments, and thereby maintain a high degree of resilience, coupled with a low propensity for organisational change. This active stance takes a number of related forms. Firstly, senior managers, often influenced by key information 'gatekeepers', interpret the ambiguous 'demands' of the environment (March and Olsen, 1976; Aldrich and Herker, 1977) and their organisation's performance within it, especially if this remains above a minimum 'satisficing' level. These interpretations offer a 'scope of choice' (Schreyogg, 1980) in strategic responses which need not involve organisational change (Child, 1973b). Secondly, organisations can, to some extent, select their environments and, having done so, react to them in particular ways, through interaction and accommodations with other organisations (Starbuck, 1976). Thirdly, organisations may manipulate or control their environment by using their resources to counteract or prevent potential threat or instability (Galbraith, 1974; Pfeffer and Salancik, 1978; Perrow, 1986; Kanter, 1990). Lastly, organisations may construct or 'enact' their environments by engaging in activities which are self-fulfilling, or by defining past activities as being environmentally determined (Hirsch, 1975; Smircich and Stubbart, 1985).

These different levels of manipulation and control apply to different aspects of the external environment. For their economic or market environments, organisations have a host of 'environmental control strategies' available (Hage, 1977). Potential competitive threats can be countered by business strategies: acquisition of or merger with competitors, price or territorial agreements, price wars, the maintenance of barriers to entry through high levels of research or advertising expenditure, product differentiation or diversification. Potential resource threats are countered by vertical integration or supply agreements.

Environmental control strategies involve cooperative, as well as competitive, actions. Increasingly, large organisations enhance their capacity to survive by pooling resources and forming alliances and partnerships with others. These partnerships take the form of 'multi-organisation service alliances', or consortia, 'opportunistic alliances', or joint ventures, and 'stakeholder alliances' (Kanter, 1990).

Potential threats of consumer volatility are countered by marketing strategies: product differentiation, advertising, promotions and public relations. All potential threats may also be countered by locational strategies – relocating to greenfield sites, expansion overseas or operating cross-subsidy through transfer pricing – or by technological strategies. Although such strategies are not always successful or unproblematic, and whilst they may entail some organisational change, particularly among and within the parties to a business alliance (Kanter, 1990), they do represent alternatives to radical reorganisation. Moreover, it is large, divisional organisations, particularly multinationals, which have the resources to pursue these strategies.

Large organisations also possess the resources to intervene in a potentially threatening political, social or legal environment to produce outcomes which, if not favourable, are not averse to their interests. These interventions include public relations, issue campaigns or corporate advertising directed at public opinion. They may be supplemented by more direct pressure on governments, either overtly through lobbying and representations, or more covertly through networks of informal contacts. Such activities can result in direct government financial assistance, state provision of infrastructural services, favourable trade and competition policy or, in extreme cases, actual political change (Sampson, 1973).

The claim that organisations must adapt to technological change and changes in the skills and attitudes of potential employees treats these changes as largely external. Large organisations are heavily involved in technological developments, much of which takes place either in their own research departments, or elsewhere (e.g. in universities) under their sponsorship and hence under their influence, if not control. Furthermore, innovation, technology transfer and patenting – translating technical advances into physical changes in proprietorial products and processes – is even more under the sway of large organisations. Consequently, they are rarely surprised by technical change.

Nor are large organisations surprised by the characteristics of those whom they employ. Large organisations expend considerable time, effort and money in attracting and selecting managers who will 'fit in': organisations recruit in their own image. Having recruited their managers, organisations are at pains to indoctrinate them with the corporate ethos; conformity is reinforced through appraisal and reward systems.

Overall, therefore, organisations go to considerable lengths to try to control, or influence, the conditions under which they operate, and large organisations have the necessary resources to enjoy a good chance of success.

Exploiting informal organisation

Because organisations employ people, amongst whom inter-personal relationships and informal groups develop, 'informal organisation' inevitably arises within the interstices of formal organisation. Such informal organisation may comprise informal systems of communications ('the grapevine') and networks of interpersonal contacts; tacit job responsibilities and rights; informal friendship groups or 'cliques'; informal payments in cash or kind and informal power and status relationships based upon personal characteristics. Arising from these informal relationships, and from relationships and affiliations outside the organisation, are a range of attitudes, values and orientations held by individuals and shared by group members.

As we saw in Chapter 5, informal organisation may modify or subvert the operation of the formal organisation, but it may also work with and reinforce it. In particular, it may be precisely the operation of informal arrangements which lend flexibility to otherwise rigid bureaucratic systems (Shamir, 1978). Informal communications may bypass hierarchical levels, people may work beyond the terms of their contract, team spirit may make up for limited responsibilities and informal contacts may improve coordination. Bureaucratic organisation, there-fore, may come to rely upon the tacit workings of the informal organisation in order to operate more flexibly. This, in turn, means that instituted flexibility, through formal decentral-isation, may be unnecessary.

Over time, informal organisation may develop a consistent character, with a prevailing, tacit, consensus among managers about appropriate forms of behaviour (norms) and desirable outcomes (values). The result is a distinctive organisational or corporate 'culture'. (We explore management through organ-isational culture more fully in Chapter 8.)

To summarise, large organisations with divisional or bureau-cratic forms of administration, in the face of change and uncertainty, can avoid radical decentralisation by controlling internal and external contingencies or exploiting informal organisation. (The argument is summarised in Figure 7.1.) However, the fact that organisations can avoid decentralisation does not of itself fully explain why they should choose to do so.

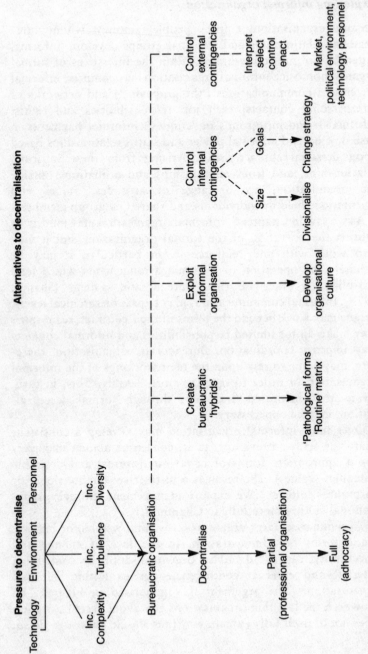

Figure 7.1 Decentralisation and its alternatives

Reluctance to decentralise

The reason for this reluctance to decentralise lies in both the nature of organisational politics and the problems associated with decentralisation. Indeed, given what decentralisation entails, the surprise is not that it occurs rarely, but that it happens at all.

Decentralisation, even in its more limited forms, means the devolution of management functions from senior to middle and junior managers. Senior managers give up some of their power to take decisions, allocate work, motivate other managers and to coordinate and control their efforts. Whilst this surrender of operational control may be compensated by an opportunity to concentrate on strategic, corporate issues (such as investments, acquisitions and external relations), the loss is nevertheless a real one. It is a sacrifice which senior managers may, for a number of reasons, be reluctant to make.

In part, reservations about decentralisation are based on the practical difficulties which accompany this form of organisation, as will be discussed later. In this case the decision not to decentralise is based on a judgement that the disadvantages of doing so outweigh the advantages. Equally, however, these problems may also be used as justification for a decision based more on vested interests. Senior managers are reluctant to give up operational control because these functions carry with them, indeed justify, the power, status and rewards of senior managers. Although these would not necessarily disappear with decentralisation, some of their *raison d'être* and therefore that of senior head office managers themselves would. Even if senior managers were immune to considerations of vested interest, the 'control mentality' which we noted in discussion of bureaucracy in Chapter 5 comes into play. Control can become an end in itself, rather than a means to an end, and senior managers may tolerate bureaucratic inefficiencies in order to retain the reassuring certainties of personal control. This is more likely the less senior managers feel able to trust their subordinates.

This reluctance to decentralise is manifested both in the rarity of radical decentralisation and in certain tendencies within decentralised structures. The first is for decentralisation to be accompanied not by a loss of senior managers' power but by a loss of middle managers' jobs. Junior managers and professional specialists are given greater operational autonomy, but are answerable to the centre, rather than to middle managers, for their performance (Drucker, 1988; Kaye, 1989; Kanter, 1990). Secondly, there are strong centralising or bureaucratising tendencies in adhocratic, professional and divisional organisation. In professional and adhocratic organisation, the autonomy of professionals and specialists is always under the threat of greater centralised control over behaviour through rules or tighter performance measures. In divisionalised organisation, tension between head office and the divisions is endemic and the possibility of more direct interference by head office in the operations of the divisions is ever present (Mintzberg, 1979).

Senior managers' lack of trust of subordinates is not simply the paranoia of the powerful. There are a number of respects in which lower-level managers may not use their increased autonomy in ways consistent with organisational goals. This is, perhaps, the central weakness of decentralisation.

DECENTRALISATION: AN OVERALL ASSESSMENT

In essence, greater individual autonomy is the key to both the strengths and weaknesses of decentralised organisation. On the one hand it is conducive to flexible forms of work, sensitivity and adaptability to particular circumstances, a greater capacity for learning and innovation and greater commitment on the part of individual managers. On the other hand, it carries the potential danger of a preoccupation with narrow concerns and interests, inconsistency, disintegration and a loss of central direction and purpose.

With operational planning and decision-making devolved to managers and professional specialists, these decisions and plans are more likely to be relevant to particular circumstances and based on appropriate forms of technical knowledge, whilst the response to change is likely to be more rapid. Furthermore, direct involvement in or 'ownership' of decisions and plans brings a greater commitment to them and a greater determination to see them through. The danger, however, is that those decisions and plans are based on a short-term, narrowly specialist or local view. Although this is partly obviated by the use of teams comprising different specialists and by sophisticated coordinating mechanisms, the possibility remains that

decisions are based on professionally sound and locally pertinent, but organisationally inappropriate, criteria. Thus, for
example, technically perfect or 'custom-built' solutions may be
developed regardless of cost. This is true the more that managers
and professionals are subject to influence from local or external
professional colleagues.

'Bottom-up', consultative strategic decision-making has the
advantages of bringing a breadth of expertise and opinion to
bear on decisions and of fostering commitment to them. On the
other hand, this form of decision-making can be slow, frus-
trating and lacking in clarity of vision and purpose. Moreover,
it can be politically charged, with a wide range of competing
views and interests. Suppression of this conflict may be neither
desirable nor possible without a reversion to centralisation.
Where, as in adhocracy, strategy is the consolidation of existing
practices, there is the danger that strategy is driven by parochial
or inappropriate considerations, rather than the 'big picture'.

The allocation of work to teams with a fluid division of
labour based on broad individual responsibilities within professional specialisms brings the advantages of flexibility and a
multi-disciplinary approach to problems, which is especially
suited to innovation and open-ended tasks. Team working
provides both the breadth of expertise and collective synergy
necessary for creativity. Challenging and varied work, coupled
with team spirit, may be a source of satisfaction for individuals,
and of commitment to tasks.

On the other hand, unpredictable, ill-defined responsibilities
and a high level of group interaction may create a stressful work
setting. Further, managers and specialists have to be equal to
the responsibilities placed upon them, and the quality of their
work is heavily dependent upon their personal and technical
qualities. For organisations, this quality does not come cheap:
appropriately skilled and qualified staff are expensive to recruit
and retain. Lastly, the focus of teams or divisions upon projects
or products means a duplication of effort which may prove
costly if functional economies of scale are lost.

Self-motivation, through internalised rules, the intrinsic
rewards of work and a strong achievement orientation, can be
very potent. Decentralisation may, therefore, reap the benefits
of managerial flexibility, high levels of job satisfaction and
greater commitment which flow from it. However, although

motivational force may be increased, its direction may not be consistent with organisational goals. Managers in decentralised organisation may be fired up to do the wrong things. Internalised professional practices or problem-solving routines may not be consistent with organisational interests. Specialists may pursue technically faultless or elegant solutions, or those which conform to professional ethics, rather than 'adequate' solutions at lower cost. Autonomy is an important determinant of the intrinsic satisfactions of work, but it may prove stressful for some whilst providing others with the freedom to do little, to work incompetently or to pursue professional interests rather than organisational obligations. Lastly, the achievement ethic, if taken to excess, can lead to a failure adequately to assess the appropriateness of particular goals, or to the pursuit of ends without consideration of the effects or ethics of the means employed. 'Can do' can become 'whatever it takes'. Divergence between professional and organisational practices, the misuse of autonomy and unreflecting commitment can lead to a form of instrumentalism, concerned more with professional advancement than loyalty to the organisation. Attempts to counter this, through greater regulation of professional work or by 'buying' loyalty through financial and career inducements, may simply demotivate professionals, stifle creativity and exacerbate instrumentalism.

Coordination is potentially the Achilles' heel of decentralisation, if individual or team autonomy lead to a fragmentation of effort. The problem is that either there are insufficient coordinating mechanisms, in which case there may be duplication or inconsistency of effort, or coordinating mechanisms are adequate, but necessarily complex. Hence the costs of preventing decentralised organisation from falling apart are high. Further, although non-hierarchical, non-directive forms of coordination have advantages – in particular, the direct involvement of the parties affected and the greater likelihood of their agreement – they lack mechanisms for resolving conflict. An absence of hierarchical authority or of ground-rules for resolving conflict is a particular problem, given that the potential for conflict between professionals is high.

As with self-motivation, self-control, through internalised professional practices and commitment to work tasks, is potentially highly effective, but its operation is problematic. Its potential lies in its immediacy – managers control their actions as they carry them out, rather than after the event – and its unobtrusiveness – managers do not work under visible external constraint. Furthermore, the team or profession reinforces this through colleague or peer control based on informal expectations and shared understandings. From the organisation's point of view, however, much depends on trust, that managers and professionals exercise control in ways appropriate to organisational goals. The danger is that control may be exercised according to localised or specialist criteria instead. Thus *ex ante* control over managerial and professional orientations through careful selection and recruitment may prove insufficient and is, in any case, costly both as a process and in terms of rewarding those selected.

The fragile nature of trust leads to an ever-present threat that external forms of control will be used to supplement managers' self-control. External performance control has some advantages. It focuses attention upon outcomes, hence upon contributions to organisational goals, and leaves managers and professionals free to choose how to meet them. The problem comes in choosing performance measures. The quality of professional or project work is difficult to measure, except in its own terms. Reliance upon more easily measurable performance, such as budgets and profits, may encourage accountability and a business orientation, but can equally lead to the narrow pursuit of short-term financial targets. Having managers participate in setting their own performance objectives (as in MBO) does not always square the circle. Consequently, there is the ever-present threat of reversion to centralised regulation and curbs on the freedom of action of managers and professionals. This, however, only creates a vicious circle of demoralisation, loss of creativity, instrumentalism and the imposition of yet further controls.

Therefore, decentralisation of management functions offers the opportunity for administration to become more flexible, adaptive and innovative and to make fuller use of managerial and specialist employees. At its heart is greater autonomy and responsibility for managers and professionals. The price of flexibility and innovation, however, is the need for elaborate mechanisms of coordination and, crucially, some loss of centralised control and direction. Radical decentralisation, therefore, is only risked if senior managers trust their subordinates, or can contrive to trust them through careful recruitment and indoctrination, or if they can subject them to effective performance controls. In the absence of those conditions, large bureaucratic organisations respond to uncertainty and change by divisionalisation, coupled with strenuous efforts to control their market, technological and socio-political environments. Rather than decentralise or die, bureaucracies find a multitude of ways to effect a stay of execution.

FURTHER READING

Descriptions of decentralised organisation are to be found in Burns and Stalker (1968), Blau (1970b), Pugh and Hickson (1976), Hage (1977), Mintzberg (1979), Morgan (1986), Drucker (1989), Handy (1989) and Kanter (1990).

Analyses of specific forms of decentralised organisation are particularly prone to a bewildering variety of labels for what are, essentially, similar concepts. On forms of professional organisation, see the analysis of 'adaptive bureaucracy' in Blau (1970c), 'personnel bureaucracy' in Pugh and Hickson (1973), 'professional bureaucracy' in Mintzberg (1979) and 'functional decentralisation' in Drucker (1989), as well as more general discussions in Perrow (1979), Esland (1980), Johnson (1980) and Rueschmeyer (1986).

On forms of radically decentralised organisation, see the discussion of 'organic' organisation in Burns and Stalker (1968) and Hage (1977), 'latently structured' organisation in Pugh and Hickson (1973), 'matrix' organisation in Galbraith (1973) and Knight (1977), 'project' organisation in Chandler and Sayles (1971), 'self-adaptive/holographic' organisation in Morgan (1986), 'post entrepreneurial' organisation in Kanter (1990) and 'adhocracy' in Toffler (1970, 1985) and Mintzberg (1979). On divisionalised organisation, see Williamson (1975), Chandler (1977), Mintzberg (1979), Hill (1984) and Drucker (1989).

On the various alternatives to decentralisation, see Child (1973b/c), Galbraith (1974), Starbuck (1976), Hage (1977), Weick (1977, Pfeffer and Salancik (1978), Schreyogg (1980), Dawson (1986), Perrow (1986) and Kanter (1990).

Chapter 8

The search for commitment and performance
Japanese management and clan organisation

In Chapters 6 and 7 we reviewed a number of alternative approaches seeking to address the problems of organisational inflexibility, low employee satisfaction and low commitment which bedevil bureaucracy and rationalised work. These solutions also engender problems of their own, one of which is common to them all: they are essentially piecemeal, in that they attempt to rectify isolated problems of employee and organisational performance by focusing upon some, but not all, elements of work organisation. Even where these alternatives are adopted, they are often 'tacked on' to existing arrangements and, consequently, fail to solve the problems which they seek to address. Fully decentralised administration remains a comparative rarity because it focuses exclusively upon decentralising formal structural arrangements, ignoring the informal practices and control of contingencies which permit those with a vested interest in centralised, hierarchical organisation to resist change. Job redesign and participation, in the name of QWL or flexibility, are equally piecemeal in that they are applied to particular jobs, work groups or organisational systems, rather than to the organisation of work as a whole. They, too, tend to be incorporated into, rather than supersede, more traditional arrangements.

Such piecemeal efforts ignore the interconnected and interdependent character of work organisation. In particular, they treat organisational inflexibility, employee dissatisfaction and poor performance as separate, bounded problems, rather than symptoms of a deeper malaise. A more holistic appreciation of the interrelatedness of different aspects of work organisation recognises, instead, that employee commitment may breed a virtuous circle of flexibility, high performance and work satisfaction. A holistic approach also recognises that commitment is the product of more than just structural arrangements: something is necessary to breathe life into formal organisational relationships and to make actual what structure only makes possible. Although structure facilitates planning, coordination and control, there must be something – actual performance of work – to plan, coordinate and control.

This chapter examines ideas which suggest that this virtuous circle is, perhaps, attainable. Firstly, we consider the approach to work organisation typical of large Japanese companies, together with their characteristic features and the effect of these upon employee behaviour and performance. In doing so, we address the central issue of the extent to which such an approach is rooted inextricably in the culture and economy of Japan, and whether it is exportable to the West, perhaps in modified form. This leads us to consider, secondly, the broad approach to work organisation and specific practices evident in certain American and British companies which represent a modified version of Japanese methods. We see that 'J-organisations' and 'clan organisations' have two key characteristics in common. Firstly, both exhibit, in addition to an identifiable set of institutional arrangements, a coherent, shared and sustained system of beliefs and values. In other words, the process of management is attempted not only through organisational structure, but also through organisational culture. Secondly, both have impressive levels of organisational performance. The implication, therefore, is that the management of work is most successfully conducted when a particular set of organisational arrangements is bolstered by a strong, coherent organisational culture.

Finally, we ask whether this model can provide a blueprint for the effective management of work elsewhere and, in doing so, offer a critical evaluation of clan organisation and the 'excellence' thesis.

THE JAPANESE APPROACH TO WORK ORGANISATION

Until the mid-1970s, accounts of Japanese work organisations were confined to occasional published monographs (e.g. Abegglen, 1958; Cole, 1971; Dore, 1973). Since the mid-1970s, however, interest in Japanese work practices has both intensified and shifted in concern away from learning about 'other ways', towards a strong desire to learn *from* them. This interest has been fuelled by the increasingly evident disparity between the spectacular success of Japanese corporations in world markets and the largely indifferent performance of their American and British counterparts. Consequently, a substantial body of literature has grown up which not only documents and diagnoses the 'Japanese miracle' but often contains a heavy dose of prognosis about how the West can effectively meet the challenge by stealing (or borrowing) the opposition's clothes (see, for example: Hayes and Abernathy, 1980; Pascale, 1991). Although different writers have emphasised different aspects of the J-organisation, together they offer a comprehensive picture, the key elements of which are generally agreed on. These are: the 'Nenko', or seniority system of tenured employment; a group-based division of labour; an obsession with quality through technical efficiency; centralised control of recruitment and performance; visible, high-profile managers and supervisors; negotiated and consultative decision-making (*Ringi-Ko*); and, finally, strong corporate cultures emphasising achievement and harmony.

The features of the Nenko Seido system of employment, and their socio-historical origins, may be summarised as follows. Essentially, managerial and non-managerial employees in large Japanese corporations are recruited through a careful and intensive selection process into lifetime employment. Over the course of this employment, which in fact lasts until comparatively early retirement at fifty-five, Nenko workers enjoy job security. An almost impervious internal labour market means that senior positions are filled exclusively from within the company, and a hierarchy of managerial and operative job titles means that both categories of employee may look forward to a career and status advancement. Promotion, however, is slow and based primarily upon seniority. Indeed, 'promotion' often takes the form of lateral transfer to work roles which are informally recognised as more prestigious or central to the work process.

Seniority, or length of service, is the predominant, though not exclusive, determinant of employee remuneration. Wage 'profiles' are steep; employees are comparatively under paid during the early years of employment, but recoup this shortfall during the second half of their employment lifetime. In addition to seniority, work performance, cost of living and workers' specific family needs also influence pay. Educational qualifications mainly serve to determine the employee's broad function, within which seniority and performance determine pay. All of these determinants of pay are insulated from the operation of free market forces: wages and salaries are determined by organisational rules.

Despite differences in relative scales of pay, there are few other differences in the trappings of occupational status. All employees enjoy similar bonus or incentive arrangements (usually group-based and linked to long-term performance), comparable pension and sick-pay schemes, and access to other welfare benefits, whilst symbolic status privileges (such as office space, parking facilities, canteen facilities and dress codes) are largely absent.

Extensive welfare benefits, such as subsidised housing and transport, loans for education and medical services, together with a wide range of extramural facilities, constitute an important element in the total reward package of the Japanese employee. Welfare provision is not only substantial and offered as of right, but is also regarded as a central element in the holistic relationship between the employee and the company.

Nenko employees are subject to continuous, extensive performance appraisal. This begins even before the individual becomes an employee, through the importance attached to educational qualifications and personal qualities during the process of recruitment. Once recruited, employees are regularly appraised on work performance, personal attributes, attitudes and general behaviour, including responsibility, creativity and, crucially, ability to work well with others. The importance of cooperation is reinforced by the involvement of the work group in the appraisal process. Either the group as a whole is appraised, in which case there is strong peer pressure upon individuals to contribute appropriately to the group, or appraisal of the individual involves some peer review. Appraisal is continuous and is based on long-term behaviour, attitudes and performance.

The system is supported and reinforced by continuous in-company training which is regarded as an investment, the benefits of which will subsequently accrue to the company. As well as acquiring technical skills, learning the 'company way' – both in terms of work practices and in terms of company philosophy – is an important component of the training process. Training, therefore, has a moral as well as a purely practical character and, once again, the work group has an important part to play.

The final piece in the interlocking Nenko jigsaw is the company union, to which all categories of employee belong. Because the union represents all Nenko workers within a company, the emphasis is not only upon general wage bargaining (rather than a concern for inter-occupational differentials) but also upon bargaining over the total remuneration package. There are regular and predictable bargaining periods, and whilst bargaining is often intense, it is conducted in a spirit of resolvable differences, rather than of confrontation. More generally, company unions are involved in a range of joint endeavours with management, such as productivity councils and the administration of welfare schemes, which proceed from an assumption of a communality of interest and acceptance of management authority.

The fact that union representation as described above is confined almost exclusively to workers within the Nenko system, and that the Nenko system is, in turn, confined to particular sectors of the Japanese economy, is an important point which forms a bridge with the second major feature of work organisation in Japan – the essentially group-based division of labour, within which there are a number of distinct, if interrelated, features. The first of these is the sharp division, within the Japanese economy as a whole, between the large corporations (*Zaibatsu*) where Nenko employment conditions obtain, and the smaller firms where employment conditions are very different. In these smaller companies, employment is highly insecure; there is no link between pay and seniority; wages are lower, often substantially so; bonuses, fringe benefits, sick pay and pensions are rare; welfare benefits are minimal; yet hours of work are longer and industrial accidents more common (Oh, 1976). These smaller firms, in their capacity as suppliers or contractors, are the flexible element of the Japanese economy upon which employment stability in the large corporations rests.

Secondly, there is also a sharp division within the large corporations between Nenko and non-Nenko workers. The latter comprise temporary, casual or part-time workers, predominantly female, retired workers or workers subcontracted from smaller firms. All of these groups have employment conditions which are inferior to those of Nenko workers – no security of employment, lower wages and few fringe benefits, representing a second element of employment flexibility upon which job security in the Nenko system rests.

The third manifestation of a group-based division of labour is task specialisation at the level of the work group rather than the individual. Employees are recruited into and remain within general work roles with flexible job specifications, rather than particular demarcated occupations. This flexibility is reinforced by training in company practices rather than specific technical skills, and by the practice of job rotation. Tasks are allocated to work teams, which function as autonomous work groups in that work scheduling, the precise division of labour and support functions (e.g. maintenance) are the responsibility of the group, albeit operating within stringent quality, efficiency and performance constraints. Japanese managers are recruited as generalists and remain so as a consequence of planned, long-term rotation through a variety of managerial positions. Within the managerial hierarchy, responsibilities are allotted to departments and teams, rather than to individuals, and there are company-wide task forces responsible for particular projects or problems. Most notable are quality circles, which are widespread and of long standing in many Japanese companies.

The final manifestation of a group-based division of labour is the predominance of the divisionalised form of corporate organisation. Most large Japanese firms are, essentially, conglomerates with semi-autonomous divisions based upon products or markets, with functional areas duplicated across each division. The divisions are held together, however, by the third major element of Japanese work organisation: stringent, centralised controls in the key areas of performance output and personnel inputs. The control of performance is effected through firstly, a detailed planning system incorporating long, medium and short-term plans; secondly, an accounting system based on key performance indicators and variance analysis by financial controllers at the centre; thirdly, stringent divisional performance reviews by head office; and fourthly, the existence of a central fund into which a proportion of divisional profits flow and from which investment funding is provided (Pascale and Athos, 1982).

Poor divisional performance is sanctioned financially and by *de facto* demotion of the divisional manager. Consequently, considerable importance attaches to the recruitment and training of managers to ensure that those entrusted with decisions of consequence for divisional performance may be relied upon to make the right decisions. Indeed, careful screening, recruitment and training extends to all core employees.

The control of quality, though effected in detail at the operational level, is guided from the centre by the existence of clear and powerful corporate values relating to customer service and product quality. This concern with quality is linked to the fourth major feature of Japanese work organisation, a close attention to technical efficiency. Within the context of corporate values exhorting efficiency and productivity as expressions of collective achievement, there are specific efficiency-oriented practices: a high proportion of engineers and technicians, resulting in highly 'engineered' production; investment in the most modern machinery; working methods which are governed by detailed technical rules; and the use of managers and supervisors as technical advisors or trouble-shooters. In addition, quality circles and productivity councils continuously monitor work methods and products. However, all these arrangements would count for little were they not infused by a consensual agreement on the importance of efficiency and 'continuous improvement' (Kaizen) among all employees.

The technical assistance rendered to work groups by managers and supervisors is also one aspect of the fifth general feature of work in Japan: a visible, 'hands-on' style of supervision. This is facilitated by an emphasis upon open, face-to-face communication and the importance attached not only to the purpose but also to the intrinsic quality of manager–subordinate relationships, a quality founded on trust, subtlety and intimacy. Supervision is comparatively 'dense' or intrusive, with managers continuously and intimately involved in not only the work of their subordinates but also their personal problems and moral welfare. Supervisors act as team leaders, functioning as group representatives, technical assistants and problem-solvers. The management of managers is no less intrusive, with managers on call at almost any time and subject to constant peer reviews and the goldfish bowl atmosphere of open-plan offices.

It would be misleading, however, to suggest that the manager–subordinate relationship in Japan was simply one of surveillance, for a sixth central feature of work organisation is the importance attached to employee consultation. The central feature is the recognition and acceptance of decision-making as an essentially 'political' process, not in the sense of bargaining but in the sense of explaining and establishing mutual understandings (*Nemawashi*) as the precondition of taking any decision. Greater emphasis is placed upon reaching an agreed decision than reaching the 'best' decision.

Consequently, decision-making is an iterative and interactive process, much of which takes place at an unofficial, informal level. Thus, in the first instance, certain broad and intentionally vague ideas are broached with all the different departments and groups concerned, often involving the circulation of formal, written suggestion cards (*Ringi-Ko*). The functions of this 'sounding' process are threefold: to test how certain ideas impact upon different interested parties, to involve all interested parties early on and to explore all the ramifications and interconnections of a course of action.

Individual departments and groups then give internal technical consideration to the ideas, repeating the informal 'sounding' process among their own sub-units. From there, reactions to and suggestions about the initial ideas begin to reverberate back up the system and across it. The process then repeats, back and forth in an iterative way until shared understandings clarify and become established. The process is essentially top-down and consultative, rather than participative.

In all this there is a constant acceptance of ambiguity, uncertainty and interdependence as unavoidable features of work organisation. There is vagueness of both intentions – by reserving or avoiding 'final' decisions, by agreeing simply to proceed, by avoiding announcements – and of communications – by avoiding blunt or confrontational language or direct approaches to an issue. There is emphasis upon both self-restraint and adaptation in interactions in order to maintain harmony, as well as the encouragement of frank, vocal disagreement, or *Waigaya* (Pascale, 1991).

Thus, decision-making in Japan is long and drawn out. The purpose, however, is to establish agreement and identification with a decision, rather than to force or buy agreement. There is a studied avoidance of both arm-twisting and horse-trading. However, once a decision is taken the question of securing agreement no longer arises and implementation is swift.

This decision-making process is much more than a set of formal arrangements. The key is not the structure but the spirit of decision-making; in particular, shared understandings about the nature, process and purpose of 'decisions'. This brings us to the final feature of Japanese work organisation: the existence of strong, pervasive corporate cultures. Within this, we may identify three distinct elements: firstly, the existence of clear corporate philosophies and value systems *per se*; secondly, the tendency for these to have, *mutatis mutandis*, a similar content and tenor; and thirdly, the mechanisms whereby these are transmitted and reinforced. In brief, we may distinguish Japanese corporate culture as a set of beliefs, values and expected behaviours which together constitute a corporate 'way of life'.

Company philosophies are enshrined in written creeds, codes, values, slogans and company songs. Most researchers on Japanese work organisation are struck by the extent to which all employees appear to interact harmoniously, sharing common understandings and feeling a common sense of collective identification with and duty to the company.

It is recognised that this homogeneity of norms and values is greatly enhanced by the content of company philosophy and the practices which express it. In Japan, all large companies promote the idea of the company as a family with mutual obligations and loyalties. But more than this, it is a family with a mission. In this way, loyalty and harmonious cooperation are given purpose and are translated into commitment. This mission is usually couched in terms of a number of aims, relating to the company as a business, as a community and as a member of a yet wider community. Thus, in addition to the pursuit of profit and market share, Japanese companies aim to promote the well-being and the development of their employees, and to act as good corporate citizens.

These 'spiritual values' are promulgated and reinforced by a multiplicity of events, actions and interactions. Some of these, such as the proliferation of wall slogans, the early morning exercises, singing of the company song and the hortatory group meetings, are explicitly concerned with the transmission of ideas. Other mechanisms, in particular the process of recruitment, training and career rotation, which are heavily imbued with a moral character, operate more subtly.

Finally, the previously enumerated structural arrangements serve to convey and reinforce corporate values. The Nenko system, for example, both creates the conditions for a stable, receptive workforce through careful selection, security and slow promotion, and also conveys implicit messages of community, reciprocity and reward for loyalty, messages which are reinforced by paternalist welfare schemes. In short, Nenko provides the material basis for a holistic relationship between employer and employee consistent with the concept of community. Further, the group basis for task allocation, evaluation and rewards reinforces the relative importance of the collectivity over the individual.

Indeed the existence of corporate culture *per se* and its characteristic value system is more than simply one aspect of Japanese work organisation. The notion of the company as a family with a mission is the ideological hub unifying an interdependent and mutually reinforcing whole, in which the sense of identity, belonging, harmony, cooperation and mutual purpose resonates in practices which foster and exemplify these qualities. These have a number of beneficial consequences in terms of employee attitudes and behaviour which, in turn, reinforce the notion of corporate community.

Loyalty and duty both to the work group and to the company arises out of a combination of job security, payment for seniority and extensive welfare benefits, reinforced by a family ethos and a prohibition on inter-company mobility. Commitment to corporate goals and values develops through training, constant exposure to peer evaluation and exhortation, reinforced by the system of long-term promotion, transfers and rotations which preserve a role for the employee and the consultative decision-making process which produces strong commitment to decisions once they are made. Commitment is coupled with the flexibility made possible by the use of non-Nenko employees, a low level of individual specialisation, the practice of job rotation, the quiescence of company unions and the acceptance of change born of job security and involvement in the change process. Flexible commitment translates into high performance through an emphasis upon technical efficiency and product quality, use of performance controls and an intense sense of competition with other companies and, indeed, other nations.

We can now summarise Japanese organisation in terms of the MTO framework. In essence, organisation entails a 'despecialised' division of labour coupled with a rationalised and formalised physical work process, held together by a bureaucratic employment relationship, a consultative planning process, centralised performance and recruitment control, extensive face-to-face supervision and, crucially, the normative power of a strong corporate culture.

In J-organisations, the management process is reintegrated into many aspects of the work process. Only ownership functions, strategic decisions about investment and disposal of the product, remain exclusively in the hands of managers. Responsibility for planning, allocating, motivating, coordinating and controlling work is shared between managerial and non-managerial employees – these principles of management are applied to all forms of work, both administrative and operational.

Planning and decision-making is consultative and decentralised, relying on information flows which are both formal and informal, vertical and lateral. Operating decisions are taken at work group level, tactical decisions at divisional level and both, in different ways, rest upon considerable informal consultation.

The allocation of work is group-based, with specialisation at the level of the division or work group based more on product or output than process. The allocation of individual tasks and responsibilities is made by the work group or managerial team, and individual job specialisation is low.

Motivation is to a large degree internalised and dependent upon normative influence stemming from the ideological power of company values. Rewards are preferential and are deferred, with career, salary and welfare benefits linked to loyalty and seniority. Rules take the form of performance, quality and technical efficiency standards.

Work is coordinated more through informal mutual adjustment than through formal liaison. There is mutual adjustment in the form of intra-group cooperation and inter-group inter-action, with team leaders playing a pivotal role. Some formal liaison comes from the activities of quality circles and project teams.

Control focuses upon the control of norms, personnel inputs and outputs rather than the regulation of behaviour. Standardised recruitment, training and performance norms are the principal forms of external impersonal control and are reinforced by personalised control in the form of face-to-face supervision, close managerial involvement in work and peer pressure from group members. Within these constraints, carefully selected and intensively socialised employees also exercise considerable self-control. Table 8.1 summarises these main points.

In essence, therefore, this approach rests upon circumscribed trust. Those responsible for executing work are permitted a high degree of discretion in planning, allocating and coordinating it and there is considerable reliance upon self-motivation and self-control. Other mechanisms exist, however, to increase the probability that this self-direction, motivation and control result in behaviour consistent with organisational goals. Firstly, there is careful, discriminating selection of an elite workforce with the desired qualifications, skills and, importantly, attitudinal dispositions. Secondly, the loyalty of this workforce is secured through lifetime employment, salary progression based on length of service and extensive welfare benefits. Thirdly, employee attitudes and values are managed to be consistent with organisational philosophy through continuous socialisation, indoctrination and peer pressure. Finally, there is tight control over performance and quality.

J-ORGANISATION, THE CENTRAL ISSUE: IS IT EXPORTABLE?

Commentators often draw sharp contrasts between the typical Japanese and Western approaches to work organisation. Dore (1973) contrasts the two employment systems; Ouchi (1981) more generally contrasts the J-organisation with the bureaucratic 'A-organisation' characteristic of the West; Pascale and Athos (1982) develop their analysis from a comparison between Matsushita and ITT which, though similar in terms of tangible

Table 8.1 Managing through J-organisation

Management process	:	Management functions reintegrated into work process. Senior managers retain ownership functions.
Area of application	:	Throughout the organisation: managerial and operational work.
Planning/decision-making		
Degree of centralisation	:	Operational decisions highly decentralised. Strategic decisions partly decentralised to divisions.
Information/communication flows	:	Omnidirectional, interactive, formal and informal.
Allocation of work		
Form of specialisation	:	Outputs/products.
Level of specialisation	:	Work group/management team.
Degree of job specialisation	:	Low: flexibility and rotation.
Motivation		
Rewards	:	Deferred (by seniority), preferential, high non-pay element.
Rules	:	Performance standards and company norms.
Rationales	:	Organisation as family with a mission.
Coordination		
Locus of responsibility	:	Internal (work group/team) + specialist (superior)
Method	:	Adjustment and consultation
Degree of formality	:	Mainly informal
Control		
Focus	:	[Values] + [Inputs/outputs]
Locus of responsibility	:	[Internal/mutual] [Self/mutual]
Degree of impersonality	:	[Personal] [Impersonal]
Degree of formality	:	[Informal] [Informal]

Mutual adjustment and specialist liaison

Self/mutual
Normative control + external recruitment and performance control

structural elements, differ markedly in terms of values and culture; and Pascale (1991) contrasts the learning processes of Honda and General Motors. The argument that Japanese management is non-exportable suggests that these differences are unbridgeable because the features of Japanese work organisation are rooted in the peculiarities of Japanese culture and society, economic history and its economy as well as the strategy of major Japanese corporations.

The links between Japanese work organisation and Japanese society are drawn at the level of culture (de Bettignies, 1973; Pascale and Athos, 1982) or social institutions (Dore, 1973). The key feature of Japanese culture which resonates in work organisation is the assumption of unavoidable interdependence and, hence, the primacy of the group. This engenders an emphasis upon loyalty, obligation, conformity, respect for authority, traditionalism, cooperation and self-restraint. Being accepted by the group and avoiding anything that would bring 'shame' on it are major motivating forces. Furthermore, the importance attached to the in-group finds expression in competition with, even hostility to, out-groups. What is, perhaps, uniquely Japanese is the way in which the company acquires the mantle of a revered collectivity, integrating material, social and spiritual needs (Pascale and Athos, 1982). The company is not simply an economic entity, but a community which is a source of social relationships and meanings to its members. Consequently, it can make a credible appeal to group loyalty and duty, as well as to more instrumental motivation.

Furthermore, the employment system dovetails with family life, with its emphasis upon the dependence of the young, the strict segregation of male and female roles and the obligations of the male to social networks outside the family. It is also consistent with a social structure marked by an absence of class consciousness and class-based political organisations. Again, companies have a clear run in their claim to be the collectivities with which Japanese must identify, owe allegiance to, and from which they may expect reciprocal obligations.

The Japanese employment system is a product of comparatively late economic development, an absence of early economic individualism, the vacuum created by the lack of state involvement in welfare schemes and the dual economy. Nenko evolved as an employer strategy for dealing, firstly, with labour shortages and high levels of labour turnover which accompanied economic expansion and, secondly, with the growth and strength of unionisation. The dual economy – the disparity between large corporations and smaller firms, and between Nenko and non-Nenko workers – also sustains the Nenko 'elite'. Crucial to this is the collusion of company unions which are confined to Nenko workers and act to protect their privileges.

All these factors seem to suggest that Japanese organisation is a non-exportable commodity, which the West may learn about but not learn from. However, some aspects of J-organisation may have a metacultural logic which renders them more generally applicable. These include an internal labour market and bureaucratised employment (Hatvany and Pucik, 1981; Weiss, 1984), the consultative and exploratory decision-making process (Howard and Teramoto, 1981) and a strong corporate culture and value system (Cool and Lengnick-Hall, 1985). There is also evidence that some Japanese methods have been successfully transplanted in the West, in particular by subsidiaries of Japanese companies (White and Trevor, 1983; Wickens, 1987).

Perhaps the most forceful argument, however, is that Japanese management as a total package may be adapted, modified and, as a result, adopted in the West. This argument turns, crucially, on evidence of American and British companies which exhibit features which are strikingly similar to those of J-organisations; these companies have also been among the most successful in their fields. (A summary of the argument thus far is presented in Figure 8.1.)

'CLAN' ORGANISATIONS AND 'EXCELLENT' COMPANIES

The identification and analysis of organisations in the West with an apparent capacity to secure commitment and high levels of performance from employees through the normative force of corporate culture has, in the space of a few years, developed from an off-shoot of other concerns to a major academic industry. From an early concern to point up similarities between Japanese organisation and the approach adopted by certain organisations in the West, attention shifted to

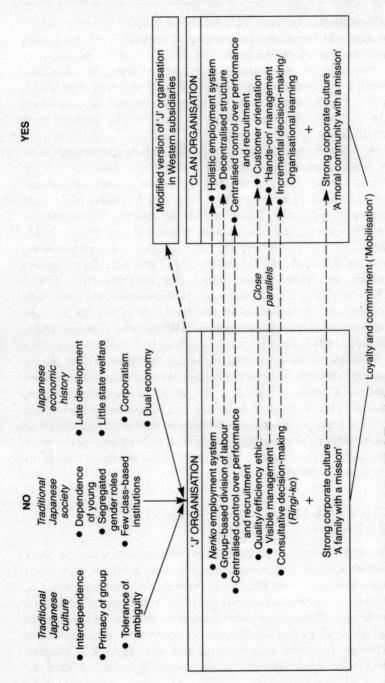

Figure 8.1 Is J-organisation exportable? The debate

organisational culture as a key variable in accounting for high levels of corporate performance (Peters and Waterman, 1982; Goldsmith and Clutterbuck, 1984; Peters and Austin, 1986).

Much of this preoccupation with organisational culture is a revival and reorientation of a form of organisational analysis which takes organisational culture as its main object of study, to which has been added the use of 'culture' as a metaphor through which organisations may be studied (Morgan, 1986). Our central concern here, however, is with culture as a manipulable element of work organisation, hence with what is referred to as 'cultural control' (Ray, 1986), or 'clan organisation' (Ouchi, 1981).

The main contours of clan organisation bear a striking resemblance to those of Japanese work organisation, namely a strong internal labour market and a holistic employment relationship; a loose, decentralised, fluid structure; an emphasis upon action, experimentation and organisational learning; consultative and participative decision-making; tight centralised control of financial performance and 'service' standards; visible, face-to-face managerial involvement in work; and a clear corporate value system transmitted through an array of institutional mechanisms. In what follows, to avoid repetition we will emphasise the main points of difference from the Japanese model and give particular consideration to organisational culture.

The main difference between the employment practices of clan organisations and the Japanese Nenko system is the extent to which the internal labour market operates as a closed system. In clan organisation, employment is relatively secure and a long-term association with the company is encouraged and rewarded, but lifetime employment is neither an obligation nor a fact. Although promotion is predominantly from within, it is not exclusively so, and it is based more upon work performance than seniority. Seniority also plays a much smaller part in the determination of employee remuneration, with pay linked more to performance than to ascriptive characteristics. Rates of pay are generally higher than elsewhere, but this premium is much less substantial than that enjoyed by Nenko workers.

There is a greater equality of employment conditions and non-monetary reward in clan organisations than in other Western companies, and a greater provision of welfare benefits. However, compared with Japan there is not the same comprehensive company involvement in the material and non-work life of employees, and welfare is viewed, more instrumentally, as conducive to employee productivity.

Although the system of employee appraisal in clan organisations is more long-term, more group-based and more focused on attitudes than in other Western organisations, it is more performance-oriented than in Japan. The use of continuous training, with emphasis upon company norms and values as well as technical skills, closely resembles the Japanese system, but, because of the looser connection between employee and employer, there is more emphasis upon the individual as the beneficiary of investment in training.

Whilst the Nenko system operates with the open support of company unions, clan organisations tend to be non-unionised, or comparatively sparsely unionised, often as the result of deliberate company policy to discourage or prohibit union membership. At the same time, clan organisations tend to offer a more equal employment relationship to all employees, in sharp contrast to the wide division between Nenko and non-Nenko workers in Japan.

In short, although clan organisations maintain a more stable workforce than other companies in the West, through the operation of an internal labour market and a comparatively holistic employment relationship, the ties that bind employees are nowhere near as tight as for the Nenko worker. Lifetime employment is merely more probable, not guaranteed; welfare provision is more extensive, not all-embracing, and the obligations and rewards for being a 'company person' are greater, but not paramount.

The loose, decentralised properties of clan organisation have points both of similarity and of difference from the group-based division of labour in Japan. Although not located within such an explicit, institutionalised social division of labour as in Japan, clan organisation is typical of larger 'core' companies which rely upon the flexibility of smaller peripheral companies as suppliers and subcontractors, and the use of part-time, temporary and subcontracted workers. In addition, whilst clan organisation exhibits a high degree of flexibility in job responsibilities, this is not as institutionalised as in Japan, and employees retain a higher degree of occupational identity. The exception to this is at managerial level, which echoes the Japanese system of planned job rotation and generalist managerial careers. Therefore, clan organisation uses both employment relationships and work allocation as sources of organisational flexibility.

Clan organisation also entails divisionalised corporate structures, with each division having relatively decentralised managerial work organisation based upon teams. Divisional managers have considerable discretion over how divisions operate, whilst the constituent work teams have a degree of autonomy within their areas of operation, resulting in 'lattice organisation' (Peters and Austin, 1986) with self-managing teams as the basic building block. Consistent with lower-level managerial autonomy, there are few permanent head office staff and comparatively few hierarchical levels. Neither the divisional nor the team arrangements tend to be permanent, however, since the emphasis is upon fluidity.

The maintenance of such a loose arrangement requires a high level of up-to-date communication flowing in all directions, facilitated by an emphasis upon face-to-face interaction. Competition, as well as communication, between teams and divisions is encouraged and reinforced by peer review and evaluation. Flexibility is pursued by avoiding excessive reliance upon structure. Instead of complex structural arrangements detailing channels of communication and reporting relationships, there is a trust that communication and cooperation will take place on the basis that all, or most, employees share a common set of goals and values.

Within these arrangements there is a greater degree of individual autonomy than in Japan. This is exemplified in the encouragement of product 'champions' or 'intrapreneurs' (Pinchot, 1985) using organisational resources to develop particular business ideas. Such encouragement flows from the third characteristic of clan organisations: a prevailing climate of action, experimentation and organisational learning.

Evolution, rather than detailed planning, is a central distinguishing feature of 'excellent' and innovating companies. This means there is a tendency to reduce projects to small, actionable 'chunks' which can be tested, modified and developed if promising, or discarded without great loss if unsuccessful. Experimentation is encouraged and occasional failures are perceived as valuable learning exercises. Ideas and projects are openly available for scrutiny and critique in an atmosphere of intense, if constructive, criticism. Whilst this open discussion of ideas closely resembles that of Japanese organisations, there is a greater emphasis upon individual initiative, risk-taking and experimentation.

Open evaluation of ideas is echoed in a participative approach to decision-making. This is particularly evident in strategic decision-making, which relies much more upon the bottom-up evolution of strategy, rather than top-down imposition. Strategy is the *post hoc* crystallisation of smaller, incremental localised changes in practices or grass-roots ideas (Kanter, 1985; Peters, 1989). As in Japan, with operating decisions there is an emphasis upon a high level of face-to-face communication of information and participation. Much of this communication and consultation is informal, unprogrammed and predicated upon a climate of openness and involvement. The main differences between participation in clan organisation and the Japanese system are fourfold: the style of communications is more direct; there is greater use of participative mechanisms such as productivity councils and consultative committees; there is greater emphasis upon negotiated agreement rather than consensus; and the process is one of participation, rather than consultation.

Such decentralised, participative arrangements could produce strong centrifugal forces. As in J-organisations, however, key centralised controls over financial performance, service quality and the recruitment and training of personnel are used to check these forces. This combination gives clan organisations their 'loose–tight' properties (Peters and Waterman, 1982).

Financial controls are stringent, and concentrate on a few key indicators. The careful screening, selection and socialisation of employees seeks to ensure that those who are trusted with decisions are predisposed to act in particular ways. In addition to these controls, however, is the influence exerted by a prevailing obsession with quality and service. This obsession is manifested in close customer involvement in product development, the importance attached to sales and after-sales service and the involvement of all grades of employee in customer-contact activities and quality control.

Control is also exercised through 'management by wandering around' (MBWA) (Peters and Waterman, 1982), the close, face-to-face involvement in work processes shown by managers and supervisors. The emphasis, however, is less upon technical guidance or problem-solving, as in Japan, but in 'transformational leadership' (Peters, 1989), the constant articulation of values through word and symbolic behaviour, and the 'shaping' of employee orientations in ways which are consistent with company goals. Managers, including senior managers, are highly visible and closely involved in the work of employees, and are concerned to use every event or activity, however trivial, as an opportunity for conveying value messages. Whilst all managerial concerns have this symbolic quality, training, monitoring and 'coaching' and the way managers use their time are especially important. Once again, it is how managers behave, as much as what they do, which is crucial. MBWA, coaching and setting an example are all ways in which the key role of the manager, as conduit of the organisation's value system, is realised. This value system is the essence of corporate culture.

Attempts to analyse corporate cultures run up against two almost intractable difficulties. Firstly, the interconnected, systemic and ubiquitous character of culture makes it resilient to adequate linear description: cultures are not a list of characteristics. Inevitably, however, they must be described so. Secondly, as Marshall and McLean (1985) point out, culture is not simply a describable phenomenon but is something essentially lived and experienced: any description of the visible, high-profile symbols of culture only scratches the surface and misses the deeper meanings and evocations of culture which give it its richness. Bearing these points in mind, we may distinguish among the content of corporate culture, its mechanisms (the actions, interactions and events which convey the meanings embodied in that corporate culture), its ramifications (the actions, interactions and events which are informed by these meanings) and the behavioural and attitudinal effects among members of the culture. Although we consider each of these in turn, it is important to recognise that they are each mutually reinforcing and sustaining.

All collectivities of interacting, sense-making human beings have some form of culture, however rudimentary. What distinguishes clan organisation is the strength, clarity and pervasiveness of their cultures. In terms of content, clan organisations are characterised by a coherent and pervasive body of ideas and values about what the organisation is and what it is for. These are values in the sense that what the organisation 'is' and does are seen as desirable and valuable. Thus, the organisation is regarded as a community or 'tribe' (Deal and Kennedy, 1982), bound by ties deeper than economic self-interest. This general perception subsumes a belief in the importance of the continued existence of the organisation and a perception of it as having an existence transcending that of its individual members. The organisation is 'sacred', in the wide sense of the term (Ray, 1986). The relationship between employee and the organisation is a holistic, 'covenental' one (Peters and Austin, 1986), with a range of mutual obligations. Thus, the organisation is a moral community whose members feel a sense of belonging and mutual rights and obligations.

Beliefs about what the organisation is for add a sense of mission or purpose to the idea of community. Clan organisations are distinguished by clear goals whose constant attainment is seen as having overriding importance and which become a singular preoccupation. These goals usually emphasise superiority or excellence in product quality, corporate integrity, technological innovation and above all, service to the customer. Customer service is usually paramount in that other values are either tributary to this (quality and innovation are ways of serving the customer better) or derivative of it (integrity comes from customer perceptions).

The second sense in which clan organisations possess strong cultures is in having an array of mechanisms which effectively transmit and reinforce the values outlined above. Firstly, there is an identifiable value *system*, in that ideas and beliefs are both shared and consistent, rather than confined to particular groups (such as senior managers) or subject to wide varieties of interpretation. Clan organisations, therefore, have a hegemonic quality: they possess a homogeneous culture, rather than a number of competing sub-cultures or counter-cultures. Secondly, managers play a central, active role in promoting and shaping values.

Heroes, rituals and communications are key mechanisms for transmitting values within clan organisations. Corporate heroes, about whom stories and myths circulate and who serve as examples, often include the founder(s) of the organisation, whose personal vision is translated into a corporate mission. Recurrent events, such as meetings, induction and training courses, have a ritualistic quality in that their manifest agendas are coupled with the more covert restatement, dramatisation and reinforcement of values. Other events have a more overtly ceremonial character. The network of formal communications – announcements, meetings, notices, newsletters – and informal communications – gossip and stories – acts as a conduit of organisational values by conveying information steeped in symbolic messages. In this network, certain key actors play a strategic role, and language, in particular any special jargon, plays an important symbolic role. However, culture is perhaps most powerfully articulated in mundane, everyday behaviour and the taken-for-granted assumptions which it expresses and reinforces.

A strong organisational culture may be underpinned by structural features of work organisation. Some of these – the internal labour market, training and socialisation, participation, lower-level autonomy and managerial involvement – have been mentioned already. In addition, we can note, firstly, the extensive use of symbolic rewards (badges, plaques, certificates, publicity) for behaviour consistent with corporate values; secondly, the symbolic use of dress, decor and organisational artefacts; and thirdly, the blurred distinction between work and non-work, which reinforces the sense of community.

The central effect of a strong organisational culture is that organisational practices and activities are conducted in a spirit consistent with corporate values. Thus the idea of community underpins a particular and identifiable treatment of employees. Values guide decision-making by acting as 'tie-breakers' (Peters, 1989), specifying what is important and hence indicating which course of action is appropriate. Finally, by giving meaning to actions, culture provides emotional or affective rewards to employees for conformity.

High levels of identification, loyalty and commitment to the organisation and its goals are generated through the galvanising force of shared values. The power of these values lies precisely in their capacity to orient employees towards the pursuit of common goals, whilst at the same time retaining a feeling of individual autonomy and freedom from overt control. The overall effect may be described as 'mobilisation' (Soeters,

1986). That such mobilisation is associated with high levels of individual and organisational performance is not altogether surprising.

We may now summarise clan organisation in terms of the MTO framework. Clan organisation obtains where the normative control exerted by a powerful corporate value system, coupled with a high level of face-to-face manager–subordinate interaction and centralised control over performance outputs and personnel inputs, permits a fluid, *ad hoc* division of labour and decentralised decision-making.

In clan organisation, elements of the management process are reintegrated into the work process. Employees 'manage' themselves, to the extent that they have responsibility for decisions, for planning and allocating their work, motivating themselves and controlling and coordinating the results. Managers, particularly senior managers, retain the ownership functions of strategic decision-making relating to investment and marketing and the promulgation of ideologies in the form of organisational values and beliefs.

The planning of work is decentralised and participative, based upon omnidirectional informal information flows. Decision-making is comparatively decentralised, with day-to-day operating decisions taken by individuals or work teams and tactical decisions taken at divisional level. Strategic decision-making remains centralised, but rests upon a participative process.

The allocation of work is based on a fluid *ad hoc* division of labour with a low level of detailed individual specialisation. Specialisation at the level of the division and the work team is based upon product, rather than process. Work groups, managerial teams and individuals are able to exercise a high level of discretion in their work.

The elicitation of effort rests upon internalised self-motivation and the normative influence of organisational values. Rationales, or ideologies, therefore, play a key motivational role. In addition, economic power is mobilised through deferred and preferential rewards linked to employee loyalty and performance, whilst rules take the form of product quality and service standards.

Work is coordinated by a combination of mutual adjustment and direct, face-to-face managerial involvement. Informal contacts between individuals and groups are more important than formal liaison devices.

Work is controlled, not through the regulation of behaviour, but by influencing the beliefs, values and performance standards of carefully recruited employees. Personnel inputs, values and outputs are therefore the focus of control. The external, impersonal controls exercised by training, indoctrination and performance targets are reinforced by the more personal external controls of MBWA and peer pressure. All these are the preconditions for a reliance upon employee self-control. Table 8.2 summarises these points.

Thus, management through clan organisation is based upon 'controlled trust': permitting employees discretion under conditions which, while they do not ensure, at least increase the probability, that this discretion will be exercised in ways consistent with organisational goals. The difference between this and Japanese management is essentially one of degree: clan organisation cannot rely upon the collectivist national culture and strong institutional features of welfare corporatism which obtain in Japan.

JAPANESE AND CLAN ORGANISATION: AN ASSESSMENT

Our evaluation of these approaches to management attempts to answer four key questions. Firstly, to what extent are these forms of organisation the critical determinants of high levels of performance? Secondly, are these approaches applicable to the organisation of work under all circumstances? Thirdly, what are their problems and unintended consequences? Finally, what are their moral implications? Thus, we assess these approaches and their effects in terms of their reality, practicality, effectiveness and desirability. (See Figure 8.2 for a summary of these arguments.)

There is good evidence for questioning any claim that these approaches to organisation are the sole explanation of corporate success. The success of Japanese companies may be equally attributable to, among other things: their relative reliance upon debt funding and interlocking equity, which encourage reinvestment and growth; tariff protection of home markets; the practice of 'technical followership' (concentrating on turning

Table 8.2 Manging through clan organisation

Management process	: Management and some ownership functions reintegrated into work process. Senior managers retain strategic ownership functions.
Area of application	: Throughout the organisation: managerial and operational work.
Planning/decision-making	
Degree of centralisation	: Operational decisions highly decentralised. Strategic decisions centralised but participative.
Information/communication flows	: Omnidirectional, interactive, predominantly informal.
Allocation of work	
Form of specialisation	: Outputs/products and services.
Level of specialisation	: Work group/management team.
Degree of job specialisation	: Low: flexibility and autonomy.
Motivation	
Rewards	: Deferred, preferential, high symbolic element.
Rules	: Quality/service standards and company norms.
Rationales	: Organisation as community with a mission, 'quality', 'service'.
Coordination	
Locus of responsibility	: Internal (work team) ⎱ Mutual
Method	: Adjustment and consultation ⎰ adjustment.
Degree of formality	: Mainly informal
Control	
Focus	: [Values]
Locus of responsibility	: [Internal/mutual] + [Inputs/outputs] ⎫ Self/mutual
Degree of impersonality	: [Personal] [External] ⎬ normative control +
Degree of formality	: [Informal] [Impersonal] ⎭ external recruitment
	[Formal] and performance control.

Argument 1	But
The structure and culture of J and Clan organisations explain their success	• Other reasons for success of J and Clan organisations • Successful organisations with different structures and cultures • Many 'excellent' companies have not remained so

Argument 2	But
The structure and culture of J and Clan organisations may be adopted by other organisations	• Many practices are exclusive or not generalisable • Particular circumstances of J and Clan organisations • Can culture be managed or changed readily?

Argument 3	But
J and Clan organisations represent an ideal model or 'best way' from the point of view of effectiveness	• Problem of inflexibility or 'tunnel vision' • Failure to innovate methods or activities • Moral rejection by employees

Argument 4	But
J and Clan organisations represent desirable forms of work organisation	• Based on elitism and exclusion • Insidious constraints on employee behaviour • Pressure on employees • Questionable ends

Figure 8.2 J and clan organisations: questioning the structure-culture-performance thesis

existing technology into marketable products, rather than engaging in basic research); close involvement with a network of suppliers and distributors; and a marketing strategy aimed primarily at increasing market share. Similarly, even the most enthusiastic reporters of corporate excellence in America and Britain claim that the management of human resources is only one determinant of commercial success and cite, additionally, a vigorous marketing orientation, emphasis upon product innovation (often coupled with technical followership) and a reluctance to diversify too far or too fast from known products and markets (Peters and Waterman, 1982; Goldsmith and Clutterbuck, 1984).

There is also evidence which questions the extent to which the 'excellent' companies remain so (Soeters, 1986; Peters, 1989; Pascale, 1991), the extent to which they, exclusively, have been the high performers (Carroll, 1983) and the extent to which clan organisation and strong corporate culture are associated with high performance in other companies (Reynolds, 1986). The evidence suggests that the link between organisational culture and high performance may be contingent and transient, rather than causal and permanent.

The practicality of clan organisation and management through organisational culture turns on three issues: first, whether this approach is generalisable, second, whether it requires particular conditions in order to be effective and third, whether culture can be managed and changed.

A number of key elements in the approach have a distinctly 'zero-sum' quality about them, in that they can only be adopted by some organisations if others fail to do likewise. For example, one cornerstone of clan organisation is selective, not to say elitist, recruitment. Employee trust is predicated upon employing only those who, by virtue of their skills and attitudes, can be trusted. This is only possible however if others recruit the less able or less enthusiastic. Any suspicion that employees in clan organisations are attitudinally 'different' in some way is supported by the fact that they are atypical occupationally. The vast majority of 'excellent' or 'innovating' companies are those with a disproportionately large white-collar labour force of managers, professionals and sales staff, occupations which have always been responsive to corporate ideologies and the ethic of commitment.

Furthermore, technical followership, or 'creative swiping' (Peters, 1989), is only possible if other companies altruistically engage in technical leadership. Strong customer orientation and a high level of service only bestow competitive advantage if there are other companies offering poorer service. Once every organisation becomes imbued with consumer sovereignty as part of its value system, all that happens is that the stakes are raised, the dance to the customer's tune becomes ever more frenzied and competitive advantage evaporates.

The development of clan organisation may also require particular, conducive circumstances, such as long-term stable membership, an absence of institutional alternatives, a high level of interaction among organisational members, the existence of certain technological or financial advantages, the support of external groups, compatibility with the wider culture and an absence of strong occupational cultures within the organisation (Wilkins and Ouchi, 1983). Where such conditions do not obtain, clan organisation is less likely to develop or work effectively.

The issue of whether organisational culture can be created, changed or 'managed' is much debated, and turns on the wider issue of whether culture is something which an organisation *has* or *is*. If culture is something which an organisation has, then it may be replaced or changed. For example, Ouchi (1981) offers a blueprint of change necessary for shifting work organisation from a bureaucratic to a clan type, whilst Deal and Kennedy (1982) and Peters (1989) argue that active 'symbolic management' can shape culture. Both of these assertions are open to the same basic objection, however. If culture is an all-pervasive system of ideas, beliefs and values, then those organisational members who might be change agents or shapers of culture are themselves creatures of that system, thus conditioned in their perceptions and understandings of whether change is necessary, and what kind of change is possible (Marshall and McLean, 1985). This perception may be restricted to changes of degree, rather than fundamental changes. Consequently, managers in bureaucratic forms of work organisation might see no reason to 'develop and implement philosophy', or to 'encourage participation' (Ouchi, 1982) and might act as if they were following 'rules for stifling innovation' (Kanter, 1985).

One pessimistic and paradoxical conclusion, therefore, might be that management through culture is only available in the short term in those organisations where it already exists. Although in the longer term cultures do change and evolve, the process is necessarily slow. A second paradox is that the power of organisational culture resides in the fact that it is not just another management 'technique' which can be applied at will, but is, rather, an influence upon behaviour which is not recognised as overt 'management'. The beliefs and values which shape employee behaviour are internalised, taken for granted and accepted as unobjectionable; therein lies their force. Culture, therefore, can exercise the most powerful and insidious form of control because it combines *de facto* compulsion with perceived freedom from coercion. Therefore, whilst the structural elements of clan organisation can be generally adopted, management through culture cannot, beguiling though it is. Two sets of reasons, one instrumental, the other moral, suggest that this is not necessarily a matter for dismay.

The instrumental reason concerns the effectiveness of clan organisation as an approach to management. Whilst it is evident that the existence of a strong culture breeds loyalty and commitment, it is questionable whether these qualities alone are always conducive to effective performance. Unless loyalty and commitment are subject to constant critical scrutiny they can easily slide into parochialism, tunnel vision and inflexibility. Beliefs, values and the behaviour which they guide may become inappropriate to changed circumstances, while at the same time obscuring the need for change. The result may be 'conditioned helplessness' (Bate, 1984; Pascale, 1991). Organisations with strong cultures may become first-rate at what they do, but they become incapable of perceiving or responding to new threats and opportunities. In this case, changing the boundaries of the organisation by incorporating, allying with or 'spinning off' other organisations (Kanter, 1990) may be a more realistic way of adapting to changed circumstances than attempting to change culture.

Of course, the content of the culture is crucial here, and a value system which sets great store by experimentation and criticism is less prone to stagnation. This is, in effect, what Kanter (1985) and Peters (1989) identify as cultures *of* change, where change is a normal, incremental, symbolic and, above all, bottom-up process. Where employees are both encouraged and empowered to experiment and innovate by working in creative teams which are subject to minimum regulation but maximum information, change takes the form of 'logical incrementalism' (Kanter, 1985): the accretion of informal, localised innovation. This requires maintaining the momentum of grass-roots innovation and crystallising these innovations, symbolically, into strategic change. In this way, organisations 'thrive on chaos' (Peters, 1989).

Alternatively, organisations may maintain an 'edge' by developing a value system which maintains a constant tension between cooperation and consensus on the one hand, and constructive conflict on the other. Adaptation, then, comes from constant questioning, with organisations becoming 'engines of enquiry' stimulating, harnessing and 'contending', rather than seeking to suppress, the inevitable conflicts and debates of organisational life (Pascale, 1991). Organisational 'resilience' comes from radical transformations, rather than incrementalism.

Here again, however, the problem is how such conditions can be created or developed if those needing to undergo a 'mental revolution' (Peters, 1989) or to 'break old mindsets' (Pascale, 1991) are themselves the intellectual prisoners of earlier organisational paradigms. Even if a culture of constant change and innovation could be instituted, the dangers might be those of change simply for its own sake, and of what might be described as 'conditioned dynamism' which regards every issue as 'no problem' and, hence, unworthy of careful consideration.

A second Achilles' heel of clan organisation is that it may sow the seeds of opposition to itself. One unintended consequence of both the structural and cultural features of the organisation as a community is a greater homogenisation of the labour force (Ray, 1986). So long as employees accept organisational goals and values, then cooperation, openness, high levels of communication, experimentation and criticism serve managerial ends. However, if these values are questioned or rejected, then collective sentiments and dispositions may become a powerful force for resistance to managerial goals. The mobilisation of employees is only a powerful management force if the mobilisation is in a positive direction.

A shift in the values of a mobilised workforce could come about as a result of a growing moral critique of the normative controls of clan organisation. Certainly it is possible to advance such a critique by pointing to a number of objectionable realities behind beguiling appearances. Firstly, there is the wider system of inequality necessary to sustain the privileged employees of clan organisation. The stable, secure, relationship of mutual obligations which they enjoy with their employers is predicated upon the structured disadvantages of other groups – non-Nenko workers in Japan or those who fail to break into the internal labour markets of 'excellent' companies. In that sense, clan organisations are not 'whole' communities, but exclusive clubs, pervaded at best by elitism, at worst by racism and sexism (Ouchi, 1981).

Although the privileged employees of such organisations might remain immune to any feeling of moral outrage, this might change if they come to realise that beneath the rhetoric of autonomy, 'empowerment', responsibility, trust and self-direction lies the reality of insidious and powerful constraints upon behaviour. The clan organisation's happy invitation to employees to 'be yourself' carries the implicit rider 'as long as you are like us', and the invocation to 'do your own thing' is qualified by 'so long as it suits us'. The warm glow of involvement, team spirit and hoopla disguises the cold reality of normative control.

This reality becomes even less attractive if questions are asked about the ends and interests which are served by such high levels of loyalty, commitment and performance. Some of the most morally repugnant organisations in history have relied upon unswerving loyalty and commitment (Bumstead and Eckblad, 1985). More mundanely, it is questionable whether it is desirable to devote so much energy, creativity and passion to the narrow confines of paid employment and its end products, particularly when the result may not be excitement and achievement, but stress and redundancy. There is also the question of whether within these narrow confines there should not be protected spaces of real personal autonomy, where, insulated from the exhortations of all the wearying enthusiasts, employees can be apathetic, miserable, cynical or angry.

Once employees of clan organisations question what all their effort and enthusiasm is for, they may conclude that they are not worth it if the products of their efforts do not demonstrably increase the sum total of human happiness (even if they do not decrease it) and do not render the human condition finer and nobler (even if they do not actually debase it). They may also conclude that their need to 'belong' is better served by other forms of association, and their need to 'achieve' better served by other endeavours.

The ideology of consumer sovereignty which imbues clan organisations is a powerful counter to such ideas. This suggests that if customers are prepared to pay for particular goods and services, then the providers of these services must do whatever it takes to satisfy them. But the fabric of this ideology is thin. Even exponents of the freest of markets concede that, on moral grounds, there are things that money cannot and should not buy. There is no reason why such prohibitions should not extend to the 'right' of consumers to make unreasonable demands upon each other as producers. Already there is evidence of this view taking hold. Younger Japanese workers are beginning to reject a lifetime of enthralment to a single employer, while in the West, badges bearing the legend 'I'd rather be dead than excellent' are in evidence, and even managers are beginning to question the work ethic (Scase and Goffee, 1989). The final paradox may be that employees of clan organisations are among the first to challenge the transposition of consumer sovereignty into consumer tyranny and to question the belief that our stimulated appetite for cheaper goods and instant service justifies a frenetic corporatist work-place. 'Excellence', like everything else, has its price.

FURTHER READING

The key sources on the features of J-organisations are Abegglen (1958), Cole (1971), Dore (1973), Oh (1976), Howard and Teramoto (1981), Hatvany and Pucik (1981), Ouchi (1981), Littler (1982), Pascale and Athos (1982), Cool and Lengnick-Hall (1985), Wickens (1987), Clegg (1990) and Pascale (1991).

Ouchi (1981) and Pascale and Athos (1982) are the main texts to draw parallels between Japanese organisation and clan organisation in the West.

On culture as a key organisational variable, see Deal and Kennedy (1982), Peters and Waterman (1982), Wilkins and Ouchi (1983), Goldsmith and Clutterbuck (1984), Kanter (1985), Lebas and Weigenstein (1986), Peters and Austin (1986) and Ray (1986).

For critiques of the thesis of culture as a manageable determinant of a high level of organisation performance, see Carroll (1983), Bate (1984), Reynolds (1986), Soeters (1986) and the revised views of Peters (1989) and Pascale (1991).

Chapter 9

Managing within organisation
Managerial work in an organisational context

So far, we have considered 'management' in two senses of the term. Chapter 1 examined management in terms of what managers do and, in particular, in terms of the common characteristics of the content and form of managerial work. Chapters 4 to 8 examined management as organisation, the institutionalised mechanisms for attempting the planning/ decision-making, allocation, motivation, coordination and control of work. In any large-scale undertaking, management in the sense of what managers do takes place in the context of organisation: managers are obliged to manage within, as well as through, organisation. It remains to be considered how these two facets of 'management' are related and, specifically, how and why managerial work varies across different organisational contexts.

Central to this analysis is the concept of 'management divisions of labour' which forms a bridge between, on the one hand, forms of management through organisation and, on the other, the characteristics of managerial work. The chapter begins with a discussion of management divisions of labour and their four key dimensions. We then examine, firstly, the way in which management divisions of labour are shaped by different approaches to the organisation of operational and managerial work and secondly, the way in which different management divisions of labour ramify into different forms of managerial jobs and different ways in which managerial work is practised. (See Figure 9.1 for an outline of these arguments.)

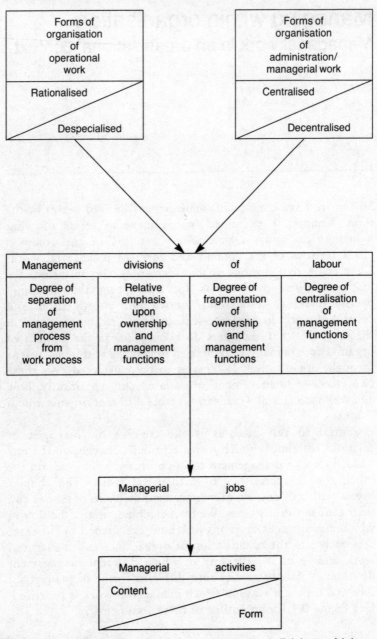

Figure 9.1 Forms of organisation, management divisions of labour and managerial work

MANAGEMENT DIVISIONS OF LABOUR

The concept of management divisions of labour builds on and extends the concepts of a 'managerial labour process' (Braverman, 1974; Knights and Willmott, 1986), a 'managerial hierarchy' (Williamson, 1975; Chandler, 1977) and the synthesis of these in Teulings' model of four distinct managerial labour processes, each with their own forms of organisation and logics of action, corresponding to four levels of management: the 'institutional', 'strategic', 'structuring' and 'operational' (Teulings, 1986). In contrast to these formulations, however, the concept of management divisions of labour recognises firstly, that whilst ownership functions have their origins in the market, management functions proper have their origins in the work process; secondly, that different management functions do not necessarily map on to different managerial levels; and thirdly, that managerial work, as well as operational work, is itself managed. Management divisions of labour arise out of the way in which management functions become separated from the work process and amalgamated with ownership functions to form an extended 'management' process. In this process, the emphasis between ownership and management functions may vary, as will the way in which both of these functions, to varying degrees, are subject to fragmentation and the separation of conception from execution. It is these variations which determine variations in management divisions of labour.

As the term implies, management divisions of labour refer to different ways in which a separate management process is dispersed among different positions, whether deemed managerial or not. As we have seen in earlier chapters, however, counter-effects of dilution, resistance and diversion have meant that separation of the management process is contingent, variable in extent and subject to reversal. Both despecialisation, through job redesign, group working and participation, and clan organisation represent, in effect, a reintegration of elements of management into the work process such that non-managers are enabled, or obliged, to manage themselves in certain respects. Therefore, the first and most basic way in which management divisions of labour vary is in the degree to which management functions are confined to positions which are deemed 'managerial'.

Management in its extended sense is an amalgamation of both ownership functions (subsuming allocation and disposal of capital, in the form of material or monetary inputs or outputs) and functions relating to the management of work. The balance between these functions is variable, and this is reflected in the relative preponderance of different kinds of managerial jobs accorded different degrees of importance, power and status.

Management divisions of labour also reflect the dispersion and fragmentation of management. Management is fragmented by the creation of specialisms dealing predominantly with one management function, rather than many, and subsequently in the creation of yet more detailed sub-specialisms. This creates different types of management work, mirrored, although not always unambiguously so, in job and occupational titles.

Just as management is, in part, the outcome of the separation of conception from execution of the work process, so management itself may undergo, to varying degrees, a separation of conception from execution. The processes of planning and decision-making, allocation, motivation, coordination and control of managerial work may themselves become separated. The effects of this separation are, firstly, the creation of positions with responsibility for managing managerial work, and secondly, a variation in the extent to which different managers are able to exercise self-management. For ownership functions, there are those managers who make decisions about investments, resource allocation, product development and marketing, and other managers who mainly provide information on which these decisions are based or who put these decisions into effect. Equally, for management functions, there are managers who decide how work is to be planned, allocated, motivated, coordinated and controlled, and those who merely provide information for these decisions or put them into effect. Therefore, some managers choose and initiate the institutional arrangements whereby the management of work is attempted (i.e. choose and initiate forms of organisation), whilst others must 'manage' within and through these arrangements. It is this differentiation which creates different levels of management (Johnson, 1980). This differentiation is a matter of degree, however, as our comparison between bureaucracy and different forms of decentralised administration showed. In centralised forms of organisation, where decisions about organisational arrangements and the management of managers are the exclusive responsibility of senior managers, lower-level managerial work, in effect, loses its conceptual elements or is deskilled.

Thus, management divisions of labour represent different ways of dividing and allocating the various ownership and management functions. As such, they are configurations of four principal dimensions:

1 The extent to which the management process is separate from the work process – hence the extent to which management is the exclusive responsibility of 'managers'.
2 The relative emphasis between ownership and management functions within management as a whole.
3 The degree of fragmentation of ownership and management functions into distinct specialisms and types of jobs.
4 The degree to which decision-making and the management of managers is centralised.

Management divisions of labour form the bridge between forms of work organisation and the character of managerial jobs and managers' work.

FORMS OF ORGANISATION AND MANAGEMENT DIVISIONS OF LABOUR

Forms of organisation shape and, to some extent, are shaped by management divisions of labour. That is, forms of organisation both give rise to different management specialisms and occupations, with varying degrees of responsibility, power and status, and are also sustained by those differences, or modified by changes in them (Armstrong, 1986). Furthermore, this relationship operates at two levels. Firstly, there is an indirect relationship in the way that the organisation of operational work necessitates certain kinds of vertical and horizontal divisions within management itself. Secondly, divisions within management also reflect the way that the management process itself is organised.

As Chapters 4 and 6 showed, 'rationalisation' and 'despecialisation' represent two broad alternative approaches to the management of operational work. These two approaches impact rather differently upon the management division of labour.

Firstly, whereas a central tenet of the rationalisation of work is the sharp segregation of management functions, despecialisation entails some reintegration, however limited, of management into the work process and, hence, a transfer of some management functions to non-managers. In both approaches, non-managers are generally excluded from ownership functions, although under some forms of despecialisation, such as autonomous work groups, non-managers may acquire limited responsibility for resource allocation (Kanawaty, 1981). The balance between ownership and management functions is also likely to be different in the two approaches, with ownership functions accorded relatively greater importance where work is despecialised because of the relative importance of market, rather than production, considerations (Kelly, 1982).

The two approaches also entail different degrees of fragmentation and centralisation within management. Where work is rationalised, management functions themselves tend to be both fragmented and centralised. There is a high degree of managerial specialisation relating to work planning, motivation systems, coordination of work and control systems, since little of this is carried out in the work process and these functions are themselves highly fragmented. Further, these functions are relatively centralised, since elaborate planning, motivational and control systems demand a sharper differentiation between policy relating to work systems and its implementation and a tendency for policy to be centrally controlled. Despecialisation, on the other hand, engenders less fragmentation and centralisation of management functions, since more of these functions have been designed into 'enriched' jobs, or have been made the responsibility of the work team. Consequently, despecialisation of work often entails a reduction in the number of junior managers/supervisors. Table 9.1 summarises and contrasts the effects of these approaches to the organisation of operational work upon the management division of labour.

As Chapters 5 and 7 showed, bureaucracy and various forms of decentralisation (professional organisation and adhocracy) are the two basic alternative approaches to organising administrative work. These also shape the management division of labour. In bureaucratic organisation, operating in stable and predictable conditions (often of their own making), management, rather than ownership functions, predominate,

Table 9.1 Management divisions of labour associated with different forms of organisation of operational work

	Rationalisation			Despecialisation/flexibility		
	Fragmentation *High*	Centralisation *High*	Exclusivity to managers	Fragmentation *Low*	Centralisation	Exclusivity to managers
Ownership functions	Ideological, resource, marketing and liaison specialisms	Senior managers take resource/ marketing decisions, junior managers implement/ assist	Yes: (non-managers excluded from resource allocation and marketing. Ideology of exclusion)	Broad responsibility for ideology, resources, marketing and liaison	*High* But work teams may take some resource decisions	Yes: but limited resource allocation by non-managers
Management functions	*High* Planning, allocating, motivational, coordinating and control specialisms	*High* Senior managers take organisational decisions, junior managers implement/ assist	Yes: (non-managers excluded from management process)	*Low* All managers plan, allocate, motivate, coordinate and control	*Low* Work teams may take organisational decisions	No: devolved to 'enriched' jobs or work teams
Emphasis between functions	Management functions predominate			Ownership functions predominate		

since ensuring a smooth work process is relatively more important than investment or marketing activities. Both sets of functions show a high degree of fragmentation and centralisation. Ownership functions are handled by specialist departments and positions, and are centralised in the sense that policy is formulated and decided at the top, even though resource allocation may be pyramidal, with 'levels' of budgetary autonomy. Equally, the management of managerial work is divided among specialists – corporate planners, personnel, management training and development, finance, control specialists, etc. – although the pyramidal structure means that line managers retain some personal responsibility for managing their subordinates directly, albeit within the framework of arrangements (e.g. appraisal systems, grievance procedures, salary scales) determined centrally.

Professional and adhocratic forms of organisation, where middle and junior managers to some extent manage themselves, give rise to a management division of labour which is less fragmented and, perforce, more decentralised. Ownership functions tend to predominate because of the volatility of the external conditions under which these organisations operate and, therefore, aspects of marketing, external liaison and resource allocation are undertaken by managers in general as well as by specialists. Furthermore, marketing decisions and, in particular, expenditure and resource allocation decisions are decentralised, albeit within budgetary or performance constraints. Although corporate strategy, external relations and large-scale resource allocation remain centralised, in the more radical forms of decentralised organisation (e.g. adhocracy), these are participative and emergent. Although decentralisation, except in its more limited forms (e.g. divisionalisation), means greater autonomy for junior managers to manage themselves (or each other), decisions relating to managerial recruitment, the development and enforcement of performance controls and resource allocation tend to remain centralised. Whilst, in general, decentralisation brings less narrow managerial specialisation, coordination remains – or becomes – an increasingly specialised function because of its importance (Lawrence and Lorsch, 1976). Table 9.2 summarises and contrasts the management divisions of labour associated with these two approaches to the organisation of administration.

Table 9.2 Management divisions of labour associated with different forms of organisation of administration (i.e. ways of managing managerial work)

	Fragmentation	Centralisation	Fragmentation	Centralisation
	High	*High*	*Low*	*High/low*
Ownership functions	Ideological, resourcing, marketing and liaison specialists	Senior managers determine ideology and external relations *High/low* Pyramidal budgeting decisions	Resourcing, marketing and liaison functions are non-specialised	Senior managers control large-scale resource allocation, corporate strategy, corporate ideology and external relations, but these may be emergent and participative *Low* Middle/junior managers have marketing and financial responsibility
	High/low	*High/low*	*Low*	*High/low*
Management functions	Planning, personnel, work flow and control specialists, but also generalist line management positions	Pyramidal/hierarchical arrangement with managers managing work of immediate subordinates. Junior managers' work is routine	All managers plan, allocate, motivate and control subordinates, but coordinate specialists	Junior managers plan, allocate, coordinate and control own work and motivate themselves and each other, but senior/HO managers control performance/resource allocation and managerial recruitment
Emphasis between functions	Management functions predominate		Ownership functions predominate	

Clan organisation, as Chapter 8 showed, differs from other approaches in that it is not only a more inclusive form of organisation, extending through both managerial and operational work, but it also relies less on formal structural arrangements and more on the informal norms and values of organisational culture. Although some ownership functions, particularly those relating to investment and marketing strategy, remain the exclusive responsibility of mainly senior managers, clan organisation generally exhibits the most wide-ranging reintegration of management functions into work itself. Not only lower level managers, but also operational employees, have some responsibility for marketing the organisation and its product through a constant customer/public relations orientation, and for some control over the use of resources, as well as some formal autonomy and opportunity to managing themselves, as individuals or teams. The strength of organisational values emphasising service facilitates this, and also means that, with the management of work less problematic, ownership functions, particularly those relating to marketing, predominate.

In clan organisation, ownership and management functions are recombined and less fragmented. There is a more diffuse responsibility for resource allocation and business decisions, linked with the encouragement of internal competition and 'intrapreneurship' (Atterhed, 1985). There is also more diffuse responsibility for articulating organisational values and ideology, and for marketing and external relations through a common 'customer-orientation' (Peters and Austin, 1986). Management functions are also less fragmented. Managerial job rotation creates generalist managers who manage the work of their teams, through close involvement or 'management by wandering around', and there is less reliance upon specialists to devise particular planning, reward and control systems. The 'loose–tight properties' (Peters and Waterman, 1982) of clan organisation mean that some ownership and management functions are centralised, whilst others are decentralised. Investment and marketing strategy are centralised, but often participative. However, operational business decisions, resource allocation, specific product marketing and external relations are devolved to front-line managers and, through consultation or job responsibility, operational staff. Equally, front-line managers have considerable autonomy in managing both their own work and that of their teams, whose members may, in turn, participate in the management process. Counterbalancing these decentralised management functions are those which remain the responsibility of senior head office managers: the construction and implementation of performance controls, resource allocation decisions, recruitment and training policy and the formulation of organisational ideology. Table 9.3 summarises the management division of labour in clan organisation.

Thus, forms of organisation shape management divisions of labour. We can now trace the effects of different management divisions of labour upon managerial work.

MANAGEMENT DIVISIONS OF LABOUR AND MANAGERIAL WORK

The observation that managerial work varies in different organisational contexts is something of a commonplace in the management literature. The nature of the relationship between the two is often only alluded to, however, rather than convincingly demonstrated. This, in part, reflects ambiguities in the use of the term 'organisation'. Organisation is seen, variously, as synonymous with particular companies, with producers of specific goods or services, or different industries. Hence it is claimed that managers in setting X work in different ways from those in setting Y. In other cases, the national culture in which an organisation operates is held to influence the nature of managerial work (Hofstede, 1980; Child and Keiser, 1981; Inkson *et al.*, 1981). Although many of these analyses are carefully constructed, here again the argument is either by implication – that differences in the cultural characteristics of employees will necessitate different forms of management and managerial behaviour – or focuses on differences in managerial 'style' rather than substance.

Others have examined the impact of organisational structure upon the nature of managerial jobs at different positions, or levels, in the structure (Child and Ellis, 1973; Stewart, 1976). Mintzberg's analysis of how managerial roles differ among basic organisational forms (Mintzberg, 1979; 1983) is closest to the analysis offered here but is not always complete and is, at times, inconsistent.

Here we are concerned with the way in which organisation as

Table 9.3 Management divisions of labour in clan organisation

	Fragmentation	Centralisation	Exclusivity to managers
	Low	*High/low*	*Some*
Ownership functions	Diffused responsibility for resource allocation/business decisions ('intrapreneurship'), articulating organisational ideology, marketing and external relations (customer orientation)	Centralised marketing and investment strategy. Devolved business decisions/resource allocation, production of organisational ideology, marketing and customer liaison	Investment and marketing strategy only, but these may be consultative. Non-managers involved in resource allocation, marketing, external relations and promoting corporate values.
	Low	*High/low*	*No*
Management functions	Generalist peripatetic managers plan, allocate, motivate and control work of subordinates (MBWA). Less reliance on specialists to devise management systems.	Autonomy for junior managers in planning, allocating, coordinating and controlling their own work and motivating themselves and each other, but senior/HO managers decide performance controls, resource allocation, recruitment policy and formulate organisational ideology.	Non-managers involved in management process.
Emphasis between functions	Ownership functions predominate		

the institutional arrangements for managing work impacts upon the specific character of managerial work. In this, it is important to bear in mind two distinctions: firstly, between managerial work as constituted (and embodied in managerial jobs) and as it is practised, and secondly, between the content and form of managerial work. Further, it is important to remember that forms of organisation, through their effect on management divisions of labour, influence managerial work only insofar as they impose structural constraints or create structural possibilities. What managers do and how they do it is also the outcome of their own skilled accomplishments.

Evidence on the way in which managerial jobs are constituted can be linked to differences among management divisions of labour (Stewart, 1976; Machin, 1982; Hales, 1987b). Where ownership and management functions are fragmented, there is a preponderance of specialist managerial and professional jobs with associated competencies or qualifications, 'logics of action' (Teulings, 1986) and career patterns, whereas where the two functions are less clearly divided, there is greater incidence of generalist managerial jobs. The degree of centralisation of ownership and management functions determines the extent to which managerial jobs vary by level. Where ownership functions are highly centralised, there is a comparatively wide gulf between the business and strategic responsibilities of senior managers and implementation of business procedures and processing of information by lower-level managers. Where ownership functions are decentralised, however, lower-level managerial jobs have a greater business component. Similarly, where management functions are centralised, there is a wider disparity between senior managers, responsible for policy on matters of organisation and staffing, and lower-level managers responsible for implementing policies and procedures and supplying control information. Where management functions are decentralised, junior managerial jobs have wider responsibility for and more autonomy in the management of people.

Managerial jobs also reflect broader features of the management divisions of labour. The number of managerial, relative to non-managerial, positions reflects the extent to which ownership and, in particular, management functions reside exclusively with managers. The power, influence and status of different managerial specialisms or professions reflects the relative emphasis between ownership and management functions (Child *et al.*, 1983; Lawrence, 1984; Armstrong, 1986).

The content of managerial work can also be linked to differences among management divisions of labour. Fragmented ownership and management functions give rise to managerial work with a relatively technical, rather than generalist, component; a concentration on specialist agendas (Kotter, 1982), specialist 'decisional' roles and externally oriented roles such as those of 'liaison' and 'spokesman' (Mintzberg, 1973) or 'involvement in workflows', and 'monitoring' (Sayles, 1964). Where ownership and management functions are less fragmented, however, managers' work typically has a more general, 'business management' component, with broader agendas, more areas of responsibility, greater emphasis on roles internal to the work group, such as 'leader' and 'disseminator' (Mintzberg, 1973) and more emphasis on human resource management (Luthans *et al.*, 1988). Less fragmentation of functions also offers managers more choice of work content or 'domain' (Stewart, 1982) and requires more 'networking' activity (Luthans *et al.*, 1988).

The degree of centralisation of ownership and management functions impacts primarily on the distribution of work activities among managerial positions at different levels. Where these functions are centralised, it is mainly senior managers whose work encompasses 'traditional managing' (Luthans *et al.*, 1988) and 'decisional', 'leader', 'liaison' and 'spokesman' roles (Mintzberg, 1973). In contrast, the work of middle and junior managers encompasses these roles and, generally, affords greater choice of content and domain, where management functions are decentralised.

The extent to which management functions reside exclusively with managers influences the extent to which differences between managers and non-managers in terms of work content are more significant than differences among managers. This, in turn, has implications for managers' self-perceptions, the distinctiveness of managerial ideologies and the strength of managerial claims to authority. The less exclusive managerial jobs are, the more managers perceive themselves simply as employees and tailor their orientations accordingly (Snape and Bamber, 1985). Managers' orientations and priorities are also shaped by the relative importance accorded to ownership and management functions. Where the former predominate, orientations are external, focused upon service or customers (Peters and Austin, 1986), whereas when management functions predominate, the focus is upon internal systems and processes.

Lastly, variations in the form of managerial work are shaped by variations in management divisions of labour. The extent to which ownership and management functions are fragmented impacts primarily upon managers' contacts and interactions. Where these functions are fragmented, managers have to accomplish their work through relatively large networks, a high level of lateral communications, many meetings and contact patterns resembling the 'hub' or 'peer-dependent' types. However, more specialist work is of a more continuous, 'project' type. In contrast, where management functions are less fragmented, managers have smaller networks, engage in more vertical communication, hold fewer meetings and exhibit 'man management' contact patterns (Stewart, 1976). Their own work, however, often involves discontinuities and rapid commuting between different but brief activities.

The degree of centralisation of management and ownership functions impacts mainly on the opportunity for proactivity and rhythms of work. Where these functions are decentralised, lower-level managers are able to take initiatives on resource allocation, marketing activities or planning, allocating, motivating and controlling the work of their subordinates, and their work more closely resembles 'system maintenance' than 'system administration' (Stewart, 1976). Table 9.4 summarises these arguments.

Different approaches to work organisation give rise, therefore, to rather different structural constraints, opportunities and experiences on the part of those designated as managers. Managing in a bureaucracy presents different prospects from managing in an adhocracy or professional organisation, just as managing rationalised work is different from managing despecialised work. In short, the process of managing *through* organisation influences, in important ways, the experience of managing *within* organisation.

Table 9.4 Impact of management divisions of labour on managerial work

MANAGERIAL JOBS		MANAGERIAL ACTIVITIES	
		Content	Form
Ownership functions			
Fragmentation			
High	Specialist: qualifications, logics of action, careers, interests	Technical: specialist decisions/ agendas; figurehead/liaison/ spokesman roles	Large network: lateral communications; many meetings Hub/peer dependent; project
Low	Generalist/homogeneous	General: leader/monitor disseminator for work group; choice of domain	Smaller network: vertical communication; discontinuity; man management
Centralisation			
High	Senior–junior differences in 'economic' decision-making	Senior managers only have entre-preneurial, resource allocation, liaison and spokesman roles	Senior managers proactive, junior manager reactive
Low	Junior 'intrapreneurship'	All managers have entrepreneurial, resource allocation, liaison and spokesman roles	Junior managers more proactive
Exclusivity to managers			
High	More managerial jobs	Managers' work evidently distinctive	Distinctively 'managerial'
Low	Fewer managerial jobs	Managers' work less evidently distinctive	Less distinctively 'managerial'

Management functions

Fragmentation			
High	Specialist: qualifications, logics of action, careers, interests	Technical: specialist decisions/agendas; figurehead/liaison/spokesman roles; external work flows/monitoring	Large network: lateral communication; many meetings hub/peer dependent; project
Low	Generalist/homogeneous	General: leader/monitor/disseminator for work group; more insular; choice of domain; networking; human resource management	Smaller network: vertical communication; discontinuity; man management
Centralisation			
High	Senior–junior differences in 'organisational' decision-making	Senior managers only have negotiation, disturbance handler, leader roles and 'traditional managing'	Senior managers proactive, juniors reactive and engage in system administration
Low	Junior managers take 'organisational' decisions	All managers have negotiation, disturbance handler, leader roles and engage in 'traditional managing'	Junior managers more proactive and engage in system maintenance
Exclusivity to managers			
High	More managerial jobs	Managers' work evidently distinctive as 'managerial'	Distinctively 'managerial'
Low	Fewer managerial jobs	Managers' work less distinctively 'managerial'	Less distinctively 'managerial'
Emphasis between functions			
Ownership	Power/status reflects proximity to finance or marketing	Market/financial management emphasis	Less fragmented
Management	Power/status reflects proximity to line management	People management emphasis	Fragmented

FURTHER READING

On variations in managerial work generally see Dubin and Spray (1964), Sayles (1964), Horne and Lupton (1965), Pheysey (1972), Child and Ellis (1973), Mintzberg (1973, 1979), Stewart (1976, 1982), Luthans and Davis (1980), Kotter (1982), Machin (1982), Lawrence (1984), Martinko and Gardner (1984), Whiteley (1985), Hales (1987b) and Luthans *et al.* (1988).

A review may be found in Hales (1986).

Chapter 10

Conclusion

Although our review of different approaches to the management of work has taken a critical stance, by seeking to evaluate rather than merely describe different organisational forms, it has striven to do so impartially and has held no brief for a particular approach. Nevertheless, in the face of this array of alternatives, together with their respective strengths and weaknesses, the question arises as to which, on the balance of the evidence, represents the most effective way of organising work. The difficulty in providing an answer, however, inheres not only in the often ambiguous and controversial nature of the evidence relating to the strengths and weaknesses of the different approaches, but also in the different circumstances to which the approaches may be applied and in divergent criteria of effectiveness. Mindful of these difficulties and hence of the possibility of rather different interpretations of the evidence, we may offer the following broad conclusions and observations.

Certainly the most pervasive and enduring approaches to organisation, both at the level of ideas and, more especially, at the level of practice, are those which employ centralised control and formal regulation to coordinate an intentionally (and, often, extremely) fragmented division of both managerial and non-managerial labour. Bureaucracy and rationalised work, in their different guises, have long endured and are not dead yet. The supposedly 'unavoidable' need for order, predictability and system efficiency underpins a continued preoccupation with unambiguous planning and decision-making, tight control and detailed regulation, even in the face of inflexible work systems, poor morale and lack of individual responsibility and initiative. In effect, an over-emphasis on 'management' as planning and control leads to the creation of forms of organisation in which management as motivation is neglected: an obsession with regulating how work is to take place spawns an inattention to ensuring that it takes place at all. Tolerance of these difficulties in the singular pursuit of order and control is fortified by the undoubted capacity of bureaucracy and rationalised work to preserve the interests of the organisationally powerful.

The reluctance of the organisationally powerful to relinquish the means by which their power is sustained, a reluctance born either of political and material interest or of a mistrust of subordinates, explains why, hitherto, decentralisation and despecialiation have taken the form of limited, cautious and often short-lived organisational experiments. Even the recent waves of interest in more adhocratic, decentralised forms of administration and flexible, despecialised operational work are more the result of a forced response to greater environmental uncertainty than of a positive desire to grant greater managerial and employee autonomy. Indeed, there is more than a suspicion that these are opportunistic reactions to 'enacted' environmental uncertainties where the real aim is a new form of rationalised work. Thus, 'flexibility' is a way of securing higher levels of productivity in the guise of meeting more variegated consumer demand which is itself largely the creation of the marketing strategies of large organisations. Equally, 'decentralisation' in pursuit of 'leaner', 'fitter' and more adaptable management is a relatively thin disguise for rationalising administration through a wholesale winnowing of middle management layers. Even so, the constant tension between the need for responsibility, initiative and problem-solving at lower levels of management and on the shop-floor, and the need to ensure that this autonomy is exercised in pursuit of centrally defined goals, means that a swing back to more centralised control and regulation is likely in the future. Autonomy for lower-level managers and employees will only continue if some other mechanism is in place for ensuring their 'responsibility' and justifying the 'trust' of senior managers.

One such mechanism is a strong, pervasive organisational culture, focused on 'quality' or 'service', and reinforced by highly selective recruitment, normative training and indoctrination and the symbolic quality of managerial behaviour, organisational ceremonies and myths. Certainly, on the evidence, variations on Japanese or clan organisation, with cultures of change and innovation, appear to be highly successful, since they are able to fuse commitment, control and change. This gives motivational force, controlled direction and flexibility to the efforts of employees. It is the combination of structure and culture that appears decisive: a decentralised structure permits individual initiative, creativity and choice, whilst a strong culture directs choices towards clear ends. This represents, therefore, the most sophisticated attempt, to date, of solving the central organisational dilemma of reconciling autonomy and control, individuality and uniformity. By instilling organisational values that employees come to regard as their own, it represents the large-scale mobilisation of normative power to evoke moral commitment.

But this approach is necessarily exclusive and rooted in particular circumstances: not every organisation can acquire, or even build, a dynamic culture, and not every organisation can 'win'. This means that, although it is much and imperfectly imitated, this approach is unlikely to be the new organisational paradigm that some claim. Furthermore, the price of its success in terms of the insidious curbs imposed upon individual freedom of action and thought, the exclusion of whole categories of possible employees as 'unsuitable', and the physical and psychological pressures placed on those who are selected for employment, make it an unlikely candidate for the most morally desirable form of organisation. It is little short of organisational eugenics and is anathema to anyone concerned about the ends, rather than simply the means, of organisational life.

Indeed, given the demonstrated capacity of bureaucracies or corporate clans to pursue, either with grinding rationality or breathless enthusiasm, narrowly defined economic ends with little heed to the quality of existence of those employed by them or to the preservation of the global environment populated by them, there is a case for more radically conceived organisational paradigms. What all the approaches to organisation reviewed in this book have in common is a concern to so manage work and the people who do it that output and effort are maximised; they differ only over how this may be attained. The conservation of resources, including human ingenuity and effort, and their liberation for use in activities beyond the narrow confines of economic production and employment, will almost certainly require very different forms of organisation. Hitherto these have been only hazily conceived and rarely implemented in recognisable forms. Whether 'reality' (in the form of human nature, the exigencies of work or the market context) truly precludes these alternative forms, or whether it is simply invoked as justification for resisting any change which challenges the material and political interests of the powerful, is an open question. If, however, reality is no more than the invention of unimaginative people, the time has come for exercising greater imagination not only in how we conceptualise organisation, but how we organise work in practice.

Bibliography

Abegglen, J.C. (1958) *The Japanese Factory*, Glencoe, Illinois: Free Press.

Aiken, M. and Hage, J. (1970) 'Organizational Alienation: A Comparative Analysis', in Grusky, O. and Miller, G.A. (eds), *The Sociology of Organizations: Basic Studies*, New York: Free Press.

Aitken, H.G.J. (1960) *Taylorism at Watertown Arsenal: Scientific Management in Action*, Cambridge, Mass.: Harvard University Press.

Albrow, M. (1970) *Bureaucracy*, London: Macmillan.

Aldrich, H.E. (1979) *Organizations and Environments*, Englewood Cliffs, N.J.: Prentice-Hall.

Aldrich, H.E. and Herker, D. (1977) 'Boundary-spanning Roles and Organization Structure', *Academy of Management Review*, April 1977: 217–30.

Aldridge, A. (1976) *Power, Authority and Restrictive Practices*, Oxford: Blackwell.

Anthony, P.D. (1977) *The Ideology of Work*, London: Tavistock.

—— (1986) *The Foundation of Management*, London: Tavistock.

Arendt, H. (1970) *On Violence*, London: Allen Lane.

Argyris, C. (1964) *Integrating the Individual and the Organisation*, New York: Wiley.

Armstrong, P. (1986) 'Management Control Strategies and Inter-Professional Competition: The Cases of Accountancy and Personnel Management', in Knights, D. and Willmott, H. (eds) *Managing the Labour Process*, Aldershot: Gower, 19–43.

Asplund, C. and Von Otter, C. (1979) 'Codetermination Through Collective Effort', in Cooper, C.L. and Mumford, E. (eds) *The Quality of Working Life in Western and Eastern Europe*, London: Associated Business Press, 258–79.

Atkinson, J. (1985) 'The Changing Corporation', in Clutterbuck, D. (ed.) *New Patterns of Work*, Aldershot: Gower, 13–34.

Atterhed, S.G. (1985) 'Intrapreneurship: the way forward?', in Clutterbuck, D. (ed.) *op.cit.*, 78–86.

Babbage, C. (1832) *On the Economy of Machinery and Manufacture*, London: Charles Knight.

Bacharach, D.B. and Lawler, E.J. (1980) *Power and Politics in Organizations*, San Francisco: Jossey-Bass.

Bachrach, P. and Baratz, M.S.A. (1962) 'Two Faces of Power', *American Political Science Review*, 56 (4): 947–52.

Baldamus, W. (1961) *Efficiency and Effort*, London: Tavistock.

Bannester, E.M. (1969) 'Sociodynamics: an integrative theorem of power, authority, influence and love', *American Sociological Review*, 34: 374–93.

Baran, P. and Sweezy, P.M. (1966) *Monopoly Capital*, New York: Monthly Review Press.

Barnard, C.I. (1938) *The Functions of the Executive*, Cambridge, Mass.: Harvard University Press.

Bate, P. (1984) 'The Impact of Organizational Culture on Approaches to Organizational Problem Solving', *Organization Studies*, 5 (1) 43–66.

Beetham, D. (1987) *Bureaucracy*, Milton Keynes: Open University Press.

Bell, D. (1960) 'Work and its Discontents', in Bell, D. *The End of Ideology*, Glencoe, Ill.: Free Press.

—— (1973) *The Coming of Post-Industrial Society*, New York: Basic Books.

Bendix, R. (1963) *Work and Authority in Industry*, New York: Harper.

Bennis, W.G. (1966) 'The Coming Death of Bureaucracy', *Think*, Nov–Dec, 1966: 30–5.

Berg, I. (1979) *Managers and Work Reform: A Limited Engagement*, New York: Free Press.

Berger, P., Berger, B. and Kellner, H. (1974) *The Homeless Mind*, Harmondsworth: Penguin.

Beynon, H. (1973) *Working for Ford*, Harmondsworth: Penguin.

Biggane, J.F. and Stewart, P.A. (1972) 'Job Enlargement: A Case Study', in David, L.E. and Taylor, J.C. (eds) *Design of Jobs: Selected Readings*, Harmondsworth: Penguin, 264–76.

Birchall, D.W., Carnall, C.A. and Wild, R. (1982) 'Work Organisation Change in a Manufacturing Process – Problems in Evaluating Outcomes', in Ondrack, D. and Timperley, S. (eds) *The Humanisation of Work. A European Perspective*, London: Armstrong, 42–58.

Blackler, F.H.M. and Brown, C.A. (1980) 'Job Redesign and Social Change: Case Studies at Volvo', in Duncan, K.D., Gruneberg, M.M. and Wallis, D. (eds) *Changes in Working Life*, Chichester: John Wiley, 311–28.

Blau, P.M. (1956) *Bureaucracy in Modern Society*, New York: Random House.

—— (1968) 'The Hierarchy of Authority in Organizations', *American Journal of Sociology*, 73, Jan.: 453–67.

—— (1970a) *The Dynamics of Bureaucracy*, Chicago: University of Chicago Press.

—— (1970b) 'Decentralisation in Bureaucracies', in M.N. Zald (ed.) *Power in Organizations*, Nashville, Tenn.: Vanderbilt University Press 150–74.

—— (1970c) 'The Comparative Study of Organizations', in Grusky, O. and Miller, G. (eds) *op.cit.*, 175–86.

—— (1981) 'Interdependence and Hierarchy in Organizations', in Grusky, O. and Miller, G.A. (eds) *The Sociology of Organizations: Basic Studies*, 2nd edn, New York: Free Press, 151–75.

Blau, P.M. and Schoenherr, R.A. (1973) 'New Forms of Power', in Salaman, G. and Thompson, K. (eds) *People and Organisations*, London: Longman/Open University Press, 13–24.

Blau, P.M. and Scott, W.R. (1963) *Formal Organizations: A Comparative Approach*, London: Routledge & Kegan Paul.

Blauner, R. (1960) 'Work Satisfaction and Industrial Trends in Modern Society', in Galenson, W. and Lipset, S.M. (eds) *Labour and Trade Unionism: An Interdisciplinary Reader*, New York: Wiley, 339–60.

—— (1964) *Alienation and Freedom: The factory worker and his industry*, Chicago: University of Chicago Press.

Boreham, P. (1983) 'Indetermination: Professional Knowledge, Organisation and Control', *Sociological Review*, 30 (4): 693–718.

Boseman, F.G. and Jones, R.E. (1974) 'Market Conditions, Decentralization and Organizational Effectiveness', *Human Relations*, 27 (5): 665–76.

Bosquet, M. (1977) 'Prison Factory', in Bosquet, M. *Capitalism in Crisis and Everyday Life*, trans. Hawe, J., Hassocks: Harvester Press, 91–101.

Brannen, P. (1983) *Authority and Participation in Industry*, London: Batsford.

Braverman, H. (1974) *Labor and Monopoly Capital*, New York: Monthly Review Press.

Brech, E.F.L. (1957) *Organisation: The Framework of Management*, London: Longman.

Brewer, E. and Tomlinson, J.W.C. (1964) 'The Manager's Working Day', *Journal of Industrial Economics*, 12: 191–7.

Bright, J.R. (1958) *Automation and Management*, Boston: Houghton Mifflin.

British Institute of Management (1984) *Survey on Current Employee Participation Practices*, London: BIM.

Buchanan, D. (1987) 'Job Enrichment is Dead: Long Live High Performance Job Design', *Personnel Management*, May, 40–4.

Bumstead, D. and Eckblad, J. (1985) 'Meaning Business: Values in the Workplace', in Clutterbuck, D. (ed.) *op.cit.*, 66–77.

Burawoy, M. (1979) *Manufacturing Consent*, Chicago: University of Chicago Press.

—— (1985) *The Politics of Production*, London: Verso.

Burns, T. (1957) 'Management in Action', *Operational Research Quarterly*, 8 (2): 45–60.

—— (ed.) (1969) *Industrial Man*, Harmondsworth: Penguin.

Burns, T. and Stalker, G.M. (1968) *The Management of Innovation*, 2nd edn, London: Tavistock.

Burris, B. (1986) 'Technocratic Management: Social and Political

Implications', in Knights, D. and Willmott, H. (eds) *op.cit.*, 166–85.

Cappelli, P. and McKersie, R.B. (1987) 'Management Strategy and the Redesign of Workrules', *Journal of Management Studies*, 24 (5): 441–62.

Carchedi, G. (1975) 'The Economic Identification of the New Middle Class', *Economy and Society*, 4 (1).

Carlson, S. (1951) *Executive Behaviour*, Stockholm: Strombergs.

Carroll, D.T. (1983) 'A Disappointing Search for Excellence', *Harvard Business Review*, 61 (6), Nov/Dec: 78–88.

Carzo, R. and Yanouzas, J.N. (1969) 'Effects of Flat and Tall Organization Structures', *Administrative Science Quarterly*, 14 (2) June: 178–91.

Cavanaugh, M.S. (1984) 'A Typology of Social Power', in Kakabadse, A. and Parker, C. *Power, Politics and Organizations: A Behavioural Science View*, Chichester: Wiley, 3–20.

Cavendish, R. (1982) *Women on the Line*, London: Routledge & Kegan Paul.

Chandler, A.D. (1977) *The Visible Hand*, Cambridge, Mass.: Harvard University Press.

Chandler, A.D. and Daems, H. (eds) (1980) *Managerial Hierarchies: Comparative Perspectives on the Rise of the Modern Industrial Enterprise*, Cambridge, Mass.: Harvard University Press.

Chandler, M.K. and Sayles, L.R. (1971) *Managing Large Systems*, New York: Harper and Row.

Child, J. (1972) 'Organization Structure and Strategies of Control: A Replication of the Aston Studies', *Administrative Science Quarterly*, 17 (2) June: 163–77.

—— (ed.) (1973a) *Man and Organisation*, London: Allen & Unwin.

—— (1973b) 'Organisation: A Choice for Man', in Child, J. (ed.) *op.cit.*

—— (1973c) 'Organisational Structure, Environment and Performance: The Role of Strategic Choice', in Salaman, G. and Thompson, K. (eds) *op.cit.*, 95–107.

—— (1973d) 'Strategies of Control and Organizational Behaviour', *Administrative Science Quarterly*, 18 (1), March: 1–17.

—— (1977) *Organisation: A Guide to Problems and Practice*, London: Harper and Row.

—— (1985) 'Managerial Strategies, New Technology and the Labour Process', in Knights, D., Willmott, H. and Collinson, D. (eds) *Job Redesign: Critical Perspectives on the Labour Process*, Aldershot: Gower, 107–41.

Child, J. and Ellis, T. (1973) 'Predictors of Variation in Managerial Roles', *Human Relations*, 26 (2): 227–50.

Child, J., Fores, M., Glover, I. and Lawrence, P. (1983) 'A Price to Pay? Professionalism and Work Organisation in Britain and West Germany', *Sociology*, 17 (1).

Child, J. and Keiser, A. (1981) 'Organization and Managerial Roles in British and West German Companies: An examination of the "culture-free" thesis', in Hickson, D.J. and McMillan, C.J. (eds)

Organization and Nation, Aldershot: Gower, 51–73.

Clawson, D. (1980) *Bureaucracy and the Labor Process*, New York: Monthly Review Press.

Clegg, C. and Wall, T. (1984) 'The Lateral Dimension of Employee Participation', *Journal of Management Studies*, 21 (4): 429–42.

Clegg, S. (1975) *Power, Rule and Domination: A Critical and Empirical Understanding of Power in Sociological Theory and Organizational Life*, London: Routledge & Kegan Paul.

—— (1979) *The Theory of Power and Organizations*, London: Routledge & Kegan Paul.

—— (1990) *Modern Organizations*, London: Sage.

Clegg, S. and Dunkerley, D. (1980) *Organization, Class and Control*, London: Routledge & Kegan Paul.

Clutterbuck, D. (ed.) (1985) *New Patterns of Work*, Aldershot: Gower.

Cole, R.E. (1971) *Japanese Blue Collar: The Changing Tradition*, Berkeley, Calif.: University of California Press.

Collins, P.D. and Hull, F. (1986) 'Technology and Span of Control: Woodward Revisited', *Journal of Management Studies*, 23 (2): 143–64.

Cool, K.O. and Lengnick-Hall, C.A. (1985) 'Second Thoughts on the Transferability of the Japanese Management Style', *Organization Studies*, 6 (1): 1–22.

Cooper, C.L. and Mumford, E. (eds) (1979) *The Quality of Working Life in Western and Eastern Europe*, London: Associated Business Press.

Cooper, R. (1974) *Job Motivation and Job Design*, London: Institute of Personnel Management.

Copeman, G., Luijk, H. and Hanika, F. (1963) *How the Executive Spends His Time*, London: Business Publications Ltd.

Cotgrove, S., Dunham, J. and Vamplew, C. (1971) *The Nylon Spinners*, London: Allen & Unwin.

Crompton, R. and Jones, G. (1984) *White Collar Proletariat*, London: Macmillan.

Crompton, R. and Reid, S. (1983) 'The Deskilling of Clerical Work', in Wood, S. (ed.) *The Degradation of Work? Skill, Deskilling and the Labour Process*, London: Hutchinson, 163–78.

Crozier, M. (1964) *The Bureaucratic Phenomenon*, Chicago: University of Chicago Press.

—— (1973) 'The Problem of Power', *Social Research*, 40 (2): 211–28.

Cyert, R.M. and March, J.G. (1963) *A Behavioural Theory of the Firm*, New York: Prentice-Hall.

Dahl, R.A. (1957) 'The Concept of Power', *Behavioual Science*, 2: 201–5.

Dalton, M. (1959) *Men Who Manage*, New York: Wiley.

Davis, L.E. (1980) 'Changes in Work Environments: the Next 20 Years', in Duncan, K.D. *et al.* (eds) *op.cit.*, 197–216.

Davis, L.E. and Cherns, A.B. (eds) (1975a) *The Quality of Working Life, Vol I: Problems, Prospects and the State of the Art*, New York: Free Press.

—— (1975b) *The Quality of Working Life, Vol II: Cases and Commentary*, New York: Free Press.

Dawson, S. (1986) *Analysing Organisations*, Basingstoke: Macmillan.

de Bettignies, H.C. (1973) 'Japanese Organizational Behaviour: A Psycho-Cultural Approach', in Graves, D. (ed.) *Management Research: A Cross-Cultural Perspective*, Amsterdam: Elsevier, 75–93.

de Crespigny, A. (1968) 'Power and Its Forms', *Political Studies*, 16 (2): 192–205.

de Kadt, M. (1979) 'Insurance: A Clerical Work Factory', in Zimbalist, A. (ed.) *Case Studies on the Labor Process*, New York: Monthly Review Press, 242–56.

Deal, T.E. and Kennedy, A.A. (1982) *Corporate Cultures: the rites and rituals of corporate life*, Reading, Mass.: Addison-Wesley.

Doeringer, P.B. and Piore, M.J. (1971) *Internal Labour Markets and Manpower Analysis*, Lexington, Mass.: D.C. Heath.

Donaldson, L. (1985) 'Organization Design and the Product Life Cycle', *Journal of Management Studies*, 22 (1): 25–37.

—— (1987) 'Strategy and Structural Adjustment to Regain Fit: In Defence of Contingency Theory', *Journal of Management Studies*, 24 (1): 1–24.

Dore, R. (1973) *British Factory – Japanese Factory*, London: Allen & Unwin.

Drucker, P. (1970) *The Effective Executive*, London: Pan.

—— (1974) *Management: Tasks, Responsibilities, Practices*, London: Heinemann.

—— (1988) 'The Coming of New Organization', *Harvard Business Review*, Jan/Feb (1): 45–53.

—— (1989) *The Practice of Management*, Oxford: Heinemann Professional Publishing.

Dubin, R. and Spray, S.L. (1964) 'Executive Behaviour and Interaction', *Industrial Relations*, 3 (2): 99–108.

Duncan, K.D., Gruneberg, M.M. and Wallis, D. (eds) (1980) *Changes in Working Life*, Chichester: John Wiley & Sons.

Earl, M.J. (ed.) (1983) *Perspectives on Management: A multi-disciplinary analysis*, Oxford: Oxford University Press.

Edwards, R.C. (1979) *Contested Terrain*, London: Heinemann.

Eisenstadt, S.N. (1959) 'Bureaucracy, Bureaucratization and Debureaucratization', *Administrative Science Quarterly*, 4: 302–20.

Elger, A.J. (1983) 'Braverman, Capital Accumulation and Deskilling', in Wood, S. (ed.) *op.cit.*, 23–53.

Elliott, D. (1980) 'The Organization as a System', in Salaman, G. and Thompson, K. (eds) *Control and Ideology in Organizations*, Milton Keynes: Open University Press, 85–102.

Elliott, J. (1984) *Conflict or Cooperation? The Growth of Industrial Democracy*, London: Kogan Page.

Emerson, R.A. (1962) 'Power-dependence Relations', *American Sociological Review*, 27: 31–41.

Emery, F.E. and Trist, E.L. (1960) 'Socio-Technical Systems', in Emery, F.E. (ed.) *Systems Thinking*, Harmondsworth: Penguin.

—— (1965) 'The Causal Texture of Organizational Environments', *Human Relations*, 18: 21–32.

Esland, G. (1980) 'Professions and Professionalism', in Esland, G. and Salaman, G. (eds) *The Politics of Work and Occupations*, Milton Keynes: Open University Press, 213–50.

Etzioni, A. (1961) *A Comparative Analysis of Complex Organizations*, New York: Free Press.

Faunce, W.A. and Dubin, R. (1975) 'Individual Investment in Working and Living', in Davis, L.E. and Cherns, A.B. (eds) *op.cit.*, 299–316.

Fayol, H. (1949) *General and Industrial Management*, trans. C. Storrs, London: Pitman.

Fein, M. (1970) *Approaches to Motivation*, New Jersey: Hillside.

Ferguson, A. (1990) 'Horticulture Hits the Brigadier Belt', *Independent on Sunday*, 8 April.

Filley, A.C. and House, R.J. (1976) *Managerial Process and Organisational Behaviour*, 2nd edn, Glenview, Ill.: Scott Foresman.

Fletcher, C. (1973) 'The End of Management', in Child, J. (ed.) *Man and Organisation*, London: Allen & Unwin, 135–57.

Folkard, S. (1987) 'Circadian Rhythms and Hours of Work', in Warr, P. (ed.) *Psychology at Work*, 3rd edn, Harmondsworth: Penguin, 30–52.

Follett, M. Parker (1941) *Dynamic Administration*, Metcalf, H.C. and Urwick, L.F. (eds), London: Pitman.

Ford, J.D. and Baucus, D.A. (1987) 'Organizational Adaptation to Performance Downturns: An Interpretation-based Perspective', *Academy of Management Review*, 12 (2): 366–80.

Ford, R.N. (1973) 'Job Enrichment Lessons from AT & T', *Harvard Business Review*, Jan/Feb: 96–106.

Fox, A. (1974) *Beyond Contract: Work, Power and Trust Relationships*, London: Faber & Faber.

—— (1985) *Man Mismanagement*, 2nd edn, London: Hutchinson.

Fraser, R. (1968) *Work: 20 Personal Accounts*, Harmondsworth: Penguin.

French, J.P.R. Jnr and Raven, B. (1959) 'The Bases of Social Power', in Cartwright, D. (ed.) *Studies in Social Power*, Ann Arbor, Mich.: Institute for Social Research.

Friedman, A.L. (1977) *Industry and Labour*, London: Macmillan.

Friedmann, G. (1964) *Industrial Society: The Emergence of the Human Problems of Automation*, Glencoe, Ill.: Free Press.

Gabriel, Y. (1988) *Working Lives in Catering*, London: Routledge.

Galbraith, J.K. (1974) *The New Industrial State*, 2nd edn, Harmondsworth: Penguin.

Galbraith, J.R. (1973) *Designing Complex Organizations*, Reading, Mass.: Addison-Wesley.

—— (1977) *Organization Design*, Reading, Mass.: Addison-Wesley.

Gartman, D. (1979) 'Origins of the Assembly Line and Capitalist Control of Work at Ford', in Zimbalist, A. (ed.) *Case Studies on the Labor Process*, New York: Monthly Review Press, 193–205.

Gaventa, J. (1980) *Power and Powerlessness*, Oxford: Oxford University Press.

Giddens, A. (1982) 'Power, the Dialectic of Control and Class Structuration', in Giddens, A. and Mackenzie, G. (eds) *Social Class and the Division of Labour*, Cambridge: Cambridge University Press, 29–45.

Glenn, E.N. and Feldberg, R.L. (1979) 'Proletarianizing Clerical Work: Technology and Organizational Control in the Office', in Zimbalist, A. (ed.) *op.cit.*, 51–72.

Goffee, R. (1977) 'The Butty System and the Kent Coalfield', *Bulletin of the Society for the Study of Labour History*, 34, Spring.

Goffee, R. and Scase, R. (1985) 'Proprietorial Control in Family Firms: Some Functions of "Quasi-Organic" Management Systems', *Journal of Management Studies*, 22 (1): 53–68.

Golding, D. (1979) 'Symbolism, Sovereignty and Domination in an Industrial Hierarchical Organisation', *Sociological Review*, 27 (1): 169–77.

—— (1980) 'Establishing Blissful Clarity in Organisational Life: Managers', *Sociological Review*, 28 (4): 763–82.

Goldman, P. and Van Houten, D.R. (1977) 'Managerial Strategies and the Worker: A Marxist Analysis of Bureaucracy', *The Sociological Quarterly*, 18 (1): 108–25.

Goldsmith, W. and Clutterbuck, D. (1984) *The Winning Streak*, London: Weidenfeld & Nicolson.

Goldthorpe, J.H., Lockwood, D., Bechhofer, F. and Platt, J. (1968) *The Affluent Worker: Industrial Attitudes and Behaviour*, Cambridge: Cambridge University Press.

Goodale, J.G., Hall, D.T., Burke, R.J. and Joyner, R.C. (1975) 'Some Significant Contexts and Components of Industrial Quality of Life', in Davis, L.E. and Cherns, A.B. (eds) *op.cit.*, 1975a, 150–4.

Gordon, D.M., Edwards, R. and Reich, M. (1982) *Segmented Work, Divided Workers: The Historical Transformation of Labor in the United States*, Cambridge: Cambridge University Press.

Gouldner, A.W. (1955a) *Wildcat Strike*, London: Routledge & Kegan Paul.

—— (1955b) *Patterns of Industrial Bureaucracy*, London: Routledge & Kegan Paul.

—— (1957) 'Cosmopolitans and Locals: Towards an Analysis of Latent Social Roles', *Administrative Science Quarterly*, 1 (2).

—— (1966) 'Metaphysical Pathos and Theory of Bureaucracy', *American Political Science Review*, 49: 496–507.

Gowler, D. and Legge, K. (1983) 'The Meaning of Management and the Management of Meaning: A view from Social Anthropology', in Earl, M. (ed.) *op.cit.*, Oxford: Oxford University Press, 197–233.

Grimes, A.J. (1978) 'Authority, Power, Influence and Social Control: A Theoretical Synthesis', *Academy of Management Review*, Oct: 724–35.

Grusky, O. and Miller, G.A. (eds) (1970) *The Sociology of Organizations: Basic Studies*, New York: Free Press.

—— (1981) *The Sociology of Organizations: Basic Studies*, 2nd edn, New York: Free Press.

Guest, D., Williams, R. and Dewe, P. (1980) 'Workers' Perceptions of Changes Affecting the Quality of Working Life', in Duncan, K.D. *et al.* (eds) *op.cit.*, 499–519.

Gulick, L. (1937) 'Notes on the Theory of Organization', in Gulick, L. and Urwick, L. (eds) *Papers on the Science of Administration*, New York: Columbia University Press.

Gyllenhammar, P.G. (1977) *People at Work*, Reading, Mass.: Addison-Wesley.

Habermas, J. (1971) *Toward a Rational Society*, London: Heinemann.

Hackman, J.R., Oldham, G., Janson, R. and Purdy, K. (1975) 'A New Strategy for Job Enrichment', *California Management Review*, 17 (4): 57–71.

Hage, J. (1977) 'Choosing Constraints and Constraining Choice', in Warner, M. (ed.) *Organizational Choice and Constraint*, Farnborough: Saxon House, 1–56.

Hage, J. and Aiken, M. (1972) 'Routine Technology, Social Structure and Organisational Goals', in Hall, R.H. (ed.) *The Formal Organization*, New York: Basic Books.

Hales, C.P. (1986) 'What Do Managers Do? A Critical Review of the Evidence', *Journal of Management Studies*, 23 (1) Jan: 88–115.

—— (1987a) 'Quality of Working Life, Job Redesign and Participation in a Service Industry: A Rose by Any Other Name?', *Service Industries Journal*, 7 (3), July: 253–73.

—— (1987b) 'The Manager's Work in Context: A Pilot Investigation of the Relationship Between Managerial Role Demands and Role Performance', *Personnel Review*, 16 (5): 26–33.

Hales, C.P. and Nightingale, M. (1986) 'What Are Unit Managers Supposed to Do? A Contingent Methodology for Investigating Managerial Role Requirements', *International Journal of Hospitality Management*, 5 (1): 3–11.

Hales, M. (1980) *Living Thinkwork: Where do Labour Processes come From?*, London: CSE Books.

Hall, R.H. (1963) 'The Concept of Bureaucracy: An Empirical Assessment', *American Journal of Sociology*, 69 (1) July: 32–40.

—— (1973) 'Professionalization and Bureaucratization', in Salaman, G. and Thompson, K. (eds), *op.cit.*, 120–33.

Hammond, V. (ed.) (1985) *Current Research in Management*, London: Frances Pinter.

Handy, C. (1981) *Understanding Organizations*, 2nd edn, Harmondsworth: Penguin.

—— (1984) *The Future of Work*, London: Basil Blackwell.

—— (1989) *The Age of Unreason*, London: Hutchinson.

Hannan, M.T. and Freeman, J. (1977) 'The Population Ecology of Organizations', *American Journal of Sociology*, 82 (5) March: 929–64.

Haraszti, M. (1977) *A Worker in a Worker's State: Piece Rates in Hungary*, Harmondsworth: Penguin.

Harbison, F. and Myers, C.A. (1959) *Management in the Industrial World: An International Analysis*, New York: McGraw-Hill.

Harris, R. (1987) *Power and Powerlessness in Industry*, London: Tavistock.

Harsanyi, J.E. (1962) 'Measurement of Social Power, Opportunity Costs and the Theory of Two-Person Bargaining Games', *Behavior Science*, 7: 67–80.

Hatvany, N. and Pucik, V. (1981) 'An Integrated Management System: Lessons from the Japanese Experience', *Academy of Management Review*, 6 (3): 469–80.

Hayes, R.H. and Abernathy, W. (1980) 'Managing Our Way to Economic Decline', *Harvard Business Review*, 58 (4): 67–77.

Hedberg, B. and Mumford, E. (1979) 'Design of Computer Systems', in Davis, L.E. and Taylor, J.C. *Design of Jobs*, 2nd edn, Santa Monica, Calif.: Goodyear Publishing Co.

Hedberg, B.L.T., Nystrom, P.C. and Starbuck, W.H. (1976) 'Camping on SeeSaws: Prescriptions for a Self-Designing Organization', *Administrative Science Quarterly*, 21 (1).

Heller, R. (1972) *The Naked Manager*, London: Barrie and Jenkins.

Hemphill, J.K. (1959) 'Job Descriptions for Executives', *Harvard Business Review*, 37 (5).

Henning, D.A. and Moseley, R.L. (1980) 'Authority Role of a Functional Manager: The Controller', in Litterer, J. (ed.) *Organizations: Structure and Behaviour*, 3rd edn, New York: Wiley, 288–96.

Herbst, P.G. (1974) *Socio-Technical Design*, London: Tavistock.

Herrick, N.Q. (1981) 'The Means and Ends of Work', *Human Relations*, 34 (7): 611–32.

Herrick, N.Q. and Maccoby, M. (1975) 'Humanizing Work: A Priority Goal of the 1970s', in Davis and Cherns (eds) *op.cit.*, Vol. 1, 63–85.

Herzberg, F. (1966) *Work and the Nature of Man*, Cleveland: World Publishing.

Heyderbrand, W. (1977) 'Organizational Contradictions in Public Bureaucracies: Towards a Marxian Theory of Organizations', *The Sociological Quarterly*, 18 (1), Winter: 83–107.

Hickson, D.J., Hinings, C.R., Lee, C.A., Schneck, R.C. and Pennings, J.M. (1971) 'A Strategic Contingencies Theory of Intra-Organizational Power', *Administrative Science Quarterly*, 16 (2): 216–29.

Hickson, D.J. and McCullough (1980) 'Power in Organisations', in Salaman, G. and Thompson, K. (eds) *op.cit.*, 27–55.

Hickson, D.J. and McMillan, C.J. (eds) (1981) *Organization and Nation*, Aldershot: Gower.

Hill, C. (1982) 'Job Redesign and the UK Insurance Industry', in Ondrack, D. and Timperley, S. (eds) *The Humanisation of Work: A European Perspective*, London: Armstrong, 115–44.

Hill, C.W.L. (1984) 'Organisational Structure, the Development of the Firm and Business Behaviour', in Pickering, J.F. and Cockerill, T.A.J. *The Economic Management of the Firm*, Oxford: Philip Allan, 52–71.

Hill, F.R. (1986) 'Quality Circles in the UK: A Longitudinal Study', *Personnel Review*, 15 (3): 25–34.

Hill, S. (1981) *Competition and Control at Work*, London: Heinemann.

Hinings, C.R., Hickson, D.J., Pennings, J.M. and Schneck, R.E. (1974) 'Structural Conditions of Intra Organizational Power', *Administrative Science Quarterly*, 19 (2): 21–44.

Hirsch, P.M. (1975) 'Organizational Effectiveness and the Institutional Environment', *Administrative Science Quarterly*, 20 (4): 327–44.

Hofstede, G. (1979) 'Humanisation of Work: The Role of Values in a Third Industrial Revolution', in Cooper, C.L. and Mumford, E. (eds) *op.cit.*, 18–37.

—— (1980) *Culture's Consequences*, Beverly Hills, Calif.: Sage.

Horne, J.H. and Lupton, T. (1965) 'The Work Activities of "Middle Managers" – an Exploratory Study', *Journal of Management Studies*, 2 (1): 14–33.

Howard, N. and Teramoto, Y. (1981) 'The Really Important Difference Between Japanese and Western Management', *Management International Review*, 21 (3): 19–30.

Hulin, C.I. and Blood, M.R. (1968) 'Job Enlargement, Individual Differences and Worker Responses', *Psychological Bulletin*, 69 (1): 41–55.

Hyman, R. (1988) 'Flexible Specialisation: Miracle or Myth?', in Hyman, R. and Streeck, W. (eds) *New Technology and Industrial Relations*, Oxford: Blackwell.

Hyman, R. and Streeck, W. (eds) (1988) *New Technology and Industrial Relations*, Oxford: Blackwell.

IDE International Research Group (1981) 'Industrial Democracy in Europe: Differences and Similarities Across Countries and Hierarchies', *Organization Studies*, 2 (2): 113–29.

Inkson, J.H.K., Schwitter, J., Pheysey, D.C. and Hickson, D.J. (1981) 'A Comparison of Organization Structure and Managerial Roles: Ohio, USA and Midlands, England', in Hickson, D.J. and McMillan, C.J. (eds) *op.cit.*, 21–36.

International Labour Organisation (1979) *New Forms of Work Organisation*, Geneva: ILO.

Jacques, E. (1976) *A General Theory of Bureaucracy*, London: Heinemann.

Johnson, T. (1972) *Professions and Power*, London: Macmillan.

—— (1977) 'The Professions in the Class Structure', in Scase, R. (ed.) *Industrial Society: Class, Cleavage and Control*, London: George Allen & Unwin, 93–110.

—— (1980) 'Work and Power', in Esland, G. and Salaman, G. (eds) *op.cit.*, 335–71.

Kakabadse, A. and Parker, C. (eds) (1984) *Power, Politics and Organizations: A Behavioural Science View*, Chichester: Wiley.

Kanawaty, G. (ed.) (1981a) *Managing and Developing New Forms of Work Organisation*, ILO Management Development Series, No. 16, Geneva: ILO.

—— (1981b) 'Introducing and Developing New Forms of Work Organisation', in Kanawaty, G. (ed.) *op.cit.*, 169–206.

Kanter, R.M. (1977) *Men and Women of the Corporation*, New York: Basic Books.

—— (1985) *The Change Masters: Corporate Entrepreneurs at Work*, London: Unwin.

—— (1990) *When Giants Learn to Dance: Mastering the Challenges of Strategy, Management and Careers in the 1990s*, London: Unwin.

Kaplan, A. (1964) 'Power in Perspective', in Kahn, R.L. and Boulding, E. (eds) *Power and Conflict in Organization*, London: Tavistock.

Katz, D. and Kahn, R.L. (1970) 'Open-Systems Theory', in Grusky, O. and Miller, G. (eds) *op.cit.*, 149–58.

Kaufman, H. and Seidman, D. (1970) 'The Morphology of Organizations', *Administrative Science Quarterly*, 15: 439–51.

Kavcic, B. (1979) 'Yugoslavia: The Concept of Self Management', in Cooper, C.L. and Mumford, E. (eds) *op.cit.*, 327–36.

Kaye, D. (1989) *Game Change: The Impact of Information Technology on Corporate Strategies and Structures*, Oxford: Heinemann.

Keidel, R.W. (1982) 'QWL Development: Three Trajectories', *Human Relations*, 35 (9): 743–61.

Kelly, J. (1964) 'The Study of Executive Behaviour by Activity Sampling', *Human Relations*, 17 (3): 277–87.

Kelly, J.E. (1982) *Scientific Management, Job Redesign and Work Performance*, London: Academic Press.

Kelly, J. (1985) 'Management's Redesign of Work: Labour Process, Labour Markets and Product Markets', in Knights, D. *et al.* (eds) *op.cit.*, 30–51.

Kelly, J. and Clegg, C.W. (eds) (1982) *Autonomy and Control at the Workplace: Contexts for Job Redesign*, London: Croom Helm.

Kerr, C., Dunlop, J.T., Harbison, F. and Myers, C.A. (1973) *Industrialism and Industrial Man*, Harmondsworth: Penguin.

Khandwalla, P.N. (1974) 'Mass Output Orientation of Operations, Technology and Organization Structure', *Administrative Science Quarterly*, 19, March: 74–97.

Kinnie, N. (1989) 'Human Resource Management and Changes in Management Control Systems', in Storey, J. (ed.) *New Perspectives on Human Resource Management*, London: Routledge, 137–53.

Knight, K. (ed.) (1977) *Matrix Management: A Cross-Functional Approach to Organisation*, Farnborough: Gower.

—— (1979) 'Introducing Participation', in Guest, D. and Knight, K. (eds) *Putting Participation into Practice*, Farnborough: Gower, 267–86.

Knights, D. and Collinson, D. (1985) 'Redesigning Work on the Shopfloor: A Question of Control or Consent?', in Knights D. *et al.* (eds) *op.cit.*, 197–226.

Knights, D. and Roberts, J. (1982) 'The Power of Organization or the Organization of Power?', *Organization Studies*, 3 (1): 47–53.

Knights, D. and Willmott, H. (1985) 'Power and Identity in Theory and Practice', *Sociological Review*, 33 (1), Feb: 22–46.

—— (eds) (1986) *Managing the Labour Process*, Aldershot: Gower.

Knights, D., Willmott, H. and Collinson, D. (eds) (1985) *Job Redesign: Critical Perspectives on the Labour Process*, Aldershot: Gower.

Kolarska, L. and Aldrich, H. (1980) 'Exit, Voice and Silence: Consumers' and Managers' Responses to Organizational Decline', *Organization Studies*, 1 (1): 41–58.

Koontz, H., O'Donnell, C. and Weihrich, H. (1984) *Management*, 8th edn, Tokyo: McGraw-Hill.

Kotter, J.P. (1977) 'Power, Dependence and Effective Management', *Harvard Business Review*, 55 (4): 125–36.

Kotter, J. (1982) *The General Managers*, New York: Free Press.

Kotter, P. (1985) *Power and Influence*, New York: Free Press.

Kraft, P. (1979) 'The Industrialization of Computer Programming', in Zimbalist, A. (ed.) *op.cit.*, 3–17.

Lammers, S.J. (1967) 'Power and Participation in Decision-making in Formal Organizations', *American Journal of Sociology*, 73 (2): 201–16.

Lamphere, L. (1979) 'Fighting the Piece Rate System: New Dimensions of an Old Struggle in the Apparel Industry', in Zimbalist, A. (ed.) *op.cit.*, 257–76.

Lawler, E.E. and Ledford, G.E. (1981/2) 'Productivity and the Quality of Work Life', *National Productivity Review*, 1 (1): 23–36.

Lawrence, P. (1984) *Management in Action*, London: Routledge & Kegan Paul.

Lawrence, P.R. and Lorsch, J.W. (1967) *Organization and Environment*, Boston: Harvard University Press.

Lazonick, W. (1978) 'The Subjection of Labour to Capital: The Rise of the Capitalist System', *Review of Radical Political Economics*, 10 (1): 1–31.

Lebas, M. and Weigenstein, J. (1986) 'Management Control: The Role of Rules, Markets and Culture', *Journal of Management Studies*, 23 (3): 259–72.

Lee, D. (1983) 'Beyond Deskilling: Skill, Craft and Class', in Wood, S. (ed.) *op.cit.*, 146–62.

Legge, K. (1978) *Power, Innovation and Problem-Solving in Personnel Management*, London: McGraw-Hill.

Likert, R. (1961) *New Patterns of Management*, Tokyo: McGraw-Hill.

Littler, C. (1982) *The Development of the Labour Process in Capitalist Societies*, London: Heinemann.

Littler, C. (1983) 'Deskilling and Changing Structures of Control', in Wood, S. (ed.) *op.cit.*, 122–45.

—— (1985) 'Taylorism, Fordism and Job Design', in Knights, D. *et al.* (eds) *op.cit.*, 10–29.

Littler, C.R. and Salaman, G. (1984) *Class at Work: The Design, Allocation and Control of Jobs*, London: Batsford Academic.

—— (1985) 'The Design of Jobs', in Littler, C.R. (ed.) *The Experience of Work*, Aldershot: Gower, 85–104.

Locke, E.A. (1976) 'The Nature and Causes of Job Satisfaction', in Dunnette, M.D. (ed.) *Handbook of Industrial and Organizational Psychology*, Chicago: Rand McNally.

Locke, E.A., Feren, D.B., McCaleb, V.M., Shaw, K.N. and Denny, A.T. (1980) 'The Relative Effectiveness of Four Methods of Motivating

Employee Performance', in Duncan, K.D. *et al.* (eds) *op.cit.*, 363–88.

Lorsch, J.W. and Morse, J.J. (1974) *Organizations and Their Members: A Contingency Approach*, New York: Harper and Row.

Lukes, S. (1974) *Power: A Radical View*, London: Macmillan.

Lund, R. (1980) 'Indirect Participation, Influence and Power: Some Danish Experiences', *Organization Studies*, 1 (2): 147–60.

Luthans, F. and Davis, T. (1980) 'Managers in Action: A New Look at their Behaviour and Operating Modes', *Organizational Dynamics*, Summer: 64–80.

Luthans, F. and Lockwood, D.L. (1984) 'Toward an Observational System for Measuring Leader Behaviour in Natural Settings', in Hunt, J. *et al.* (eds) *Leaders and Managers*, Pergamon: New York, 117–41.

Luthans, F., Hodgetts, R.M. and Rosenkrantz, S.A. (1988) *Real Managers*, Cambridge, Mass.: Ballinger Publishing Co.

McCall, M.W. (1979) 'Power, Authority and Influence', in Kerr, S. (ed.) *Organizational Behaviour*, Columbus, Ohio: Grid.

McGregor, D. (1960) *The Human Side of the Enterprise*, New York: McGraw-Hill.

Machin, J.L.J. (1982) *The Expectations Approach*, Maidenhead: McGraw-Hill.

McNeil, K. (1978) 'Understanding Organizational Power: Building on the Weberian Legacy', *Administrative Science Quarterly*, 23 (1): 65–90.

Mandel, E. (1975) *Late Capitalism*, London: New Left Books.

Mangham, I. (1986) *Power and Performance in Organizations*, Oxford: Basil Blackwell.

Mansfield, R. (1973) 'Bureaucracy and Centralization: An Examination of Organizational Structure', *Administrative Science Quarterly*, 18 (4): 477–88.

Mansfield, R., Todd, D. and Wheeler, J. (1980) 'Structural Implications of Company–Customer Interface', *Journal of Management Studies*, 17 (1): 19–33.

Mant, A. (1977) *The Rise and Fall of the British Manager*, London: Macmillan.

—— (1983) *Leaders We Deserve*, Oxford: Martin Robertson.

March, J.G. and Olsen, J.P. (1976) *Ambiguity and Choice in Organizations*, Oslo: Universitetsforlaget.

March, J.G. and Simon, H. (1971) 'The Dysfunctions of Bureaucracy', in Pugh, D.S. (ed.) *Organization Theory*, Harmondsworth: Penguin, 30–41.

Marchington, M. (1988) 'The Four Faces of Employee Consultation', *Personnel Management*, May: 44–7.

Marglin, S.A. (1976) 'What Do Bosses Do? The Origins and Functions of Hierarchy in Capitalist Production', in Gorz, A. (ed.) *The Division of Labour*, Brighton: Harvester, 13–54.

Marshall, J. and McLean, A. (1985) 'Exploring Organisation Culture as a Route to Organisational Change', in Hammond, V. (ed.) *op.cit.*, 2–20.

Martin, M. (1970) 'Operational Research: A New Discipline', in

Tillett, A. *et al.* (eds) *Management Thinkers*, Harmondsworth: Penguin, 140–65.

Martin, R. (1977) *The Sociology of Power*, London: Routledge & Kegan Paul.

Martinko, M.J. and Gardner, W.L. (1984) 'The Observation of High-Performing Educational Managers: Methodological Issues and Managerial Implications', in Hunt, J.G. *et al.* (eds) *Leaders and Managers*, Pergamon: New York, 142–62.

Marx, K. (1976) *Capital, Vol I*, Harmondsworth: Penguin.

Maslow, A.H. (1970) *Motivation and Personality*, 2nd edn, New York: Harper and Row.

Mayo, E. (1975) *The Social Problems of an Industrial Civilisation*, London: Routledge.

Mechanic, D. (1962) 'Sources of Power of Lower Participants in Complex Organizations', *Administrative Science Quarterly*, 7 (3): 349–64.

Merton, R.K. (1966) 'Bureaucratic Structure and Personality', in Coser, L. and Rosenberg, B. *Sociological Theory: A Book of Readings*, 2nd edn, London: Collier-Macmillan.

Meyer, M.W. (1968) 'The Two Authority Structures of Bureaucracy', *Administrative Science Quarterly*, 13: 211–28.

Meyer, M.W. and Brown, M.C. (1977) 'The Process of Bureau-cratization', *American Journal of Sociology*, 83 (2): 364–85.

Meyer, J.W. and Rowan, B. (1977) 'Institutionalized Organizations: Formal Structure as Myth and Ceremony', *American Journal of Sociology*, 83 (2): 340–63.

Michels, R. (1970) 'Oligarchy', in Grusky, O. and Miller, G.A. (eds) *op.cit.*, 25–43.

Millar, J.A. (1978) 'Contingency Theory: Values and Change', *Human Relations*, 31 (10): 883–904.

Miller, D. (1981) 'Towards a New Contingency Approach: The Search for Organizational Gestalts', *Journal of Management Studies*, 18 (1): 1–26.

Miller, E.J. and Rice, A.K. (1967) *Systems of Organization: The Control of Task and Sentient Boundaries*, London: Tavistock.

Mintzberg, H. (1973) *The Nature of Managerial Work*, New York: Harper & Row.

—— (1979) *The Structuring of Organizations: A Synthesis of the Research*, New York: Prentice-Hall.

—— (1983) *Power In and Around Organizations*, Englewood Cliffs, N.J.: Prentice-Hall.

More, C. (1983) 'Skill and the Survival of Apprenticeship', in Wood, S. (ed.) *op.cit.*

Morse, J.J. and Lorsch, J.W. (1970) 'Beyond Theory Y', *Harvard Business Review*, May–June.

Mouzelis, N. (1975) *Organisation and Bureaucracy* (revised edn), London: Routledge & Kegan Paul.

Mumford, E. (1972) 'Job Satisfaction: A Method of Analysis', *Personnel Review*, Summer.

Murray, F. (1988) 'The Decentralisation of Production – The Decline of the Mass-Collective Worker?', in Pahl, R. (ed.) *On Work*, Oxford: Blackwell, 258–78.

Nadler, A.A. and Lawler, E.E. (1983) 'Quality of Work Life: Perspectives and Directions', *Organizational Dynamics*, Winter: 20–30.

Nadworny, M.J. (1955) *Scientific Management and the Unions, 1900–32*, Cambridge, Mass.: Harvard University Press.

Nash, M. (1983) *Managing Organizational Performance*, San Francisco: Jossey Bass.

Nath, R. (1968) 'A Methodological Review of Cross-Cultural Management Research', *International Social Science Journal*, 20 (1): 35–62.

Nelson, R. and Winter, S. (1982) *An Evolutionary Theory of Economic Change*, Boston: Belknap Press.

Nichols, T. (1980) 'Management, Ideology and Practice', in Esland, G. and Salaman, G. (eds) *op.cit.*, 279–302.

Nichols, T. and Armstrong, P. (1976) *Workers Divided: A Study in Shopfloor Politics*, London: Fontana/Collins.

Nichols, T. and Beynon, H. (1977) *Living With Capitalism*, London: Routledge & Kegan Paul.

Offe, C. (1976) *Industry and Inequality*, trans. and with an introduction by J. Wickham, London: Edward Arnold.

Oh, T.K. (1976) 'Japanese Management – A Critical Review', *Academy of Management Review*, 1, Jan: 14–25.

Ondrack, D. and Timperley, S. (eds) (1982) *The Humanisation of Work: A European Perspective*, London: Armstrong.

Ouchi, W.G. (1981) *Theory Z: How American Business can Meet the Japanese Challenge*, New York: Addison-Wesley.

Palloix, C. (1976) *The Labour Process: From Fordism to Neo-Fordism*, CSE Pamphlet No. 1, The Labour Process and Class Struggle, London, 46–67.

Palmer, B. (1975) 'Class, Conception and Conflict: The Thrust for Efficiency, Managerial Views of Labour and the Working Class Rebellion 1903–1922', *Review of Radical Political Economy*, 7: 31–49.

Parsons, T. (1964) 'A Sociological Approach to the Theory of Organizations', in Parsons, T. *Structure and Processes in Modern Society*, Glencoe, Ill.: Free Press.

—— (1970) 'Social Systems', in Grusky, O. and Miller, G. (eds) *op.cit.*, 75–82.

Pascale, R. (1991) *Managing on the Edge: How Successful Companies Use Conflict to Stay Ahead*, Harmondsworth: Penguin.

Pascale, R.T. and Athos, A.G. (1982) *The Art of Japanese Management*, Harmondsworth: Penguin.

Paul, W., Robertson, K. and Herzberg, F. (1969) 'Job Enrichment Pays Off', *Harvard Business Review*, March–April.

Peabody, R.L. (1970) 'Perceptions of Organizational Authority', in Grusky, O. and Miller, G.A. (eds) *op.cit.*, 319–28.

Penn, R. (1983) 'Skilled Manual Workers in the Labour Process 1856–1964', in Wood, S. (ed.) *op.cit.*, 90–108.

Pennings, J.M. (1975) 'The Relevance of the Structural-Contingency Model for Organizational Effectiveness', *Administrative Science Quarterly*, 20: 393–410.

Perrow, C. (1970) 'Departmental Power and Perspectives in Industrial Firms', in M.N. Zald (ed.) *op.cit.*

—— (1971) *Organizational Analysis: A Sociological View*, London: Tavistock.

—— (1972) *Complex Organizations: A Critical Essay*, Glenview, Ill.: Scott, Foresman & Co.

—— (1974) 'Is Business Really Changing?', *Organizational Dynamics*, 3 (1): 31–44.

—— (1979) *Complex Organizations: A Critical Essay*, 2nd edn, Dallas: Scott, Foresman.

—— (1986) *Complex Organizations: A Critical Essay*, 3rd edn, New York: Randon House.

Peters, T. (1989) *Thriving on Chaos*, London: Pan.

Peters, T.J. and Austin, N. (1986) *A Passion for Excellence: The Leadership Difference*, Glasgow: Fontana/Collins.

Peters, T.J. and Waterman, R.H. (1982) *In Search of Excellence: Lessons from America's Best-Run Companies*, New York: Harper & Row.

Peterson, M.F., Peterson, S. and Macy, B.A. (1982) 'Study of a Quality of Work Life Program: Organizational Control, Experienced Influence and Objective Involvement', *Group and Organizational Studies*, 7 (4): 476–84.

Pettigrew, A.M. (1972) 'Information Control as a Power Resource', *Sociology*, 6 (2): 187–204.

Pfeffer, J. (1981) *Power in Organizations*, Boston: Pitman.

Pfeffer, J. and Leblebici, H. (1973) 'The Effect of Competition on Some Dimensions of Organization Structure', *Social Forces*, 52 (2): 268–79.

Pfeffer, J. and Salancik, G. (1978) *The External Control of Organizations: A Resource Dependency Perspective*, New York: Harper & Row.

Pfeffer, R. (1979) *Working for Capitalism*, New York: Columbia University Press.

Pheysey, D.C. (1972) 'Activities of Middle Managers – A Training Guide', *Journal of Management Studies*, 9: 158–71.

Pinchot, G. III (1985) *Intrapreneuring*, New York: Harper & Row.

Piore, M.J. and Sabel, C.F. (1984) *The Second Industrial Divide: Possibilities for Prosperity*, New York: Basic Books.

Pollard, S. (1968) *The Genesis of Modern Management*, Harmondsworth: Penguin.

Poole, M. (1986) *Towards a New Industrial Democracy: Workers' Participation in Industry*, London: Routledge & Kegan Paul.

Presthus, R. (1979) *The Organizational Society*, revised edn, London: Macmillan.

Pugh, D.S. (ed.) (1971) *Organization Theory*, Harmondsworth: Penguin.

—— (1973) 'The Management of Organization Structures: Does Context Determine Form?', *Organizational Dynamics*, Spring: 19–34.

Pugh, D.S. and Hickson, D.J. (1973) 'The Comparative Study of Organizations', in Salaman, G. and Thompson, K. (eds) *op.cit.*, 50–66.

—— (1976) *Organizational Structure in Its Context*, Farnborough: Saxon House.

Pugh, D.S., Hickson, D.J., Hinings, C.R. and Turner, C. (1968) 'Dimensions of Organization Structure', *Administrative Science Quarterly*, 13: 65–105.

Pugh, D.S. and Hinings, C.R. (eds) (1976) *Organizational Studies: Extensions and Replications*, Farnborough: Saxon House.

Ramsay, H. (1980) 'Participation: The Pattern and Its Significance', in Nichols, T. (ed.) *Capital and Labour: A Marxist Primer*, Glasgow: Fontana, 381–94.

—— (1985) 'What is Participation For? A Critical Evaluation of "Labour Process" Analyses of Job Reform', in Knights, D. *et al.*, *op.cit.*, 52–80.

Raven, B. (1965) 'Social Influence and Power', in Steiner, I.D. and Fishbein, M. (eds) *Current Studies in Social Psychology*, New York: Holt, Reinhart and Winston.

Ray, C.A. (1986) 'Corporate Culture: The Last Frontier of Control?', *Journal of Management Studies*, 23 (3): 287–97.

Reed, M. (1989) *The Sociology of Management*, Hemel Hempstead: Harvester Wheatsheaf.

Reeves, T.K. and Woodward, J. (1970) 'The Study of Managerial Control', in Woodward, J. (ed.) *Industrial Organisation: Theory and Practice*, Oxford: Oxford University Press.

Reif, W.E. and Luthans, F. (1972) 'Does Job Enrichment Really Pay Off?', *California Management Review*, 15 (1): 30–7.

Reimann, B.C. (1973) 'On the Dimensions of Bureaucratic Structure: An Empirical Reappraisal', *Administrative Science Quarterly*, 18 (4): 462–76.

Reynolds, P.D. (1986) 'Organisational Culture as Related to Industry, Position and Performance: A Preliminary Report', *Journal of Management Studies*, 23 (3): 333–45.

Rice, A.K. (1963) *The Enterprise and its Environment*, London: Tavistock.

Robson, M.P. (1981) *Worker Participation in the UK*, Bradford: MCB Publications.

Robson, M. (1984) *Quality Circles in Action*, Aldershot: Gower.

Roethlisberger, F.J. and Dickson, W.J. (1939) *Management and the Worker*, Cambridge, Mass.: Harvard University Press.

Rose, M. (1988) *Industrial Behaviour: Theoretical Developments Since Taylor* (new edition), Harmondsworth: Penguin.

Rose, M. and Jones, B. (1985) 'Managerial Strategy and Trade Union Responses in Work Reorganisation Schemes at Establishment Level', in Knights, D. *et al.* (eds) *op.cit.*, 81–106.

Roy, D. (1952) 'Quota Restriction and Gold-Bricking in a Machine Shop', *American Journal of Sociology*, 57, March: 427–42.

—— (1955) 'Efficiency and "the Fix": Informal Intergroup Relations in a Piece-work Machine Shop', *American Journal of Sociology*, 60: 255–66.

—— (1969) 'Making Out: A Counter System of Workers' Control of Work', in Burns, T. (ed.) *Industrial Man*, Harmondsworth: Penguin, 359–79.

—— (1973) 'Banana Time: Job Satisfaction and Informal Interaction', in Salaman, G. and Thompson, K. (eds), *op.cit.*, 205–22.

—— (1980) 'Fear Stuff, Sweet Stuff and Evil Stuff: Management's Defences Against Unionisation in the South', in Nichols, T. (ed.) *op.cit.*, 395–433.

Rueschmeyer, D. (1986) *Power and the Division of Labour*, Cambridge: Polity Press.

Rus, V. (1980) 'Positive and Negative Power: Thoughts on the Dialectics of Power', *Organization Studies*, 1 (1): 3–19.

Salaman, G. (1979) *Work Organisations: Resistance and Control*, London: Longman.

—— (1980) 'Roles and Rules', in Salaman, G. and Thompson, K. (eds) *op.cit.*, 128–51.

—— (1981) *Class and the Corporation*, Glasgow: Fontana.

—— (1982) 'Managing the Frontier of Control', in Giddens, A. and Mackenzie, G. (eds), *op.cit.*, 46–62.

Salaman, G. and Thompson, K. (eds) (1973) *People and Organizations*, London: Longman/Open University Press.

—— (1980) *Control and Ideology in Organizations*, Milton Keynes: Open University Press.

Salancik, G.R. and Pfeffer, J. (1977) 'Who Gets Power – and How They Hold On To It. A Strategic Contingency Model of Power', *Organizational Dynamics*, 5, Winter: 3–21.

Sampson, A. (1973) *The Sovereign State*, London: Hodder & Stoughton.

Samuel, Y. and Mannheim, B.F. (1970) 'A Multidimensional Approach Towards a Typology of Bureaucracy', *Administrative Science Quarterly*, 15 (2): 216–28.

Saunders, G. (1984) *The Committed Organisation: How to Develop Companies to Compete Successfully in the 1990s*, Farnborough: Gower.

Sayles, L.R. (1964) *Managerial Behaviour*, New York: McGraw-Hill.

Scase, R. and Goffee, R. (1980) *The Real World of the Small Business Owner*, London: Croom Helm.

—— (1989) *Reluctant Managers: Their Work and Lifestyles*, London: Unwin Hyman.

Schein, E.H. (1979) *Organizational Psychology*, 3rd edn, Englewood Cliffs, N.J.: Prentice-Hall.

Schreyogg, G. (1980) 'Contingency and Choice in Organization Theory', *Organization Studies*, 1 (4): 305–26.

Schull, F.A., Delberg, A.L. and Cummings, L.L. (1970) *Organizational Decision Making*, New York: McGraw-Hill.

Seashore, S. (1975) 'Defining and Measuring the Quality of Working Life', in Davis, L.E. and Cherns, A.B. (eds) *op.cit.*, 105–18.

Selznick, P. (1948) 'Foundations of the Theory of Organizations', *American Sociological Review*, 13: 25–35.

—— (1949) *TVA and the Grass Roots*, Berkeley, Calif.: California University Press.

—— (1957) *Leadership in Administration: A Sociological Interpretation*, New York: Harper & Row.

—— (1966) 'An Approach to a Theory of Bureaucracy', in Coser, L. and Rosenberg, B. (eds) *Sociological Theory: A Book of Readings*, 477–88.

Shamir, B. (1978) 'Between Bureaucracy and Hospitality – Some Organisational Characteristics of Hotels', *Journal of Management Studies*, Oct: 285–307.

Shetty, Y.K. (1978) 'Managerial Power and Organisational Effectiveness: A Contingency Analysis', *Journal of Management Studies*, May: 178–81.

Siehl, C. and Martin, J. (1984) 'The Role of Symbolic Management: How Can Managers Effectively Transmit Organisational Culture?', in Hunt, J.G., Hosking, D., Schnesheim, C.A. and Stewart, R. (eds) *Leaders and Managers: International Perspectives on Managerial Behaviour and Leadership*, New York: Pergamon, 227–39.

Silverman, D. (1970) *The Theory of Organisations*, London: Heinemann.

Silverman, D. and Jones, J. (1976) *Organisational Work: The Language of Grading, the Grading of Language*, London: Collier-Macmillan.

Simon, H. (1960) *The New Science of Management Decision*, New York: Harper & Row.

Sloan, A.P. (1965) *My Years With General Motors*, London: Sidgwick & Jackson.

Smircich, L. (1983) 'Concepts of Culture and Organizational Analysis', *Administrative Science Quarterly*, 28, Sept: 339–58.

Smircich, L. and Stubbart, C. (1985) 'Strategic Management in an Enacted World', *Academy of Management Review*, 724–36.

Snape, E. and Bamber, G. (1985) 'Analysing the Employment Relationship of Managers and Professional Staff', in Hammond, V. (ed.) *op.cit.*

Soeters, J.L. (1986) 'Excellent Companies as Social Movements', *Journal of Management Studies*, 23 (3): 299–312.

Starbuck, W.H. (1976) 'Organizations and Their Environments', in Dunnette, M.D. (ed.) *Handbook of Industrial and Organizational Psychology*, Chicago: Rand McNally, 1069–123.

Stark, D. (1980) 'Class Struggle and the Transformation of the Labour Process: A Relational Approach', *Theory and Society*, 9 (1): 89–130.

Stein, B.A. and Kanter, R.M. (1980) 'Building the Parallel Organization: Toward Structures for Permanent Quality of Work Life', *Journal of Applied Behavioural Science*, 16, July–August–Sept: 371–88.

Stewart, R. (1967) *Managers and their Jobs*, Maidenhead: McGraw-Hill.

—— (1976) *Contrasts in Management*, Maidenhead: McGraw-Hill.

Stewart, R., Smith, P., Blake, J. and Wingate, P. (1980) *The District Administrator in the National Health Service*, London: Pitman.

—— (1982) *Choices for the Manager*, Englewood Cliffs, N.J.: Prentice-Hall.

—— (1983) 'Managerial Behaviour: How Research has Changed the Traditional Picture', in Earl, M. (ed.) *Perspectives on Management: A Multidisciplinary Analysis*, Oxford: Oxford University Press, 82–98.

Stinchcombe, A.L. (1965) 'Social Structure and Organizations', in Marsh, J.G. (ed.) *Handbook of Organizations*, Chicago: McNally.

—— (1969) 'Social Structure and Invention of Organizational Forms', in Burns, T. (ed.) *op.cit.*, 153–95.

—— (1970) 'Bureaucratic and Craft Administration of Production', in Grusky, O. and Miller, G. (eds) *op.cit.*, 261–71.

Stone, K. (1974) 'The Origins of Job Structures in the Steel Industry', *Review of Radical Political Economics*, 6 (2): 113–73.

Storey, J. (1980) *The Challenge to Management Control*, London: Kogan Page.

—— (1983) *Managerial Prerogative and the Question of Control*, London: Routledge & Kegan Paul.

Susman, G.I. (1975) 'Technological Prerequisites for Delegation of Decision-Making to Work Groups', in Davis, L. and Cherns, A.B. *op.cit.*, Vol. I.

Tannenbaum, A.S. (1968) *Control in Organizations*, New York: McGraw-Hill.

Taylor, F.W. (1912) 'Testimony to the House of Representatives Committee', in Taylor, F.W. *Scientific Management*, New York: Harper & Row.

—— (1947) *Scientific Management*, New York: Harper and Row.

Taylor, J.C. (1979) 'Job Design Criteria Twenty Years Later', in Davis, L.E. and Taylor, J.C. *Design of Jobs*, 2nd edn, Santa Monica, Calif.: Goodyear Publishing Co., 54–63.

Terkel, S. (1973) *Working*, Harmondsworth: Penguin.

Terreberry, S. (1968) 'The Evolution of Organizational Environments', *Administrative Science Quarterly*, 12 (4): 590–612.

Teulings, A.W.M. (1986) 'Managerial Labour Processes in Organised Capitalism: The Power of Corporate Management and the Powerlessness of the Manager', in Knights, D. and Willmott, H. (eds) *op.cit.*, 142–65.

—— (1987) 'A Political Bargaining Theory of Codetermination – An Empirical Test for the Dutch System of Organizational Democracy', *Organization Studies*, 8 (1): 1–24.

Thackray, J. (1988) 'Tightening the White Collar', *Management Today*, July.

Thibaut, J.L. and Kelley, H. (1959) *The Social Psychology of Groups*, New York: John Wiley.

Thompson, E.P. (1968) *The Making of the English Working Class*, Harmondsworth: Penguin.

Thompson, J.D. (1967) *Organizations in Action*, New York: McGraw-Hill.

Thompson, K. (1980) 'The Organisational Society', in Salaman, G. and Thompson, K. (eds) *op.cit.*, 3–23.

Thompson, P. (1983) *The Nature of Work: An Introduction to Debates on the Labour Process*, London: Macmillan.

Thompson, P. and McHugh, D. (1990) *Work Organisations: A Critical Introduction*, Basingstoke: Macmillan.

Thorsrud, E. (1981) 'The Changing Structure of Work Organisation', in Kanawaty, G. (ed.) *op.cit.*, 3–40.

Tillett, A., Kempner, T. and Wills, G. (eds) (1970) *Management Thinkers*, Harmondsworth: Penguin.

Toffler, A. (1970) *Future Shock*, London: Bodley Head.

—— (1985) *The Adaptive Corporation*, London: Pan.

Tornow, W.W. and Pinto, P.R. (1976) 'The Development of a Managerial Job Taxonomy: A System for Describing, Classifying and Evaluating Executive Positions', *Journal of Applied Psychology*, 61 (4): 410–18.

Touraine, A. (1971) *The Post-Industrial Society*, New York: Random House.

Trist, E.L. (1981) *The Evolution of Socio-Technical Systems: A Conceptual Framework and Action Research Programme*, Toronto: Ontario Ministry of Labour.

Trist, E.L. and Bamforth, K.W. (1951) 'Some Social and Psychological Consequences of the Longwall Method of Coal Getting', *Human Relations*, 4 (1): 3–38.

Udy, S. (1959) 'Bureaucracy and Rationality in Weber's Organizational Theory: An Empirical Study', *American Sociological Review*, 24: 791–5.

Urwick, L. (1952) *Notes on the Theory of Organization*, New York: American Management Association.

US Dept of Health, Education and Welfare (1973) *Work in America*, Cambridge, Mass.: MIT Press.

Van Assen, A. and Webster, P. (1980) 'Designing Meaningful Jobs: A Comparative Analysis of Organizational Design Practices', in Duncan, K.D. *et al.* (eds) *op.cit.*, 237–52.

Van Fleet, D.D. and Bedeian, A.G. (1977) 'A History of the Span of Management', *Academy of Management Review*, 2 (3): 356–72.

Vroom, V.H. (1974) 'A Normative Model of Managerial Decision-Making', *Organizational Dynamics*, 1974, 5: 66–80.

Vroom, V.H. and Deci, E.L. (eds) (1973) *Management and Motivation*, Harmondsworth: Penguin.

Walker, C.R. and Guest, R.H. (1952) *The Man on the Assembly Line*, Cambridge, Mass.: Harvard University Press.

Wall, T.D. and Lischeron, J.A. (1977) *Worker Participation: A Critique of the Literature and Some Fresh Evidence*, London: McGraw-Hill.

Walsh, J.P. and Dewar, R.D. (1987) 'Formalization and the Organizational Life Cycle', *Journal of Management Studies*, 24 (3): 215–31.

Walsh, K., Hinings, R., Greenwood, R. and Ranson, S. (1981) 'Power and Advantage in Organizations', *Organization Studies*, 2 (2): 131–52.

Warner, M. (ed.) (1977) *Organisational Choice and Constraint*, London: Saxon House.
— (1984) *Organizations and Experiments: Designing New Ways of Managing Work*, Chichester: John Wiley.
Warner, W.L. and Low, J.O. (1947) *The Social System of the Modern Factory*, Newhaven, Conn.: Yale University Press.
Warr, P. (1987) 'Job Characteristics and Mental Health', in Warr, P. (ed.) *Psychology at Work* (3rd edn), Harmondsworth: Penguin, 247–69.
Warr, P. and Wall, T. (1975) *Work and Well-Being*, Harmondsworth: Penguin.
Warwick, D. (1974) *Bureaucracy*, London: Longman.
Watson, T.J. (1977) *The Personnel Managers*, London: Routledge & Kegan Paul.
— (1986) *Management, Organisation and Employment Strategy: New Directions in Theory and Practice*, London: Routledge & Kegan Paul.
Webb, G.H. (1975) 'Payment by Results Systems', in Bowey, A. (ed.) *Handbook of Salary and Wage Systems*, Epping: Gower, 229–40.
Weber, M. (1964) *The Theory of Economic and Social Organization*, New York: Free Press.
Weick, K.E. (1979) *The Social Psychology of Organizing*, Reading, Mass.: Addison-Wesley.
— (1981) 'Enactment and Organizing', in Grusky, O. and Miller, G. (eds) *op.cit.*, 265–79.
Weinshall, T. (ed.) (1972) *Culture and Management*, Harmondsworth: Penguin.
Weir, M. (ed.) (1976) *Job Satisfaction*, Glasgow: Fontana.
Weiss, A. (1984) 'Simple Truths of Japanese Manufacturing', *Harvard Business Review*, 62 (4) July/August: 119–25.
Westergaard, J.H. (1970) 'The Rediscovery of the Cash Nexus', in Miliband, R. and Saville, J. (eds) *The Socialist Register 1970*, London: Merlin.
White, M. and Trevor, M. (1983) *Under Japanese Management: The Experience of British Workers*, London: Policy Studies Institute/ Heinemann.
Whiteley, W. (1985) 'Managerial Work Behaviour: An Integration of Results from Two Major Approaches', *Academy of Management Journal*, 28 (2): 344–62.
Whyte, W.H. (1961) *The Organization Man*, Harmondsworth: Penguin.
Wickens, P. (1987) *The Road to Nissan*, London: Macmillan.
Wilensky, H.L. (1970) 'The Professionalization of Everyone?', in Grusky, O. and Miller, G.A. (eds) *op.cit.*, 483–501.
Wilkins, A.L. and Ouchi, W.G. (1983) 'Efficient Cultures: Exploring the Relationship between Culture and Organizational Performance', *Administrative Science Quarterly*, 28, Sept: 468–81.
Williamson, O.E. (1975) *Markets and Hierarchies*, New York: Free Press.

Wilson, D.C., Butler, R.J., Cray, D., Hickson, D.J. and Mallory, G.R. 'Breaking the Bounds of Organization in Strategic Decision Making', *Human Relations*, 39: 309–32.

Wood, S. (ed.) (1983) *The Degradation of Work? Skill, Deskilling and the Labour Process*, London: Hutchinson.

—— (1989a) *The Transformation of Work? Skill, Flexibility and the Labour Process*, London: Hutchinson.

—— (1989b) 'The Transformation of Work?', in Wood, S. (ed.), *op.cit.*, 1–43.

Wood, S. and Kelly, J. (1983) 'Taylorism, Responsibile Autonomy and Management Strategy', in Wood, S. (ed.) *op.cit.*, 74–89.

Wood, S. and Manwaring, A. (1985) 'The Ghost in the Labour Process', in Knights, D. *et al.* (eds) *op.cit.*, 171–96.

Woodward, J. (1965) *Industrial Organisation*, Oxford: Oxford University Press.

Wrong, D. (1979) *Power: Its Forms, Bases and Uses*, Oxford: Basil Blackwell.

Zald, M.N. (ed.) (1970) *Power in Organizations*, Nashville, Tenn.: Vanderbilt University Press.

Zimbalist, A. (ed.) (1979) *Case Studies on the Labor Process*, New York: Monthly Review Press.

Index

A–B models of power 19–20, 20
absenteeism 138
achievement ethic 168, 170, 184
action, climate of 205–6
'action' account of
    rationalisation 74–5, 78
activities, management 12–13,
    14; management divisions of
    labour 236–7
activities, organisational 153,
    174–6
adaptation, internal 155
adhocratic organisation 165–71,
    171–2, 182, 228
administrative adhocracies 170–1
administrative authority 91
administrative knowledge 22,
    23, 24
age, organisational 152
Albrow, M. 87
alienative compliance 30, 32, 39
alliances 177
allocation of work: bureaucracy
    95, 96; clan organisations
    210, 212; concept of
    management 2–3;
    decentralisation 158, 159,
    183, adhocratic organisation
    168, 169, professional
    organisation 163, 164;
    despecialisation 120, 121,
    126; group working 126, 128;
    job redesign 125, 126;
    J-organisations 197, 199;

MTO framework 52–4;
    rationalisation 69, 70, 71;
    separation of management
    process 5–6
appraisal, performance 190
'aura' of managers' position 41
authority 18, 28, 89; managerial
    41–6; see also power
automobile production 65
autonomous work groups
    127–8, 133; see also group
    working; team working
autonomy: clan organisations
    205; control and 240–1;
    decentralisation and 160,
    182, 184; and work
    satisfaction 136; see also
    discretion

Babbage principle 66
batch production 116
Bedaux system 64
Beetham, D. 87
behaviour modification 19;
    culture and 216; see also
    control; influence; power
'best way' 64; flexible work
    methods 117–18;
    sustainability of concept 81
boundary roles 55, 149
Braverman, H. 62; post-
    Braverman debate 71–9
Burawoy, M. 76
bureaucracy/bureaucratisation